ALWAYS YOURS, BEE

MIA HAYES

FINNSTAR PUBLISHING

Always Yours, Bee is a work of nonfiction. Some names and identifying details have been changed.

Book cover designed by Letitia Hasser of RBA Designs

For my greatest gifts, K, F, B.
And D, thank you for helping me find my voice.

AUTHOR'S NOTE

To write this book, I relied heavily on my and my husband's Facebook posts, our family photographs, my blog entries (that I've since deleted), the legal documents, my family, and my admittedly flawed memory. It is important to note that when writing about events pertaining to my immediate family, I did inquire about their differing memories of the same situations, and I used these blended recollections to better flesh out what actually happened.

I have changed the names of most of the individuals in this book, and in some situations, I obscured details to preserve anonymity. I have also created composite characters in the case of my friends, as writing about every friend individually would become unwieldy. Any event and person I felt did not contribute to the substance of the story, I omitted.

While writing this memoir, I learned the stories I told myself publicly and privately were more complicated than I realized. I've attempted to be truthful with myself, even when that truth is ugly, and I believe I've written the truest form of my story and memories that I can.

"You can't go back and change the beginning, but you can start where you are and change the ending.

~anonymous

PROLOGUE

November 2004

Lemonade light filtered through the fog, casting a warm, golden tone across us as we watched Ryan run down the empty beach, a kite string clenched in his tiny fist.

November usually brought rain to San Francisco, but this particular day was clear, and we wanted to take advantage of the sun— even if it was chilly and damp out. Surfers bobbed off the coast, waiting for their ride, and gulls skittered along the shoreline. Later, after we ate our picnic lunch, we planned on exploring the tide pools.

James snapped a picture of Leo and me snuggled into a fleecy blanket. I waved him over to us, and he settled into the sand, his jean-clad leg touching mine. He tossed his arm over my shoulder and hugged me close.

"This is nice," he said. Ryan had stopped running to inspect something on the beach, and Leo crawled off my lap into the sand. "But this is more fun." James turned and tried to tickle me through my layers of bulky clothes.

We laughed and smiled and were so very happy.

That's how I want to remember us.

Golden.

THE ACCIDENT

November 23rd, 2010

Why wasn't my phone ringing? She said seven thirty.

Relentless late-November rain battered the trio of windows behind me. It was nearly eight in the morning, two days before Thanksgiving, and I sat in the tiny family room of my San Francisco flat trying not to envision every reason why my phone was silent. Had she realized I was a hack and changed her mind?

Relax, no one is ever on time.

I opened the well-worn notebook in my lap and studied the questions my husband, James, and I had excitedly crafted the night before. Earlier that year, I had signed with a New York literary agent, and now an editor wanted to talk to me.

My writing had been squeezed in during sports practices and after the boys went to bed. James traveled frequently for work, and I often stayed up well past midnight to write despite long days of work, volunteering, and mothering.

I hadn't mentioned my new passion to James until I received three offers of representation the day I submitted the manuscript to agents. He had been baffled that I had had time to write a full-length novel but not surprised that I had *actually* written a novel. As he put it, it was a very me thing to do.

I stared at my blank phone screen. *Why hadn't she called?*

In an explosive burst of boy-noise, Ryan, my nine-year-old son, sprinted into the room and flopped on the end of the couch. His Catholic school uniform shirt was untucked, and his two blond cowlicks stuck straight up. I glanced at his feet. No socks or shoes.

"Can Grandma get me a bagel?" He gave me a hopeful, missing-tooth smile.

I set my notebook aside. "Did you ask Grandma?"

"She said if it was okay with you. I'll even ask her to get one for Tate and Leo, too."

I chuckled. "Do you really think Grandma would walk you all to school, get only you Boudin's, and leave your brothers hungry?"

Ryan shrugged.

"Go finish getting ready, and if you have time, Grandma can get all of you bagels."

Ryan leaped off the sofa and raced past James standing in the doorway of our family room.

"Hey! No hugs?" James called after Ryan.

"Sorry!" Ryan threw his arms around James's torso. "Love you!"

James rubbed the back of Ryan's head. "I love you, too."

Ryan broke free and his footsteps thundered down the stairs. "We can get bagels!"

Our front door slammed, followed by my in-laws' door closing. They lived in the flat below and often helped care for the boys. My mother-in-law, Molly, worked at their Catholic school —the same one both she and James had attended.

I was immensely proud that my boys were the fifth generation of James's family to live in our three-story house, and I planned on never leaving. James had grown up there and so had Molly, and now it was the boys' turn. Molly and Joe, my father-in-law, lived in the second-level flat, and my family lived in the third level. The garage and a small in-law unit occupied the ground floor.

James's family roots ran deep in San Francisco, a park was even named after them, and I wore it as part of my identity. We were the Doyles from 11th Avenue (even though we were now the Suttons), and that meant something in our small community.

Molly and Joe were good sports about allowing me to put my own stamp on the house, going along with whatever my current obsession was. When I said I wanted to be a modern home-steader and turn our deep backyard into an organic city farm with fruit trees, bees, and chickens, they didn't blink, and they let James buy me a chicken coop for our anniversary.

No matter what my current obsession was—like starting an online shopping site, becoming a personal shopper, or taking on the task of revamping our school and church's annual festival— James supported me. I was a whirlwind, and he was the calm hand that steadied the ship.

"I'll call when I get to work. I want to know how everything goes." James's Chelsea boots clomped against the hardwood floor as he walked toward me. He wore dark jeans and a black leather bike jacket that showed off his trim figure, and the olive-green messenger bag I had given him for Christmas bounced off his hip. He hadn't bothered to do his messy, brown hair because he'd fix it at work after he took off his motorcycle helmet. I teased him that he carried more beauty products in his bag than I did, but really, I gave him a hard time because he was more pulled together than me.

Unlike James, my days consisted of mom things like going to the park and dust-bustering Cheerios off the floor. I did, however, shower, dress, and do my makeup every day after running a 5K at 5 a.m. The other moms marveled that I always managed to look presentable with three kids under the age of ten. I'd laugh and say it was my secret weapon, Molly, but the truth was the thought of anyone seeing me less than perfect bothered me.

"Are you sure you don't want a ride? It's pouring." A mist of grayness swirled outside. Driving James meant I would have to take the call in the car, but I needed to offer. After all, he would have insisted on driving me.

"I'll be fine." James flashed a reassuring smile. "I don't mind getting a little wet, and you need to focus." Every day, James rode his cherry-red Vespa downtown. Taking Muni was an exhausting, smelly experience that took three times as long, and parking a scooter was cheaper than parking a car. It had been a great solution.

The rain had eased into a gentle sprinkle. Really, it was no more than the heavy fog that normally hung over the Richmond District. "We should get you a rain shield."

"Probably." James checked his phone's weather app. "If I go now, I should be okay."

"Are you positive you don't want a ride?" I nervously tapped my notebook. Everything I had worked for was coming to fruition, and I didn't want to mess it up.

"Positive." James placed three kisses on my forehead–one for each of the boys. "You're going to do great, Bee. Just be you. Everyone loves you."

"But do they love my book?"

"The editor wouldn't call you if she didn't." James playfully pat my cheek, cupping my face on the last tap. He lifted my chin and stared into my eyes. A sense of calm ran through me. "It's going to be great, just like everything else you do."

I loved making James proud. He worked hard for us, and

even though he constantly told me my job of being a mother and wife was more important than his, I felt I should do more, contribute more, be more.

My phone rang, and I startled. James mouthed, "I love you."

Unlike every other day, I didn't sing out my normal, "Be good. Be careful. Don't do bad things. I love you," as he disappeared down the hallway. My phone was already to my ear.

The house shuttered when James slammed the front door.

I never saw that version of my husband again.

———

I peeled the phone away from my ear. An unknown number had been calling for five solid minutes, and I was annoyed. Thankfully, the editor and my agent couldn't hear the beeps, but it made focusing difficult.

"So, that's all I have," the editor said. "What do you think?"

I pushed the strange number from my mind. "Sounds great! When do you want the changes?"

My agent, Kathleen, laughed. "We'd rather you do them right and not rush."

"So . . . timeframe?" I hated open-ended deadlines. Everything needed a beginning, middle, and end. It was logical.

"Well, first I'll send over an edit letter. Read through it with Kathleen, and if you have any questions, just ask." The editor had a pleasant, young voice. She was probably under thirty, which made me feel ancient at thirty-four.

"So, no timeline?" I asked.

"Nope."

Wonderful. The publishing world couldn't be more different

than the tech world I lived in where everything needed to happen yesterday.

My phone beeped again, and I held back my huff. "I look forward to getting your letter," I said. "I love your ideas."

When I hung up, my phone rang again. Thinking it was Kathleen, I didn't look at the number as I stared out the window. The heavy rain had flooded the back garden, leaving a pond-sized puddle in the middle.

"Hey! That was great! I loved her ideas!" I was still unsure about the appropriate agent-author relationship and struggled with feeling either too friendly or too businesslike.

"Ummm . . . hi. This is . . ."

Sirens blared in the background, drowning out the man's wavering voice.

"Can I help you?" I asked. Rain slammed into the side of the house, and beads careened down the windows.

"I picked up his phone. There was an accident. I think it's the guy's who was hit?"

My heart stopped. "Hit? Who was hit?"

"A guy. Yeah. He was riding a scooter, and a truck hit him."

The room dimmed, and I blinked my eyes. Did the power go out? "Where?"

"Van Ness and Geary."

Breathe, just, breathe. James is most likely at work by now. You've been on the phone for forty minutes. He's always to the office by nine. Call him. I stared at the microwave clock. It was 9:10 a.m. James wanted to know how my call went.

"Is he okay?" I don't know why I asked. What I should have been doing was calling James, not chitchatting with a stranger.

Another siren wailed. "I . . . I don't know." The man sounded like he was on the verge of tears. "He's in the ambulance. They're working on him. It was bad. He . . . he got caught under the truck. Under the tire. They're taking him to the hospital."

James rode a scooter, and he always went through that intersection. A burning dullness filled my ears as my brain tried to protect me from the man's words.

"Hello?" the man said. "Are you still there?"

"Which hospital?"

"I don't know."

"Ask!"

There was a long pause. "The ambulance just left. I'm sorry."

"Was his name James?" The room spun, and I steadied myself against the sofa. *Say no. Please say no.*

"I don't know. I just picked this phone up off the street, and this number was listed as his in case of emergency contact."

"Then why didn't you call from that phone?" I asked. Maybe this was a terrible prank?

"I don't know," the man said.

I hung up on him and called James's cellphone. The man answered.

"Why do you have my husband's phone?" I shouted. "Why?"

"I'm going to let you go now. I hope he's okay."

With concrete feet, I ran my hands along the hallway walls until I came to the steep, curving staircase. Halfway down, my knees buckled, and I slid to the bottom.

Screams pierced the air, and I pressed my hands over my ears, trying to block the horror of James being hit from my mind.

Molly flung the glass front door open, and I crumbled at her feet. She would know what to do. She'd fix this.

My youngest son, Tate, hid behind her and stared at me with deep-brown eyes that looked like James's.

James. I needed to find James.

"What's wrong?" Molly asked calmly as she stooped down next to me. She was our family rock, and nothing rattled her.

"James was hit by a truck. I don't know if he's okay. He was taken to the hospital." The words sounded foreign. How were they coming from my mouth?

Molly hauled me into her flat. "What hospital?"

I shook my head, afraid to speak in front of Tate. He, however, seemed unaware of the possible tragedy unfolding and karate chopped a block tower. When it tumbled to the ground, he stared first at me, then at the rubble. I didn't respond, and he kicked the blocks across the room with a laugh.

Molly shoved a worn phonebook into my hands and scooped Tate up.

"Take a breath and start with General. I'll call CPMC. We'll find him." Molly placed Tate next to her on the couch, flipped her phonebook open, and punched the hospital's number into the house phone. Like James, she was always calm and level-headed in a crisis.

I was learning I was not.

I thumbed through the tissue-thin pages until I found the number for General. I had to find James. He had to be okay because I would know if he wasn't, wouldn't I? I'd feel my soul shatter. I'd feel the void of losing him.

General had no report of him. No hospital did. Hours ticked by, and I called and called and called, but not a single hospital in San Francisco had a record of James.

"Where the hell is he?" I couldn't control my fear any longer. "Where is he?"

"Keep calling." Molly led Tate to the kitchen for lunch, and I slipped off the floral couch and onto the pink-carpeted floor. I lay prone, staring at a crack in the also-pink coved ceiling. It ran across the ceiling and down the wall with mini cracks radiating away from it. One crack had led to many smaller fractures.

I rolled my head to the side and kept my focus on the spiderweb of cracks. James loved me. He wouldn't leave me. He wouldn't dare.

Everything about us happened fast, including our wedding. We knew each other only six weeks before he proposed. There was no ring, just a promise that when he returned from college in December, we would get married. It wasn't the proposal of my dreams, but it felt inevitable, because if I knew anything at twenty-one, it was that James and I were meant for each other.

Who else would know where James is?

The ambulance company.

After my third call, an angel answered. "Honey," the gentle voice said, "he'd be at General if he's a trauma. They most likely haven't processed him yet. Everyone gets admitted under an alias until the hospital can confirm identity."

"He's at General." I sprinted down the short, narrow hallway to the microscopic kitchen. Tate and Molly sat at the mail-strewn table, and Tate picked at a plate of red grapes. "I'm going to get him."

Molly shook her head. "Wait for Joe. He's on his way home. He'll drive you."

But I couldn't wait. James needed me, and I needed to be with him.

There's a song, "An Olive Grove Facing the Sea" by Snow Patrol, that will forever be seared into my brain. It played on repeat as I weaved my car from the west side of San Francisco over pothole roads to the southeast side. I couldn't turn the song off because my phone was in the glove box and not easy to reach.

At a stoplight on Divisidero, my phone buzzed. I hesitated

before diving across the seat. Answering it meant knowing. Did I want a world without James?

No.

It rang again, louder, like an order for me to answer. I ripped the glove box open and disconnected the phone from the charging cord.

"Hello?" I whispered.

Please, please, please don't say it. Don't say it.

"Is this James Sutton's wife?"

"Yes."

"Can you come to San Francisco General? He's been in an accident."

My minivan's windshield wipers beat in frantic unison with my pounding heart. "Is he okay?"

"I'm sorry, I can't give that information over the phone. You'll need to speak to a doctor."

He was dead.

I rested my head against the car seat. Someone honked, and I tapped the gas too hard, launching my minivan into the intersection.

"I'm coming now." I had no tears; my brain was focused solely on being with my husband. "Tell James I'm coming."

I waited in a line five-people deep to find out if my husband was dead. I waited to find out if everything I had ever wanted had ended.

Hushed conversations swirled around me, and I strained to hear them through my mind's protective veil.

I would be okay. James would be okay. Everything was going to be okay.

"Name?"

"Jordan," a burly man answered.

Click-clack. Click-clack.

"The doctor will be out in a minute. Have a seat."

A blast of cool air hit me from behind and blew the protective veil off. An uncomfortable numbness spread from my head to my toes, and I shuffled forward one step.

The woman in front of me had thin streaks of silver sparkled throughout her dark, bra strap-length hair. When she moved forward, her hair swayed against her back.

I need to tell James's work he won't be in today.

I stared at my phone. Who should I call? Who would care that James wouldn't be in today? The only name I could think of was the CEO's assistant who I had met a few times, and she seemed to like James. When she answered, I told her James had been hit, and she asked about his condition.

"Maybe dead." Only the enormous pit in my stomach kept me from crying.

She gasped.

"It's my turn." I hung up.

The desk attendant typed James's name into her computer and refused to meet my focused gaze. "A doctor will be out in a minute."

As I stumbled toward an orange, plastic bucket seat, Joe and Molly burst through the sliding glass doors. At six foot two, Joe towered over tiny Molly, and he often barreled into rooms, leaving Molly to trot behind.

"Is he here?" Joe's booming baritone filled the packed waiting room. He taught high school English at an all-girls school. Had he left in the middle of the day? Had James and I inconvenienced him?

I pressed my lips together and exhaled through my nose. "I'm waiting for the doctor."

We huddled together on the chairs. Molly squeezed my hand, and Joe stared off into space. James was their only child, but most importantly, he was the glue that held us all together. Everything Molly and Joe did was for James, and by default me and the boys.

"Where's Tate?" I realized my son was missing.

Molly tried smiling, but the corners of her mouth didn't pull up enough, and her hazel eyes were flat. "Mr. Hanley has him. He'll keep Leo and Ryan, too." Mr. Hanley was our Catholic school principal, a big man with a bigger heart, who Molly had worked with for years. Outside of our family, there was no one I trusted more with my children. "He promised to take them to Hamburger Haven for dinner."

"They'll like that." The boys always begged me to take them to the greasy spoon, and I always refused out of disgust.

The heavy, metal door separating the waiting room from the ER swung open, and a middle-aged doctor with tightly pulled-back hair assessed the room.

"Sutton?" She scanned the room, and her gaze zeroed in on me. "Sutton?"

Molly gently pushed on my back but didn't get up herself. When Joe started to stand, she held him back. "Let her go first."

If James were dead, I didn't want to know. I wanted the possibility of him for as long as I could hold onto it. I didn't move.

"Mrs. Sutton?"

I blinked in confusion. I wasn't Mrs. Sutton, that was Molly. Did they want to talk to her first?

Molly prodded me forward, and I stumbled toward the doctor. The door softly closed behind us as we entered the cold, sterile hallway where a strung-out man lay handcuffed to a bed, and a woman yelled from deep inside the bowels of the hospital.

My shaking legs refused to hold me. I leaned against the cold wall and fought to calm my ragged breath.

I couldn't do it. I couldn't walk toward something I didn't want. The need to run away from the tragedy rushing toward me grew. If I walked out the exit, could I restart the day? I'd tell James I loved him and insist on driving him to work. I would fix things if I could just get a do-over.

The doctor backtracked to me. "Your husband sustained multiple injuries, but he's going to be okay."

He wasn't dead? I shut my eyes tightly, trying to process the doctor's words. James was alive? My exhale came out in a rush, and when I inhaled, relief settled into all the empty places, but I still couldn't move.

"He's going to be okay, I promise," the doctor said softly.

"Okay how? Okay as in never walking? Okay as in a few scratches?" Was it greedy that I wanted him returned the way I had sent him off that morning?

"He hurt his wrists, dislocated both his shoulders, has severe road rash, and received thirty stitches on his backside, but he'll be fine." The doctor stopped outside an open door. "He's resting, but he'll be okay. It looks scarier than it is." She tapped her head. "He's lucky he had on a helmet. If he hadn't, we'd be having a different conversation."

I inched closer to the doorway, and the doctor gave me a confused look. "He may have a mild concussion," she said. "But I don't think it's anything too serious. The nurse will walk you through the symptoms and care."

I stared past her into the room and gasped. My whole world was on a cold, sterile table under a crisp, white sheet. Bright lights glared down at James, and dozens of machines whirled around him.

In that moment, I knew my life had changed, because all my

supposed strength, all the bullshit type-A stuff I did, failed me. I failed James, and I failed us.

From the day we met, James had been my life, and me his. We'd occasionally let other people in, like the boys, but at the end of the day, it was always only us. The boys would one day grow up and leave to start families of their own, but James and I had chosen each other forever.

In that hospital room, we were given a chance at a longer forever.

My chin trembled, but I didn't cry. James hadn't left me, and he was going to be okay.

"You can go in," the doctor said with a twinge of confusion.

"No."

"I know it looks scary, but he's fine. Really." She motioned me forward, but my leaden legs held me in place. "Is anyone else with you? Should I get them?"

I trapped my sobs behind clenched teeth and nodded.

The doctor walked away, leaving me clinging to the door frame. James's chest rose, and I sank to my knees, a guttural sob ripping from my throat. He was alive. Broken and bruised, but alive.

Molly touched my back. "He's going to be okay."

I wiped my face with my sleeve and moved so she could pass by. In another life, Molly would have been a nurse. Through all three of my awful pregnancies, she had cared for me by changing my sheets, emptying my puke bowl, and making sure I ate what I could.

Joe lumbered behind her, and after collecting myself, I joined them in the room. James's unfocused eyes fluttered open before closing again. His clammy, pale skin matched the white sheet, and his hair stuck up at strange angles.

James hadn't left me.

Relief battled with horror inside me. I wanted to wrap James in my arms and never let go, but James did not look fine. He looked broken, fragile, and nothing like the strong, solid husband I knew. If I touched him, would I break him?

"I'll get the discharge papers ready," the doctor said.

I drew my brows together. "Already? He looks awful."

"He'll be okay with rest and time."

"But don't you think—"

"He's going to be fine, Mrs. Sutton."

While we waited for the discharge papers, Molly fussed over James. I let her gingerly change his clothes into leftovers from the hospital Lost and Found. I watched as she helped James shuffle toward the car because his stitches prevented him from sitting in a wheelchair. I waited as Joe arranged James, stomach side down, in the backseat of their sedan.

I did nothing to help my husband.

As I drove home alone, with a plastic bag of James's shredded belongings, I blared "An Olive Grove Facing the Sea" and fought the sinking feeling that, despite the doctor's reassurance, James wasn't okay.

How could anyone be run over by a truck and be okay?

2

November 2010

There are moments with James that I want to hold on to forever. Moments I knew, before they even happened, that would undoubtedly change the trajectory of my life. Many have grown fuzzy and distant, filtered through the lens of time, becoming feelings rather than concrete events. There are also moments I've tried to purge, but they stick with me like festering sores. I pick at them, thinking it will make them heal, but they remain, scarring my heart.

That Thanksgiving, two days after James's accident, I will never forget. In hindsight, I wish I'd done things differently—made my concerns more known or possibly told James 'no.'

My failures that day are perfectly clear, their lines and shapes crisp in my mind against a background of normal Thanksgiving busyness. When I close my eyes, I can still smell the mingled scent of cranberry meatballs and green bean casserole; I can feel the warmth of the fireplace and the damp chill of San Francisco fog licking at the windows; I can hear the boys running around downstairs at my in-laws and the moan of the sofa as James shifts and tries to find a comfortable position. But above all else, I feel my franticness and my desire to make everything like it had been a few days earlier.

In the moments and hours after James's accident, I changed. When the medics peeled James off the rain-flooded street, pieces of me were left behind, too. My belief in my inner strength had been shattered, and the security I had once possessed had vanished.

Death seemed to be everywhere, waiting, and I had never grasped the way it prowled around seemingly ordinary lives, waiting to pounce. It had attacked and retreated, leaving me scared and confused, because if I couldn't see death, how was I supposed to protect my loved ones from it?

I couldn't. I had no control over it. Death would come when it wanted with no notice, and the realization terrified me.

Exhaustion dogged me as I stood in the kitchen chopping and baking. The night before, James had anchored himself to me as nightmares invaded his dreams. I rubbed his back and soothed him as if I alone could prevent the nightmares flashing through his mind. In those dark hours, I believed I had that power, and that my loyal dedication and love was all he needed to move past what happened.

James was strong. His body would heal, and the nightmares would end.

On the sofa, James moaned, and I startled, dropping the knife on the counter. "Are you okay? Do you need something?" I rushed across the tiny room, past the kitchen table, not knowing what to do. "Do you need more painkillers? Some water?"

James lay on his side because the stitches across his butt hurt, and he did a weird side-crunch to look up at me. "I'm fine, Bee."

"Are you hungry?" I searched his face for signs of distress. An unfamiliar five-o'clock shadow darkened his jawline. "I have

17

some appetizers ready and was going to bring them downstairs, but I'll leave a few up here if you want."

Our family was letting James rest by staying downstairs at my in-laws' until dinner time. Our Thanksgivings were small affairs, just our family of five, Molly and Joe, and James's aunt and uncle. James was not only an only child but he also lacked cousins, so everything revolved around us and the boys. I loved his family's closeness, something mine lacked, and when I had married James, I embraced his family traditions and celebrations.

"Are the meatballs ready?" James asked.

"I'll get you some." He hadn't had much to eat over the previous two days, so this was an improvement. I hurried back across the room, got a bowl, and spooned cranberry-sauerkraut meatballs into the dish.

"Here you go." I handed him the bowl over the back of the couch.

He grimaced when he propped up on his elbow and positioned the bowl on the sofa. "This is going to be tough."

I scooted around the brown sofa and knelt next to him. "Let me help you." I took the fork and cut off a piece of meatball.

James's mouth dropped open. "You don't need to feed me."

"I'm helping," I said. "You said it was going to be hard, so I'm helping."

"Bee, it's okay." He took the fork from me. "I'm okay." He was lying to make me feel better. I was sure of it. Or maybe he was trying to convince himself.

James hadn't told me anything about the accident, and a silent understanding passed between us during those first days: I wouldn't push him too hard, and he'd only tell me what he thought I could handle. By trying to protect each other, we inadvertently created our first breakdown in communication that would haunt us for years.

"Get dressed, Bee. I'll be okay." James pointed at the terry cloth bathrobe I had thrown on after a fast shower. "I promise to not choke on the meatballs."

I didn't move, paralyzed by the thought of leaving him for even a few moments. "Are you sure?"

He gave me his are-you-serious look. "The bedroom is twenty feet away. We don't even own a baby monitor. I promise, if I choke to death, you'll hear me."

"Choking is silent."

James rolled his eyes. "Go."

I didn't shut the bedroom door as I changed. A football game blared from the TV, and instead of my normal annoyance over the TV being too loud, I smiled. It was a reassuring sound, one that reminded that James was still with me.

When I returned to the family room, James had placed the half-eaten bowl on the ground and rested his head on a throw pillow. My invincible husband looked sallow and fragile.

"Who's winning?" I sat on the end of the couch. I had a list of dishes to finish making, but they could wait.

"Not the Lions," James answered. "Your dad's going to be pissed." James and my dad had a close relationship, nurtured over the past thirteen years by lengthy trips to visit my family in upstate Michigan. My dad only had non-sports-loving daughters, so having James around gave him someone to commiserate the Lions' losses with.

I studied James while he watched the game. His eyes were foggy from the painkillers I insisted he take, and he moaned anytime he tried to move. I had helped sponge bath him earlier, but his hair was undone, and unlike his normally stylish self, he wore oversized sweatpants and a baggy T-shirt.

Pain twisted its way across James's face. His jaw clenched, and his lips pressed together.

"Are you okay?"

19

James nodded. "I'll be fine."

"That's not what I meant." I touched his foot through the blanket. "Are you okay?"

He darted his gaze past me, toward the fireplace. "I want to go on our trip."

Every year, James spent the weeks around Thanksgiving and Christmas traveling between New York, San Francisco, Europe, and Asia filming the c-suite executives of his company. We had saved money for a year so I could join him and his videographer on the European leg that year, and we were supposed to leave Saturday, only four days after the accident.

Going was out of the question. If James couldn't leave the couch to go downstairs and socialize, how would he fly nine hours to Europe?

I fought the disappointment creeping into mind and tucked the fleecy blanket tighter under his toes. "As much as I want to go, it's not a good idea."

"I need to." He flicked off the game. "I want to."

"No one will be upset if you don't go. Work will understand."

Getting James to stay home from work the day after the accident had been easy—he had been too drugged up to protest. It never occurred to me that he'd want to go back to work on Monday, let alone carry on with the trip.

James held out his hand, and I squeezed it. "Bee, I can't stay here. I need to get away. I need to forget."

The desperation in his voice ripped at me. "You think you feel okay because of the painkillers." I rubbed my thumb over his ring finger, settling on the smooth groove encircling it. His wedding band had gone missing in the accident. "You can barely walk. How are you going to carry luggage all over Europe?"

"You and Owen will help me." His eyes pleaded with me. "I want to go. I need to, and we already have the tickets."

I was selfish, that's the only explanation. I wanted to go to

Europe. Full stop. I had dreamed of this trip for a year and had bought a winter wardrobe just for it (we had little need of heavy coats in San Francisco). I had arranged for my mom and in-laws to share looking after the boys. Plane tickets were bought, hotels booked, and restaurants reserved.

It would be a shame not to go.

In my pre-accident dreams, James and I would walk along the Seine, eat on Brick Lane, and do some shopping in Milan. It was to be our first trip without the boys, and when I realized earlier in the day that James wouldn't be able to go, I had cried in the shower.

That was the problem: I wanted to go more than I wanted to acknowledge something could be seriously wrong with James. When he said he was going, I convinced myself that agreeing to his plan was the right thing to do. James needed me to make sure he took his medicine and to help carry his filming equipment. He needed me to get him through the nightmares.

I knew it wasn't a good idea. "I think you should ask about postponing a bit. Maybe wait until later in December so you have time to heal."

"I can't. The videos are for an event at the end of January. If I don't do them now, they won't get done."

"No one else can do them?"

"No."

"Oh." I bit my bottom lip, letting it hurt a little. James loved his job and took tremendous pride in it. "You need to go?"

"I do."

If he had to go, then the least I could do was be there for him.

It was insane.

"Okay." I struggled with my excitement. Part of me wondered if James insisted on going because he didn't want to let me down, but I pushed it aside. "We'll go."

He gave a closed-lipped smile. "Good."

Against all better judgments, it was decided. James announced it over dinner, after we shared stories about Great-Grandma Rose and Great-Grandpa Bill throwing dinner rolls down the table, and Great-Great-Grandma Egger's mashed potato mountains with perfect spirals of butter melting from the top down. He waited until his family had imprinted their happiest memories on our boys, memories I later learned he had mostly lost in the accident.

"We're going on the trip," James said, cutting up pieces of turkey for Tate. He handed Tate his fork and ladled cranberry sauce over the meat. Tate promptly scraped it off, having recently developed a dislike of his food touching. James should have known that; we had discussed it earlier that day.

Molly's eyes met mine, but I busied myself with Leo. I couldn't bear for her to see the truth: that I hadn't tried hard enough to change James's mind. Like me, she'd been hovering since the accident, and like me, she held her tongue.

We continued our celebration, and no one questioned James's announcement, but later, while washing the dishes, Molly asked me if I thought it was a good idea.

"Is it too soon?" She handed me a plate to dry. "He can't walk, how is he going to sit for hours on an airplane?"

"I don't know, but I think it would be good for him to get out of town. He feels like the accident is all around him here."

Molly handed me the last dish. "If that's what he thinks he needs."

The uncertainty I felt faded a little. If Molly was okay with it, then there was no reason to worry.

3

August 1998

Edinburgh's gray, stony castle loomed over us, and misty air dampened our hair and clothes. I trudged up the hillside toward the arched gate, but James lagged behind me in the wave of tourists.

"C'mon," I said. Cool air rushed around me, and I wished I had a scarf. "The line's getting long."

James held up his hand. "Can we stop for a minute? I don't feel well."

I dodged a man wearing a Yankees cap and skirted around a woman snapping a picture of the castle. "You okay?" James's face was flushed, and his eyes were glossy. I pressed my hand against his forehead. "You're burning up."

James leaned against the stone wall. "I think I need to go back to the B&B. I really don't feel well."

"Okay."

We'd spent the previous week of our honeymoon exploring the English countryside before driving up to Edinburgh for the Fringe Festival. We had tickets for a play later that evening, but James was so hot, I wasn't upset about missing it.

23

We wound our way back down the hill and to the bus stop, and when we arrived at our B&B, James passed out in a restless, feverish heap.

The ibuprofen and cool cloths I pressed against his head didn't work, and the owner of the B&B fetched a doctor out of concern. James barely moved during the examination.

"Influenza," the doctor said. "He needs rest, water, and sleep."

"When will he get better?" I asked. "We need to return to London tomorrow."

"He can't travel for three to four days." The doctor closed his medical bag, and James shivered and moaned in his sleep. "When do you leave for the States?"

"In five days."

"You can stay as long as you need," the B&B owner said. "We'll keep your room for you."

After they left, I tamped down the worry that James wouldn't be well enough to fly home and sat at his bedside with his travel notebook. I replanned our trip, cutting out most of our London plans, and I took all my meals in our room so I could watch over him. I gave James his fever reducer on time, helped him take sips of broth, and forced him to drink water.

On the third day, his fever broke, and he insisted on taking the train to London. I objected, but he insisted.

He didn't want to ruin the last two days of our honeymoon.

November 2010

I am not a natural caregiver. In fact, until James's accident, I was terrible at it. I suppose it was a matter of our different upbringings. In my rambling family of biological, half, and stepsiblings, and more cousins than I could count, we all fended for ourselves. When I was sick, my stepmom would leave me with a glass of Vernors and saltines while she went to work, and my dad absolutely never stayed home with sick kids—he worked at the steel mill and couldn't afford to.

My parents only took us to the doctor's if we were near death. Coughs were treated with whiskey and honey and sore throats by gargling lukewarm saltwater. Fevers were sweated out under piles of blankets, and we often went to school sniffling and hacking. We were tough and self-sufficient, and we didn't need outsiders to tell us how to manage our lives.

Early in our marriage, I realized things were different for James. Not only was his grandfather a pediatrician, but nothing made James happier than making my life easy. The first year we were married, I attended an expensive private college full-time as an honors student while working a forty-plus hours a week retail job. My parents weren't in a position to help me, and I only received minimal financial aid.

I didn't have free time, and James tried to elevate my stress by bringing me dinner at work and helping me study French, politics, and art history. He did all the laundry and errands in addition to working full-time for a California assemblywoman. When I said I felt like I didn't do enough for our family of two, James repeatedly said my only job was to graduate and make enough money to cover my tuition.

We were college student-level poor living in Silicon Valley right before the dot-com boom, and Molly would give us Safeway gift certificates for groceries. I felt guilty about this and like a failure, but James assured me that it made Molly happy to help us.

The concept was foreign to me, and I refused to let James use the certificates. We would have to eat more simply, and we'd pay for it ourselves. My fierce independence didn't know how to accept her generosity until two years later when my pregnancy with Ryan left me on bedrest with preterm contractions.

While I was confined, Molly would visit with me every day for a few hours. She had dreamed of a large family for herself but had suffered numerous miscarriages and a stillbirth. Maybe this is why she treated me as if I were her own daughter. In fact, when the boys were preschool-aged, the other parents assumed she was my mother because we were both petite, had blonde hair, and large hazel eyes. But mostly they thought that because of how we treated one another.

Like Molly, helping people made James happy, even if it was just changing sheets in the middle of the night. He often expressed guilt over the amount of time he worked, so when he was home, he threw himself one hundred percent into being a dad and husband.

Everything changed after the accident. I suddenly had to care for James and the boys, and I didn't know how to do it alone. I found myself copying James's past actions, but nothing felt natural or right. So, when he said he felt fine, even though I could tell he didn't, I latched onto his words with relief. Whatever I had done worked, and I was given a reprieve.

James and I arrived in London during an epic snowstorm that should have closed the airports but hadn't. It was as if even the weather knew the trip was a bad idea, but like the rest of us, was cheering James on in his miraculous, stubborn recovery.

When the local production assistant James hired failed to show up, I was thrust into the role. I didn't mind, because the thought of not being with James caused my heart to race, and I had convinced myself that if I were with James, I could make sure he took his medicine and didn't push himself too hard. I could protect him.

The truth was I couldn't bear to be away from him.

The videographer, Owen, and I set up the filming equipment in a room overlooking the Tate Modern. James shuffled around the room, fielding calls, and disappearing for long minutes. During one of his absences, Owen asked quietly, "Is he okay?"

"He's fine," I said, even though I had doubts. We had flown business class, and James had lain on his stomach most of the flight. Since arriving in London, I had been forcing painkillers on him and wasn't sure how he hadn't passed out. "Working is good for him. You know how he is."

"Yeah, but is he okay?" Owen tapped his head. "He seems off."

"He's jetlagged and on painkillers. You'd be groggy, too." I didn't feel bad pushing back against Owen. He was a friend, and we had had dinner with him and his wife not too long before the accident.

Owen shook his head but didn't bring it up again.

Once my setup job was done, I sat in a conference room and ate cookies while poring over the edit letter I had received the day before. My mind whirled with literary possibilities, and for a moment, I forgot about the accident and immersed myself in my imaginary world.

Around lunch time, James popped his head into the room. "How's it going?"

I glanced up. He still couldn't stand upright and leaned against the doorframe. "I'm making good progress."

"Am I ever going to read this mysterious manuscript?"

"Maybe." Despite James's pleas, I hadn't let him read my book. My writing was the first thing I had ever kept from him, and it felt odd not talking to James about it. It wasn't that I wanted to hide my newfound passion, but rather I didn't want to disappoint him. He was so proud of me for writing a book and getting an agent, and if he thought my teenage dystopian fantasy book was silly, it would crush me.

After filming wrapped, we needed to catch a flight to Dusseldorf. James's dislocated shoulders ached from the accident, so Owen and I piled all the bags onto ourselves and schlepped to the taxi line. We carried thousands of dollars' worth of video equipment along with our personal backpacks. James could barely keep up with us, and we stopped frequently so he didn't fall behind.

At one point, James blew up at Owen for moving slowly. "Owen! You've got to be efficient. Stop fucking with the equipment."

Both Owen and I stared at him. "We're all doing the best we can given the circumstances," I said. Owen and I were carrying the bulk of the luggage, and neither of us mentioned that we snailed along because of James. "We're not going to miss our flight. We have plenty of time."

When James turned his back, Owen raised his eyebrows. I shrugged in answer.

Our German hotel room was modern but dark and over-looked a snow-covered school courtyard. James didn't need my help filming that day, so I stayed in and slept. In the late afternoon, when James didn't return my texts, I tried Owen. He told me they'd been busy all day, but he'd have James call me during their next break.

Feeling unsettled, I set out to explore Dusseldorf on my own. I had never been to Germany, and my one quarter of college German only taught me to count to five. I felt exhilaratingly terrified. At home I was never alone—my boys or James were always with me, or I was with Molly. I never went anywhere by myself, let alone in a foreign country, and wandering the shopping district solo felt reckless, but strangely freeing.

I stopped by the river and leaned over the railing. Soft

snowflakes drifted from the sky and stuck to my navy peacoat. Behind me, a Christmas market had sprung to life and the smell of roasted chestnuts filled the air. I should have been happy. Thankful. I should have been so damn thankful that I was on a European adventure with my husband and not planning his funeral.

But I wasn't.

I was worried. In our thirteen years together, James had never seemed fragile, and I had never questioned his judgment. I knew he was in pain and that he was most likely jetlagged, but I'd never witnessed him losing his temper the way he had over the past few days. He was pretending to be fine. But why? I saw his nightmares and the way he limped. Even Owen suspected something was wrong.

If James couldn't admit he understandably hurt physically, what else was he hiding? I frowned. Was Owen right? Was something wrong with James's brain?

No. It was the stress of the insane trip. We were rapidly hopping cities throughout Europe, and it was exhausting even for me, and I hadn't been run over. James, however, worked all day without complaint and wanted to go out at night, so maybe I was reading the situation wrong. Maybe he had been right and getting out of San Francisco was exactly what he needed.

A barge slogged down the river. It was a slow, cumbersome thing gaining momentum. As it passed me, I leaned against the rail and held my arms wide. The snow fell heavier and stuck to my hair and lashes, but it wasn't cold. I sighed, letting my anxiety rush out in one long breath.

A woman said something to me in German.

"No Deutsch," I answered.

"Are you okay?" she asked in perfect English. "You seem troubled."

I stepped away from the railing. "I'm fine, thank you."

My phone buzzed in my pocket. It was James telling me where to meet him and Owen for dinner. I asked the woman for directions, and she pointed me toward the Christmas market. I hurried through the celebrating Germans and found the restaurant without any more help.

At dinner, James chose the easiest seat to get in and out of. He grimaced occasionally and shifted his weight side to side. I assumed his stitches were aching but didn't want to say anything in front of Owen.

I frowned when he ordered a beer and used it to chase his painkillers. James didn't drink, and we didn't keep alcohol in our home. For me, not drinking was mostly a habit—I'd been pregnant, nursing, or child-tending for the past nine years. For James, it was survival. He was always the one who got up with the boys in the middle of the night to change diapers and chase monsters.

I raised my eyebrows after the second drink. "You shouldn't mix alcohol with your meds."

James's glare sliced through me. "If I want a beer, I'll have a beer. Or two. Or maybe even three."

James had never spoken to me like that, and embarrassed at his public tongue lashing, I sat silently the rest of the meal and poked at my food. Owen tried making conversation, but mostly we finished up in silence.

Later that night, James reeked of beer when he climbed into bed.

"Did you brush your teeth?" I wrinkled my nose at the unfamiliar, sour smell radiating from him.

"Yeah." He wrapped his arms around me and pulled me in tight. The scent of beer oozed from him. "I love you, Bee. More than anything, I love you."

"I love you, too." I snuggled into his side until his traumatized body stopped jerking and relaxed into sleep. When he snored softly, I untangled myself, rolled onto my back, and stared into the darkness as tears slid quietly down my face.

I should have been overcome with relief that my husband, even in his injured state, was still with me, but the image of him lying stone still on the hospital table had lodged in my mind. My chest tightened until I felt like the air was being squeezed from my lungs, and I clung to the side of the bed, trying to still the quiet sobs rocking my body. I didn't want to wake James.

I needed to be stronger and not dwell on things I couldn't change. James wasn't dead. He was traveling around Europe and working. So what if he had a few beers? So what? I needed to be grateful, not upset that the European adventure we were on looked vastly different than I had imagined.

Eventually, I calmed myself, got my laptop, and spent the rest of the night immersed in my edit letter.

Europe ground to a halt. A massive snowstorm hovered over the continent, making travel nearly impossible, but James refused to give up on Paris. He had promised me a few extra days there once he finished work, and he was desperate to make it happen.

At the Milan airport, Owen and I guarded our luggage while James worked with the airline staff to change our flights into train tickets. He hobbled along the counter line, unable to stand upright because of his stitches. His excruciating movements underscored what a terrible idea this trip was.

I should have pushed back harder and insisted he cancel. So why hadn't I? Was it selfishness, or had I not wanted to see the extent of James's injuries? After all, the doctor said he'd be fine, but I could see he was hurting. His nightmares had worsened, his temper had shortened, and he was drinking.

Yet, I wholly believed love and time would fix him.

James limped toward Owen and me. "The airline will send our checked bags to the hotel." He fanned out train tickets. "Let's get to the station. I want to see if I can move us to first class because there's only standing room in coach."

"There are no seats?" I asked in confusion. "Then what do we do?"

"Stand." James shuffled toward the exit and motioned for us to follow him.

We couldn't upgrade our tickets, and fifteen hours later, after a detour to Munich, we arrived in Paris past midnight, exhausted and crabby.

James hailed a taxi and waited for me to give the hotel address to the taxi driver. My fuzzy brain fought the transition to French, a language I knew well, but was hesitant to speak even under the best circumstances. I mumbled something semi-intelligent, and we were whisked through the snow-laden Parisian streets to a cute boutique hotel a few blocks from the Champs-Élysées.

After saying good night to Owen, James and I settled into our cozy room. As I climbed onto the ridiculously high bed, I realized that in the busyness of city-hopping, we hadn't called home once.

"Can we call the boys?" I asked. My phone wasn't set up for international calls.

"They're in school," James snapped. "They won't know."

I paused. James always called the boys when he traveled. In fact, he always called every night. It was strange he hadn't mentioned calling at least once.

"We could leave a message." I pulled the stiff, white sheet

over me and topped it with the duvet. The radiator clanged and blew out lukewarm air. "They're probably wondering—"

"I guarantee they don't care." James sank into the fluffy pillows and flicked off the side table light. "Go to sleep."

"But—"

"Tomorrow." He spoke more gently. "We'll call tomorrow after I'm done working."

I marked his foul mood up to being tired and let it go. He was right. We could call tomorrow before the boys left for school. After all, the nine-hour time difference made timing difficult.

The next morning, the luggage still hadn't arrived, and James was furious. I lay on the bed, trying to read *Anna and the French Kiss* while he yelled into the phone.

"How can no one know where six bags are?" James shouted. I held my finger to my lips, telling him to speak softer. He glared at me and yelled into the phone again.

This had to be his work mode: the side of him I never saw because he saved all the good bits for us. But Owen, who he worked closely with, also seemed confused by this version of James. It had to be the stress of the trip mixing with jetlag mixing with painkillers and his injuries. There was no other explanation.

James tossed the phone on the bed. "The airline says the train company has the bags, and the train company says they never received them."

"Oh." I turned my book over in my lap. "What are you going to do?"

"Owen and I have to find loaner equipment." James bashed his fist into the bed. I recoiled, unused to this type of anger. "Why the fuck did he check the expensive-ass equipment? That's idiot move 101."

"Babe, cut him some slack. This isn't Owen's fault."

He waved me off and disappeared into the bathroom. I climbed off the bed and assessed the luggage situation. If I could fix part of that, maybe James would calm down.

We'd been wearing our clothes for over twenty-four hours and had no toiletries. I didn't even have my hairbrush, and a ratty bun sat high on my head. If our luggage didn't arrive soon, no shower was going to help our clothes' rank smell.

James emerged from the bathroom and put yesterday's clothes back on. His tense shoulders had relaxed during the shower, and he seemed calmer. He gave me a slight smile. "Have fun today."

All he needed was a shower. He just needed a moment to regroup and realize how worked up he was.

I smiled back at him. "I think I'm going to pick up a few necessities for us just in case the luggage is lost for good."

"That's fine, but don't go crazy." James's earlier foul mood had evaporated, and he tugged on his winter jacket. I helped him put his shoes on, and when I stood, James gave me my three kisses. "I'll see you tonight."

After he left, I quickly showered, put on my dirty clothes, and twisted my filthy hair into a low bun. I stared at my makeup-free reflection and dark eye circles and was surprised to see how ragged I looked. Granted, I hadn't slept well for days because James's nightmares kept me awake and my own brain wouldn't shut off, but this was something more. Fear, maybe? Or confusion?

James was fine. This trip would be hard even if he weren't injured.

I pulled my wool peacoat over my sweater, grabbed my crossbody bag, and headed toward the Champs-Élysées.

Despite my promise, I did go a little crazy, and when I finally met my friend Victoria at Ladurée, I was laden in shopping bags. We double kissed, and I arranged the shopping bags at my feet. I was going to need a new suitcase to get everything home.

"How are you?" Victoria exclaimed once we were seated. "Are you enjoying Paris?"

She didn't know about James's accident, and I decided to not say anything, which, in a way, made everything feel like a dirty secret.

"We got in late last night, but so far, I love it."

Ladurée's waiters performed careful dances around each other with silver trays balanced high over their heads, and patrons laughed while drinking tea and eating delicate pastries and macarons. A blend of languages surrounded us, and I felt like I had dropped into a movie scene.

Victoria nodded. She now lived in Paris with her family, but we had met a few months earlier while our sons were on a photoshoot in San Francisco. Over the course of two days, she had confided she wanted to be a writer and planned to move to Paris after her divorce.

And here we were seated in Ladurée, in the most beautiful city in the world.

Things changed so fast.

When the waiter handed us menus, Victoria asked if I wanted her to order for me, but despite my nervousness, I gave ordering a try and felt accomplished when the waiter understood me.

"What are your plans while you're here?" Victoria asked.

I almost said, "Keep my husband from being upset," but instead, I rattled off restaurants and museums James and I wanted to go to after Owen returned home.

"What are you doing these days?" I asked, enjoying the normalness of the conversation.

Victoria told me about her new life—the art, the culture, the people she had met—and she beamed happiness. Moving to

Paris had been the right decision, and she felt that she had an exciting new page to fill.

She was brave and adventurous and everything I was not. I barely left my San Francisco neighborhood and would never move across the world let alone with three young children.

After tea, we kissed good-bye and made promises to see each other again, but I knew that unless Victoria came back to San Francisco, she would just be someone I once met.

I didn't recognize it as a moment that would change the trajectory of my life.

It doesn't matter who you are or what time of year it is, Paris is transformative. There's a gentle, comforting ease to the city that says, "Your worries don't exist here," and that's how it was for James and me after Owen left. Paris soothed us. My franticness disappeared, James's nightmares stopped, and everything felt normal.

As hazy, afternoon light faded into dusk, I dragged James through the nearly empty streets of the Marais. When we popped into shops where perfectly styled French women greeted us with "Bonsoir!" I discovered I was afraid to speak French and would whisper phrases into James's ear. He had no qualms butchering the language, and the saleswomen were pleased he tried.

We followed ancient, twisting rues until we crossed a busy street and found the empty courtyard of Place des Vosges. Snow-laden tree branches hung precariously low, and footprints dotted the perimeter.

James pointed at a snow-covered bench. "Want to sit? We've been walking for hours."

"Can you sit?" I asked.

James laughed, and I lapped up the sound. "Only if I get to sit with someone as pretty as you."

I playfully hit his arm. "Stop."

"I mean it. You look beautiful in your hat and big coat with snowflakes in your hair."

My heart swelled. This was the James I knew. Kind James. Loving James. Sweet James. That other version had been Work James, but now that work was done, he'd returned to normal.

I hopped on James's footprints through the snow and waited as he cleared the bench with a gloved hand. When I sat, he pulled two macarons from a white paper sack and offered me a choice.

I picked the vanilla, leaving him with his favorite, pistachio.

"We could live here." He spoke slowly, between bites, like he'd been mulling it over. "You'd like it."

I nodded, thinking of Victoria and her new life. I was mildly jealous of her. "Can you imagine the boys here?" Excitement spilled into my words. "Our little French boys. It would be fun!"

James clasped his hand over mine. "I mean it. We could."

Along the far side of the courtyard, a mother pushed a stroller, and I imagined walking around Paris with my boys. I'd teach them French, and we'd spend weekends doing oh-so-European things like going to museums and having drinks at cute cafés. Maybe in the summers we'd even vacation in the south.

That life was filled with newness and excitement. It wasn't something I had thought possible before this trip, but James had brought it up, so maybe we could have it?

James had closed his eyes and rocked back and forth in a slow, soothing way.

"James?"

His eyes opened. "What?"

"Why do you think we should move here?"

He hesitated. "You always talk about moving abroad. It would be an adventure."

Something wasn't right. I was the one with the crazy ideas, not James. He was a stay-the-course guy; I was the one constantly pushing him to try new things. It was how we worked.

"You don't want to go back to San Francisco, do you?" I asked.

"Not really." He sighed. "I don't know if I can go through that intersection again."

That made sense, but moving away from the entire city? Still, I was unwilling to let go of the dream James had seeded, and I played along. "What about your job? Could you work here?"

"I might be able to." He crumbled the paper bag. "I'd have to look into it, but I think it would be good for you."

That struck me as odd since he'd said he wanted to get away from San Francisco, but I didn't point that out.

I nibbled my macaron, wanting to savor its sugary sweetness for as long as possible. There was no one else in the courtyard now, and James offered me his hand, but I stood on my own.

When he threw his arms around me and pulled me close, I clenched my teeth to fight back tears. My husband was alive. That should have been enough. He was alive and with me in Paris, so why did my heart pound and my mind race? Why was I so scared?

A strange sadness hung over me as we walked to the Métro. We had had a nice conversation, a vacation conversation, the type everyone has when they're charmed by the prospect of doing something different, but I would never be adventurous like Victoria and move to Paris.

4

July 1997

"Pick a day." James's words tickled my ear. I rolled over on the twin bed so that our chests touched, and my leg draped over his. Even though we were both fully clothed, it was intimate.

"Why?"

James untangled himself from me and stood. His childhood bedroom had a collection of baseball caps hanging from the picture rail, and his dad had taken over half the room with a computer desk and precariously stacked cardboard boxes. It had a strange storage shed feel.

He pulled a calendar off the pale-blue wall and fanned the pages. His eyebrows shot up, and he smiled. "Do you have a date?"

I folded my arms. "You're not going to tell me why?"

"Give me a day, and if it's a Saturday, I'm going to ask you to marry me."

My heart stopped. We'd been dating for six weeks, and the summer had sped by in a haze. The day after I met James, I ended a three-year relationship to be with him. I knew how I felt, but until that moment, I wasn't sure his feelings were as strong as mine. After all, we were only twenty.

"August 1st, next year," I answered and then prayed, prayed, prayed I picked correctly.

He turned to the back of the calendar and cocked his head. "It's a Saturday."

"Liar." I tossed a pillow at him, and he ducked. It hit the dresser and fell in a lifeless lump to the floor.

"No, really." James glanced nervously at me, and my heart sank. He didn't really want to get married. It was a silly game. He crossed the room and sat down next to me on the bed. He took my hand and squeezed. "Do you want to?"

It wasn't the proposal of my dreams, but it felt inevitable because if I knew anything, it was that James and I were meant for each other.

November 2010

After two more lovely days in Paris, James and I had to leave. We had an early morning flight and still needed to pack, and snow flurried around us as we strolled toward our Parisian hotel.

Our stomachs were full, and James hadn't winced in pain once as we visited the Musée d'Orsay and ate our way around town. It was a perfect ending to our trip. The accident, while still fresh, seemed fuzzier and less real. If it weren't for James's hobble and his need for painkillers, I may have forgotten about it completely.

We waited under a streetlight as cars and scooters zoomed past us in a blur. James tightened his grip on my gloved hand, and I turned my head to smile at him. In that single moment, a scooter spun out next to us, dragging the rider into the intersection. Horns blared.

James tensed. He yanked at my hand like he wanted to get away from me.

The rider stood and righted her scooter, seemingly unhurt, and continued on her way.

James's eyes went blank, like he was somewhere else, and he folded into himself, rocking back and forth. His hands went to his head, and he grasped it hard as if trying to pull something horrible out.

"I should have died."

"What?" I reached for him, but he backed away until he pressed against the stone building behind him. With nowhere else to go, he slumped to the wet, snowy street, and his hands tore at his hair.

What had happened? Why was James saying he should have died? "James? Sweetheart, are you okay?"

His vacant eyes didn't focus on me. "I should be dead," he muttered. "I should be dead."

"No." I pushed away my confusion, knelt next to James, and embraced him tightly. "No, you absolutely shouldn't be dead." I pulled his hands away from his hair and pressed my hand to the back of his head, the way I did with the boys when they were scared or hurt. "You are meant to be alive. We all need you."

James's body sagged against mine, and a long sob tore out of him. There was no one on the street. Just us. Sitting in the snow on a Paris rue. Clinging to each other, unsure what we were supposed to do.

I drew in a breath to clear my mind. I needed to get James back to the hotel. It was only a block away. "Can you stand?"

He kept staring at the spot where the scooter had been.

"James?" I shoved my arms under his and hefted him up. "I need you to walk with me. It's not far, okay? We're almost there."

He didn't fight me, and when we arrived at the hotel, I hurried him upstairs to our room.

"I'm sorry." James's face twisted. "Oh, God, I'm so sorry. I don't know what's wrong with me."

I didn't either, but I was going to stop it. "It's okay. I'm here."

Because his shoulders still ached, I helped James out of his coat. Then I bent and untied his shoes, another task he couldn't do, before removing my own outerwear.

James lay down on his side on the bed and pulled a pillow over his head. Sobs shook his body, and I stretched out next to him, my hand on his back, trying to keep the fear swirling in me at bay. James was the one who wiped my tears, but I now needed to comfort him, and I didn't want to do it wrong.

I wished I could ask Molly. She'd know how to fix everything, but I knew James wouldn't want me to tell her. He wouldn't want to worry her.

I lay there for hours, holding my husband and trying through sheer will to make whatever haunted him go away. I decided that if James couldn't be strong, I'd dig deeper and carry both of us. After all, I had promised in sickness and in health, and for better or worse.

I wouldn't let James down again.

In the morning, before the sun peeked through the small window, I quickly dressed and packed before waking James. He had slept soundly without a nightmare, which felt like a victory, but I knew he was not well. As I checked for forgotten items, James waited silently on the bed. I tried making him laugh by singing some kiddie song, but he only stared.

My unease swelled. James had slipped away into some dark corner of his mind, and I had no idea how to reach him.

"You're home!" Leo sprinted across the room toward us. Worried he may hurt James, I blocked Leo and picked him up.

He was tiny for a seven-year-old and still loved when I held him. I nuzzled his copper-brown hair, and he giggled.

"I missed you!" I said, giving him a kiss on the cheek. "Where are your brothers?"

"They went with Grandma to get French bread."

Ryan and Tate were also ecstatic to see us, and I couldn't get enough of their hugs and kisses. We'd been gone ten days, but it felt like years. I could never travel the way James did. I would miss Ryan, Leo, and Tate too much.

"Sit down." I pointed at the sofa. "Dad and I have presents for you."

The boys ran to the sofa, knocking into each other, and settled into a pile. James and I often commented that we were lucky because our boys genuinely loved each other and never physically fought. Maybe it was because I had told them a new brother brought more love into our family, or maybe they were simply well-mannered kids, but their bond was strong.

James eyed the boys carefully like he was making a serious assessment of them. I held my breath. He'd barely spoken on the flight home, and I worried about what would tumble out. "Leo," James said. "I see you're trying to grow a beard."

Leo roared with laughter. "I'm seven!"

"Ummm." James squinted. "Ryan, have you been going on dates?"

"No!"

I giggled. This was how things should be. James's breakdown in Paris was a release of the stress he'd been carrying, and now that he got it out, he'd be fine.

"Mom?" James turned to me. "Do you think they deserve presents?"

"Well, Grandma said they've been very good."

The boys squealed, and James stuck his hand into a bag I had retrieved from the kitchen table. He handed each boy candies and a small souvenir. While the boys examined their gifts, James shuffled across the room to the kitchen table and leaned against it.

"Do you have my pills?" he asked.

"That bad?" I dug around in my handbag where I had kept his painkillers and deposited the bottle in his hand.

James grimaced. "I'm sore from the flight."

We hadn't discussed what had happened with the scooter, and I didn't know how to approach it. I believed James would talk to me when he was ready, but as I watched him dry swallow his pills, I realized I had no idea what he was thinking, and it struck as strange. I had always been confident in my ability to know James's mind, but now I felt adrift.

It was close to bedtime, and Molly had already given the boys dinner and baths. James stretched his arms over his head. "Whose turn is it to pick the story?"

Leo jumped up and down. Of the three boys, he resembled James the most with dark-brown hair, deep-brown eyes, and honey-colored skin. I always thought James favored him over Ryan and Tate, not blatantly, but just enough for me to notice.

When James was home, Leo was his constant companion, wanting to help him with everything. Leo was, in many ways, a mini-James not just in looks but also in personality. We referred to Leo as our family spokesperson because he would talk to anyone about anything. His kindergarten teacher had suggested finding him an agent, so we did, and Leo had been in several TV commercials and print campaigns. James loved showing off Leo's *Pottery Barn Kids* covers.

But that night, James skipped over Leo and pointed at Ryan. "What do you want to read?"

44

Leo's face fell. "Daddy, it's my turn."

Ryan's gaze ping-ponged between his brother and James. "It's Leo's turn, Dad."

With a frown, James rolled his shoulders back. "And I said you get to pick, so go pick."

I placed a hand on my husband's arm, eager to calm him down. "What are you doing? Everyone agrees it's Leo's turn."

James huffed. "Either Ryan picks, or there's no story."

Leo's chin quivered, and I stared slack-jawed at James. "I'll read the story," I said, hoping to defuse the situation. "Leo, go pick."

He dabbed his eyes with tiny fingers and ran down the hallway to the room he shared with Tate. He came back with a well-loved copy of *Captain Underpants*, and I took the book before arranging myself on the couch so the boys could sit around me.

As I read, I occasionally caught a glimpse of James scowling at the four of us. Eventually, he stormed off to our room.

After I finished tucking the boys in, I checked on James. He sat on the edge of the bed with his head in his hands.

"What's going on?" I asked. "You seem annoyed with Leo."

His eyes were red from crying. "You guys don't need me."

"Why do you think that?" I straddled him as he leaned back and rested my hand on his smooth cheek. "Of course we need you."

James shook his head. "They didn't want me to read the story."

I tossed my hands up in frustration. "You wouldn't let Leo pick the story, and it went sideways from there."

James blinked slowly. "What?"

"You don't remember?"

"I . . . I saw you take the book, and the boys sit down with

MIA HAYES

you, and I realized that I'm not that important. Anything I do, you can do better."

I drew my brows together. "This is crazy. The boys adore you, and we all need you."

James didn't say another word. He rolled out from beneath me and buried his face in the duvet. His ribs rose and fell for a minute until he was asleep. I had no idea what had happened during story time, but his behavior hadn't been normal since we saw the scooter spin out.

It's just jetlag, I thought, trying to calm the persistent feeling that James wasn't okay. *That's all it is. James is exhausted.*

Next to me, James snored softly. I changed my clothes and climbed into bed. I needed a way to show him how much he mattered to us, but nothing I did was helping, and he seemed to be getting worse.

I picked up my phone. The doctor said James might have a mild concussion, but what if it was more severe? What would those symptoms look like? I spent the night in a Google rabbit hole, researching concussions and making a plan to fix James.

5

December 2010

We were only home two days before James boarded a plane for Japan. The Asia portion of his trip would last two weeks and have him hopscotching from Tokyo to Beijing to Shanghai and, eventually, to Hong Kong. My heart knotted at the thought of him walking out the door for fourteen days, but I couldn't leave the boys again even though Molly and Joe both assured me I could.

The boys, Molly, Joe, and I watched James drive away in the taxi from our front porch. After he was gone and the boys had run off, I stood there trying not to cry. How could I keep James safe from himself if I weren't with him? I had briefly considered asking Owen to look out for him but decided James wouldn't want coworkers to know he was struggling.

After I finished my evening routine, and the boys were tucked into bed, I dove back into my edit letter, desperately trying to focus my mind on something other than James.

I never slept that night. I paced the house, folded laundry, watched bad TV, and messed around online. When the boys woke up, I gave them breakfast, made their lunches, and got them into their uniforms. Molly had offered to take the boys to school, but I wanted to do it. I hadn't seen my schoolyard friends since before the accident, and I wanted them to know that James was fine. He survived, and we had had a wonderful time in Paris together after a grueling week of work.

When we arrived in the schoolyard, Laurie immediately zeroed in on me. "Hey! How was Paris? How's James?"

"It was great, and he's doing well." I paused. "He left for Asia last night. The man never stops!"

Roselyn joined us. Her red hair was pulled back tightly, and she bit at her lip like she was trying not to say something.

"What?" I asked.

Laurie shook her head.

"What?" I said again.

Roselyn sighed. "I saw the accident. On Van Ness." She covered her mouth with her hand. "If I had known it was James, I would have stopped. I really would have."

"Oh." My chest heaved.

"It was raining so hard, and there were police and ambulances everywhere." Roselyn's voice hitched up like she was holding back a sob. "I'm so happy he's okay. It really is a miracle."

It was a miracle. James could have died. I had been avoiding that truth. My husband nearly died.

"He was wearing a helmet." I tapped my head and forced a smile. "It's what saved him."

"With only a few bumps and dings," Laurie added. "You both are so lucky."

Kids darted around us, waiting for the bell to ring. Their shouts and laughter filled my head as I stared blankly, trying to stop the whirling of my heart and the pounding of blood in my ears. Roselyn had seen the accident and felt it was a miracle James survived. Was it worse than I allowed myself to believe?

"You know, I have to run." I took a step back. "Errands before Tate gets out of preschool."

I raced home, fighting the red-hot whooshing noise in my head. With trembling legs, I climbed the two flights of stairs to my flat and crumbled onto the couch.

Fear, confusion, worry, and relief swirled inside me until the storm erupted. James's thrashing nightmares and my own imagination had created graphic scenes in my mind, but Roselyn confirmed what I had refused to acknowledge: James shouldn't have walked away.

I cried until my throat ached and my eyes were sandpaper-rough.

I didn't know how to help James, but even worse, I didn't know how to stop the frantic feeling consuming me. Death had poked fun at us and left a long trail of confusion.

When I calmed down, I splashed water on my face and reapplied my eye makeup. I was no good to anyone like this, and I had to get Tate from school. I had errands to run and boys to raise. Life was going to go on whether I felt scared or not.

The rest of James's trip passed quickly, and I kept myself busy, so I didn't think. The boys went to school and sports practice, and I ran errands, visited with friends, and chugged ahead. If I could keep going, I wouldn't think, and if I didn't think, I wouldn't worry, and if I didn't worry, I could stop the images in my mind.

Just keep going.

Every afternoon around one, I'd walk downstairs to visit Molly. Strangely, we rarely discussed James. To me, it felt like a betrayal to bring up my concerns. Instead, Molly and I stuck to easier topics, like arranging childcare so I could attend the PTO meeting or recipes we saw on Martha Stewart's show. The fluid movement of our family between flats should have sparked some sort of conversation about James's strange behavior, but neither Molly nor Joe broached it with me.

Every night, James called to say good night to the boys and to catch me up on his day. He was eager to get home and watch Ryan play on the fourth grade basketball team, but he never asked about Tate or Leo, so I told him funny stories about them. It was Ryan, however, that James fixated on, and when I called him out on it, he replied, "Well, he's the one who actually does interesting stuff."

James, despite his fondness for Leo, had never overtly shown a preference for one of the boys before, and I gasped. "Don't ever let them hear you say that."

"Right."

"Right?" I asked. "What does that mean?"

"Nothing."

It felt like we were veering close to an argument, and the thought chilled me. James and I never fought, and if we disagreed, we talked things through calmly. Neither of us were yellers or dwellers, and our conflicts were always handled swiftly and without grudges.

Hoping to turn the conversation, I said, "I can't wait to see you tomorrow."

I missed James more than anything, but really, I wanted him home because not knowing if he was okay at all times had turned me into an emotional mess.

"Bee?"

"Yeah?" I kept my voice upbeat.

"I love you."

James came home a few days before Christmas, more exhausted and grumpier than when he'd left. But all of us— Molly, Joe, the boys, and myself—ignored the red flags and focused on the miracle of James being alive.

We celebrated Christmas with our tiny, extended family and spent New Year's Eve alone, watching the ball drop on TV. As the clock struck midnight, relief settled over me. 2010 was behind us. The accident was behind us. James was okay, the boys were healthy and happy, and I was on the verge of launching a writing career. James's accident was a blip that wouldn't carry over into the new year.

We needed a fresh start, and I clung to the public version of James's recovery: he was miraculously fine. Since the day in the schoolyard with Laurie and Roselyn, I had told the story so much that it had become my murky truth.

In mid-January, my agent, Kathleen, asked me to come to New York to meet with editors. The editor who had originally expressed interest on the day of James's accident had brought my book to her editorial board, but they passed. Now, Kathleen wanted me to meet a few editors in person. She thought it could make a difference.

James and I arranged for me to tag along on his next business trip. He warned me we wouldn't see much of each other— just a nice dinner one night—so I made plans to meet up with friends when I wasn't running around New York with Kathleen.

After a long day of meetings, I returned to our room. It was near midnight, and James wasn't back. He hadn't called or answered my texts, and at first I convinced myself it was because he was busy at the conference, but as the clock ticked closer to one, my stomach churned.

I waited. And waited. And waited. I paced the small space in front of the TV and fought the growing unease in my gut.

I tried calling James again, but it went straight to voicemail. He had warned me about the late nights, but this seemed excessive. And why wasn't he answering his phone?

My chest constricted as I tried to draw a breath, and I bent over, hands on my knees. Where was he? What if he was trapped in the elevator? There's no phone service in those. I staggered toward the unmade bed and tears stung my eyes. I knew my reaction was not rational, but I couldn't stop the tightness in my chest. Something had happened to James.

Memories of him lying on a hospital table overwhelmed me. James had been pale. So pale. And eerily still. And I couldn't go to him. I couldn't walk into the hospital room until Molly forced me.

I failed him.

My vision blurred and the room swayed. What the hell was wrong with me? Why couldn't I breathe? Why was it suddenly so hot? I clasped my phone and tried calling James again. When he didn't answer, I stumbled toward the closet and put on my shoes. I would find him even if it meant searching the entire hotel. He wouldn't be left on a cold table alone again.

A key card clicked against the door, and James crept into the room. I let out a long, relieved wail.

"What's wrong?" He rushed across the room to me. "Bee, baby, what's wrong?"

"I . . ." Images of James lying dead somewhere flashed through my mind again, and I struggled to draw a breath. "I thought something had happened to you," I stammered. "You were gone for a long time, and you didn't call or text and—"

James tucked a loose hair behind my ear. "I'm here, and I'm okay." My crying shook my body, and James caught my face between his palms. "Hey. I'm okay. Nothing bad happened."

"I'm sorry. I just . . . I don't know why I'm like this." I lied, maybe not intentionally, but deep down, I knew why I agreed to Kathleen's request to come to New York, and why I left the boys again. I could not bear to be away from James. I was constantly on edge, and I couldn't relax when I didn't know where he was.

I sniffed. "You should get ready for bed. You're probably exhausted."

"Oh, Bee. Honey, I'm sorry. I didn't mean to take so long. Time got away from me." James sat next to me on the bed and stroked my back. The faint smell of something alcoholic tickled my nose.

"Were you drinking?" I asked.

James stopped rubbing my back and dropped his hand. "It's a work conference. We drink at those."

"Oh." In Europe I had discovered Work James was different than Home James, so why was I surprised? "Do you always drink?"

He shrugged. "Yeah. It's part of the job." He ran his hand to the base of my neck. "Don't worry, I'm not drunk."

I frowned. I didn't disapprove of the drinking, I just felt cut off from a part of James's life. Other than late work nights and drinking, what else did he keep from me? I studied the side of his face as he focused on the shabby carpet. I had no idea what James was thinking. I had, strangely, believed I knew James inside and out, but this revelation that he had a separate life, one that didn't include me, was startling.

My stranger-husband squeezed my hand. "You're okay now, right?"

"I think so."

"That's my girl." James kissed my forehead. "Thanks for understanding." He stripped down to his boxer briefs and dropped his clothes on the desk chair. "Bed?"

I climbed under the sheets and let him wrap his arms around me. As his body jerked to sleep, I fixated on James having an entire world, one I only had little glimpses into, outside of me and the boys.

Maybe I didn't know him as well as I believed.

Saturday morning, a snowstorm threatened to shut down the airports, but James hailed a cab, tucked me inside, and placed a kiss on my forehead. He would be home Monday, but I needed to get back to the boys.

"Are you sure you'll be okay?" he asked. It was a fair question. Even though we flew frequently, I always traveled with James.

I chuckled. He worried about me too much. "I can manage."

As I walked through the airport, a weird sense of being untethered settled over me. I had forgotten I was capable of doing things without James, and I didn't like it. James or the boys were always with me, so this feeling of aloneness was like a shrunken wool sweater stuck around my head—uncomfortable —and I couldn't wait to take it off.

As I settled onto a chair at my gate, a thought hit me: when James went away, did he feel lonely? Or did he feel free? And if he did, did he like it?

Throughout the rest of the winter, James didn't travel much —just a quick trip to New York to meet with a new communications contractor. But other than that, he was home with us. Our lives resumed the smooth rhythm we had before the accident, but James was different, and so was I. He spent more time alone and struggled with his memory; I stopped socializing and quit my writing group. Even the boys had changed. Their play was quieter and less raucous because I had explained that James startled easily now and loud noises scared him.

We all tiptoed and danced around James until shortly after my birthday in March. James's mood was increasingly sour and his nightmares more frequent. In desperation, I asked him to see a therapist.

James agreed but never took action, so I reached out to a school mom who was a therapist. Theresa sent me a few names, and I called each one to find someone who could see James. All but one therapist were booked for months, and I quickly scheduled a late afternoon appointment for the next day.

James roared when I told him what I had done. "You told Theresa?"

I had been prepping dinner and held a chef's knife in my hand. I turned around. "She's a therapist. She can help."

"Put the knife down." James took a step back. "Put it down."

I dropped it on the counter and stared at him in confusion.

"She's going to tell everyone." James clenched his jaw.

I wiped my hands on my jeans. "Tell them what?"

James refused to look at me.

"What are you afraid she'll tell them? Everyone knows about your accident." I hugged him and rested my head against his chest, listening to his steady heartbeat. His arms, which would normally embrace me, hung limply at his sides. "Everyone is amazed you walked away. I think it's understandable that you may need a little help to get through this."

He yanked away from me. "I'm not weak."

"I didn't say you were. I just want you to check in with someone, okay? Can you do that? Your nightmares are keeping me up, too." I played the card I thought James would respond to most: impacting me.

He let out a long breath. "Okay. I'll go."

"Thank you." I turned around and picked up the knife again. I gathered a bunch of green onions in a pile and chopped them. "If it's horrible, you don't have to go back."

There was no response. I glanced over my shoulder. James was gone.

J une 2009

I sat in the middle of my office, labeling and sorting merchandise. I'd been awake nearly twenty hours and had no desire to sleep. My new company's launch was the next day, and I wanted to make sure everything was perfect. A space had been booked, invitations had been sent, press was coming, and I had to —absolutely had to—nail this.

"Bee, you need sleep." James stood in the doorway. "Or at least have dinner. When did you last eat?"

I shrugged. "Breakfast maybe. I think I had an apple or a bar or something."

James glanced around the room. "And gallons of Coke from the look of it."

"That too." I straightened my aching back and stretched. "Do you think it's going to go well?"

"Absolutely. The site is fantastic." James moved boxes out of the way and sat on the floor next to me. For the past six months, he'd encouraged my lastest endeavor—launching an e-commerce site focused on San Francisco style. I had been a wardrobe consultant and stylist but having a store had been my dream, and now I was doing it.

"But, babe"—he touched my arm—*"you need to sleep. You can't keep on like this. You're not superhuman."*

The thing was, I often stayed up for days and never felt tired. I chaired PTO fundraisers, ran three to five miles a day, owned a business, parented, and was a wife without dropping a ball.

"Admit it, I'm a little bit superhuman," I teased.

James rolled his eyes. "I'll admit it if you come upstairs and go to bed."

"I'll rest after the launch party." I stuck a sticker on a package.

"Promise?"

"Promise."

April 2011

James was depressed and suffered from PTSD. That was the official word from the therapist. Our tiny bathroom counter now displayed a variety of antidepressants—some that seemed to work, some that didn't. Ever the eager student, I threw myself into learning everything about both conditions and decided that, in addition to therapy and drugs, James needed healthier food.

I could control that.

James needed organic foods grown in perfectly balanced soil, so the boys and I spent hours planting, tending, and harvesting our garden. Until that point, I'd grown whatever I felt like, but now I had a mission. Grocery store organic labels couldn't be trusted; I wanted a year-round producing garden that would provide all our vegetable needs. James needed vitamins and antioxidants and low-metal loads.

Every meal I made was balanced to have the best brain-healing properties. I banished gluten and soy and stretched our food budget to include grass-fed organic meats and milk deliveries to the house. Our small flock of chickens provided our daily eggs, and the boys loved tending to them. I made caring for James into a game: Daddy's brain broke, and we were going to put it back together.

But no matter what I did, the James I knew—the sweet, loving, devoted husband and father—faded away. He isolated himself from us, and his once-beautiful smile grimaced when he thought I wasn't looking. I still wrapped him in my arms when he had nightmares and calmed him when he grew frustrated by small tasks, but it often felt as if he existed in a different dimension than the rest of us.

Many things I had previously explained away now made sense: James's fight or flight reflex, his inability to tolerate loud noises, his subtle pulling away from not only me, but the entire family. One of the stranger side effects was that he became a blurter, saying things he shouldn't. Like the time he walked up to Laurie in the school yard and told her she had amazing tits. Everyone laughed because it was so unlike James, and I laughed too, but inside I knew it wasn't funny, and his growing list of symptoms worried me.

Mental illness wasn't a phrase ever spoken in my family growing up, but my mother had been erratic with a famous temper and was often unpredictable and prone to crying. James's behavior reminded me of her, and I worried about my boys being exposed to the chaos I had lived my early years in.

Through this, I tried to keep things as normal as possible for the boys. After school, they'd do homework and have snacks. James mostly (although, he'd recently started coming home later and later) arrived home before six, and we'd eat at six thirty. Then Molly and Joe would give the boys baths at their flat, and I'd tuck them in at seven thirty. Before the accident, James and I loved this routine because it gave us several hours of alone time, but he had started retreating to the bedroom after dinner, leaving me alone in the evenings.

One rare night, James joined me in the family room after the boys had gone to bed. I hadn't expected him and was stretched out on the sofa waiting for *Game of Thrones* to begin. James lifted my foot and set it on his lap. For a few minutes, he gently kneaded the ball of my foot.

"That feels nice," I said. James had barely said two words to me since coming home from work.

He grunted and rub my foot harder until it felt painful.

"What?" I yanked my foot away.

He stared at me with flat and lifeless eyes. It was like he wasn't really there.

"Are you okay?" I asked.

He inhaled for a moment before exhaling through his mouth. "I don't remember anything."

"Oh!" I said. "Well, in the last episode—"

"No." James dropped my foot. "I don't remember anything. Like the kids. Or you."

"What?" I furrowed my brow. "You know who we are."

His eyes were vacant. "I know you're my wife, and they're my kids, but I don't know how we got here." A strange, strangled sound escaped his lips. "I don't remember marrying you."

Something heavy pressed against my chest, crushing my lungs. "I'm not sure I understand." I gulped at the air. "You have amnesia?"

James dropped his head like a man confessing his deepest secret. "My therapist thinks I may have a brain injury."

The room dimmed and my ears buzzed. *Go to him.*

I crawled down the couch toward James. "You do remember us. I know you do." I embraced James, and he relaxed against me. "It's in there. I know it is."

"It's not just you, Bee. I'm struggling at work. I can't

remember shit. I have to write notes on everything or things get forgotten."

Was this the reason he engaged with us less and less? "Do you . . ." I paused, trying to find the right words. "Love us? At all?"

"I think so." James rested his chin on my shoulder. It was sweet and intimate; how could he not love me? "I want to."

He wanted to love us. I clung to that.

"How do we find out if it's a brain injury?" I needed something concrete to work with.

"There are tests, but it's going to cost a fortune."

Immediately after the accident, we had briefly discussed suing the driver of the truck, but he was only nineteen and made a bad decision. James survived, and we didn't want to ruin the kid's life.

"We could sue." I leaned back to better see James's reaction.

His glossy eyes stared off at the corner of the room. "I've already reached out to a lawyer."

"Oh." He always consulted me on major things, and this felt major. Why hadn't he mentioned it earlier? "Have you found someone?"

He nodded. "She's arranging for the tests. She thinks I have a strong case, but it will take a year or more to pursue."

"A year?"

"Or more." James flicked the TV off. "I'm going to bed."

"Don't you want to watch *Game of Thrones*?" I needed some sense of normalcy. Something to take away the shock of his admission.

He didn't respond.

"Do you want me to come with you?" I swung my leg off the couch to stand, but James blocked me with his arm.

"I want to be alone." His monotone words were devoid of emotion.

"But—"

He bristled. "You don't need to babysit me. Your hovering is driving me crazy."

"But—"

"Please. Just stop." He set his jaw hard. "This isn't about you."

"How can you say that?" Confusion swirled inside me. Everything about James was about me, too. We were a team, and his emotions often became mine also. "My husband doesn't remember me or our children. Of course this is about us, too."

"The boys will be fine." James waved his hand dismissively. "They don't need to know."

"Kids pick up on things. Trust me."

"Then you need to protect them." Despite his unnerving calmness, his words tore at me. Was he asking me to protect the boys from him? And if that were the case, was he worried about hurting them?

"You have depression and PTSD. If we told them, it would explain so much." I studied his blank face. "Trust me, being honest with the boys will help all of us."

James kicked the throw blanket that had fallen to the ground. "I'm going to bed. You can watch *Game of Thrones*. I'll see you in the morning."

"Please," I begged. "Please let me come with you."

"I need to be alone." He stomped away.

I fell back on the couch. James didn't remember us, and he believed his behavior was going unnoticed by the boys. His ugly actions were more understandable, but they still hurt.

I curled up on the couch, trying not to cry. My parents divorced before I was five, and their fights filled my earliest memories along with trips to court, sitting in judges' chambers, and screaming matches between my new stepmom and mother. Those arguments resulted in assault and battery charges and restraining orders.

I didn't want that for my boys. They deserved better. They deserved to feel loved by both James and me, something he claimed he couldn't do.

I stared at the steel beams crisscrossing the cathedral ceiling of the family room. My parents' fights crept into my mind, but one altercation stood out. My dad had pulled up in front of our home, and my mom had barred the door. I'm not sure how long it had been since I last saw Dad, but I missed him. As he and my mom screamed at each other through the screen, I pushed a chair to the backdoor, undid the deadbolt, and ran down the driveway. Dad hugged me tightly before pushing me into the car.

I stayed with him after that, and my sister joined us after the judge granted Dad sole custody. To this day, my mom points to a decision I made at age five as one of my greatest flaws: I chose my dad over her. Her lack of custody forced her to move from Detroit to San Francisco, leaving my sister and me behind. She left, but in her eyes it was, and remains, my fault.

I had lived with the guilt of driving my mom away my entire life, and I refused to make the same mistake with James. I couldn't deny he felt smothered. He wanted space, but I didn't know how to do that, and the more he resisted my attention, the more I persisted. He needed to know how much I loved him, and everything I had read about depression said to not give up on the patient. Sometimes all the sufferer needed was prodding and consistency.

But what did James mean by not remembering us? Was this a new development, or something he'd hidden for months? My brain churned through facts. He knew me in Paris and New York, but after that trip, he had begun to retreat into himself.

He was also constantly panicked and frantic. He could no longer remember where he put his keys or his bag, or even conversations we had just had. For months, I'd overlooked all this and covered for him when he'd forget a good friend's name or where he was in a conversation.

Without me realizing it, my life had become running in front of and behind James, trying to keep him—and us—together.

Emily wasn't what I expected from a personal injury lawyer. She was young—around my age—and perky. As we sat in her spotless office, she explained that the lawsuit would be a drawn-out process full of additional testing for James, and our lives would be open to scrutiny.

She said we needed to ask for $750,000.

Optimism battled with worry as we walked out of the office. James would be required to give the details of the accident over and over again—something he refused to talk about, even with me. Could he handle it?

James slipped his hand in mine as we walked toward the car and gave it a squeeze, a hand hug as we called it. "I think we should do it," he said. "I want to."

"Are you sure?" I asked. "It's a little overwhelming."

He unlocked the car. "I need to do this for us. We're swimming in medical bills."

I never saw the bills anymore because James would grab them from the mailbox and drop them into his work bag before I had a chance to look. Before his accident, I had handled our finances, but now James insisted on being in charge. He claimed it was to take a few household chores off my plate, but he also refused to discuss anything financial with me. I now had a meager monthly allowance for groceries and household expenses, and often had less than ten dollars in my account.

Being in medical debt worried me. I still hadn't been able to sell my book despite interest from numerous publishing houses, and the belief I didn't contribute enough to our family dogged me. When I expressed my concern, James always reassured me that staying home with the boys was the most important job I could do.

"I could get a part-time job," I said. "Your mom would help with the kids. I don't mind."

James pulled my door open. "You are not getting a job. That's embarrassing."

"What?" Two years earlier he had no problem with me opening a business. In fact, he had been my biggest cheerleader. "How is me having a job embarrassing?"

He hardened his jaw. "I make plenty of money. We don't need additional income."

"But if we are swimming in debt—"

"You're not getting a job." The sharp lines of his face softened. "Besides, when would you write?"

James loved telling people I was an author, and it had become a central part of our public image. If I stopped writing, we wouldn't be as interesting as a couple. Still, I'd go get a job if it would help.

"I wouldn't write." I pretended like the thought didn't upset me. "Or, I'd just have to make time between everything else. It's not a big deal."

"Don't be crazy. You love writing." James walked to his side of the car and opened the door. "It's going to be okay. Trust me, we're not poor."

"We're going to sue?" I wasn't completely onboard with his decision. It felt wrong to go after a teenager, even though Emily explained that it would be two lawsuits: one against the driver's insurance company and one against his employer's.

"We need to." James backed out of the parking spot and tore out of the garage.

We needed to. We weren't poor. Everything was going to be okay. It didn't add up, but I didn't raise my questions out of fear of upsetting James.

When we got home, James immediately called Emily and told her to proceed.

7

M
ay 2004

James climbed the stage stairs as I reached around Leo to clap my hands. My nine-month-old mimicked me and smacked his pudgy fists together. "That's Daddy," I said, kissing the top of his slightly bald head. "Daddy did this for us."

From the seat next to me, Molly reached over and squeezed Leo's chubby thigh. "He loves all of you very much."

It hadn't been our plan to have two kids while James was in law school, but that's what happened. To support our family, he worked full-time during the day and drove an hour each way to school at night. After Ryan was born, we decided that I should stay home because daycare in San Francisco was too costly. It had been a four-year grind.

After his grad party, I surprised James with a limited edition Panerai watch. Before having the boys, James and I backpacked around Italy, and he fell in love with the brand in a Florence shop. It seemed like a fitting present for a law school graduate, and for three years I saved money each month to afford it.

James hefted the heavy watch from the box and stared at me in disbelief. "Are you serious?"

"You deserve it."

He set the watch down and took my hand. "Would you be mad if I didn't practice?"

"What? Why would you not practice?"

"I want to see my family. I don't want to miss any more of the boys' lives, and if I work for a big firm, I'll never be around."

I leaned against our bed and stared up at him. "What was it all for then?"

"If you want me to practice, I will." His shoulders drooped, heavy from the years of working himself to death.

He didn't want it, but he'd do it for us.

I couldn't ask that of him.

June 2011

It had been nearly seven months since the accident. Our dream of moving to Paris had been forgotten, and life took on a familiar rhythm that comes with work and kids. The anxiety I felt when separated from James lessened, and I began going out with my friends and volunteering again—but only when Molly was home to help. I worried that the boys would exhaust James, and he'd lash out at them.

As a couple, we went to dinner parties, attended every sports game together, and presented a unified front. Aside from my closest girlfriends, no one ever asked about James's health, and when they did, I would pivot the conversation. Instead of confiding in anyone, I wrote happy blog posts and upload enviable pictures to Facebook most days, making sure we always looked perfect to the outside world.

Privately, James and I were struggling. I couldn't admit it to anyone because he had asked me not to, and I wanted to respect his privacy. James worried that if people found out he had PTSD, it could impact his job. It was a fair concern given how small our community was and how many of our friends were in overlapping professional fields.

Because of my lies, our friends and family heralded James's recovery as a miracle. Everyone was impressed by how fast he bounced back, and I found myself reciting the same story over and over again: he was hit by a white pickup truck making an illegal left turn from the center lane. His head bounced off the concrete, and he was hooked to the undercarriage. It dragged him twenty feet. His left wrist was saved by the Panerai he wore. We were blessed.

We pressed forward and refused to acknowledge how precarious the situation had become.

One weekend in mid-June, we escaped fog-drenched San Francisco for a day at Johnson's Beach on the Russian River. Leo and Ryan kayaked up and down the dammed river while James splashed with Tate along the bank. I lounged under an umbrella and nibbled on an ice cream bar while looking at my camera.

Every once in a while, I snapped a picture. My obsession with photos had grown since Facebook had become a thing. My friends and I broadcasted the minutiae of our lives on the website, and it was an effective way to chronicle the parts of my life I wanted to remember. I'd snap and delete, snap and delete, until finding a picture that captured the mood I wanted.

When I landed on a picture of a widely smiling James floating in an inner tube, my heart swelled. He rarely smiled even though he'd been taking antidepressants for nearly ten weeks. I studied the picture—it was definitely Facebook-worthy.

James carried Tate toward me and plopped him down on the blanket at my feet. Tate was a preschooler now, and I had baby fever even though my doctor told me to never get pregnant again. Each pregnancy had been increasingly difficult, and Tate's had left me on bed rest for seven months while hooked to a backpack of IV fluids to combat hyperemesis. Because of this, James elected to have a vasectomy six weeks after Tate's birth; he didn't want to risk my health. A baby, no matter how hard I willed it, would never happen.

"Want to go for a walk into town?" James rubbed more sunblock over Tate's rosy skin. "Maybe grab something from the sandwich shop?"

"Let me get the boys." Johnson's Beach sold hotdogs and hamburgers and all kinds of sweets that we had already fed the boys. I waved at Ryan and Leo, beckoning them into shore. "Ryan can watch Tate and Leo for a few minutes."

Ryan was nine, Leo seven, and Tate four. They had all inherited James's mellow personality, and I never worried about them misbehaving. If I told them to do something, they did it without question. We left them sitting under the umbrella and eating ice cream, even though they'd already gorged on junk food.

Town sat outside the entrance to the beach. There wasn't much to it, just a few small shops and a real estate agency. We stopped at the agency window, and I pointed at a cute house. "It's only $350,000."

James touched the window, pointing at another house. "I like this one better."

I had dreamed of buying an easy-to-escape-to retreat. Guerneville was a short hour north of San Francisco and more affordable than homes in the city. In my mind, we would spend summers and holidays along the bank of the Russian River. Usually, James gave me an absent-minded bob of the head when I started up about it.

"We wouldn't be able to go to Palm Springs as much," he said. A few years earlier, we'd bought into a year-round time-share and spent every free minute soaking up the dry desert heat. "Could you give that up?"

"Yes," I answered before saying the unmentionable. "When we settle this damn lawsuit, I think we should seriously look into buying here."

James's body went rigid. I'd said too much.

"I have another evaluation this week," he said, carelessly, as if it didn't matter.

"Oh?" He had never mentioned it.

"I hate them." In order to proceed with the lawsuit, James was subjected to endless psychological tests and depositions that dominated our life. They left him exhausted, and it wasn't unusual for him to sleep for a day afterwards. He refused to tell me anything about them—not even his doctor's name—so I did my best to be supportive with the limited information he gave me, but if I had known the toll the lawsuits would take on both of us, I never would have agreed to suing.

"Is it the last one?" I asked. Emily warned us of how taxing it would be, but now that we were living it, it seemed unfathomably harder. Plus, we both desperately wanted to put the accident behind us and move forward. James needed to forget and reliving the accident during therapy and endless tests wasn't helping him.

"I hope so." James tugged at my hand, and I smiled. The day had been perfect and felt like our pre-accident life. "Let's get sandwiches before the kids wonder what happened to us."

I glanced at the picture of the house James liked. "You like that one?"

"I can see us there." He winked at me.

James saw a future with us, and I naively believed it meant things were getting better.

Like everything else during that time, every step forward resulted in three back.

The next round of evaluations confirmed James's therapist's suspicion that James had a previously undiagnosed traumatic brain injury which impacted his ability to retain new information and recall parts of the past. The ER had never performed a brain scan and instead had diagnosed him with a possible mild concussion. At the time, I had been reassured he'd be okay because he'd been wearing a helmet. A TBI had never occurred to me.

Even though the diagnosis was devastating to James, it brought me relief. I now had something to fix, and like with PTSD, learning about TBIs became my obsession. I took notes and compared James's symptoms to typical ones: headaches, anger, confusion, inability to follow conversations, and so on. My free time was spent researching treatments and speaking to doctors.

Over dinner one night, I eagerly shared my latest promising research. James stared out the window as he ate and ignored me.

"James?" I asked.

He blinked as if trying to focus on my face. "What?"

"Don't you want to get better?" The boys had finished eating and had run down to Molly's for their baths, leaving James and me alone.

He scowled, an expression I still wasn't used to. "I'm fine. This is who I am now. Like it or leave."

It was a slap across my face. "No. You're wrong. I found a doctor in Houston who—"

James shoved away from the table. "No one can fix me. You need to accept that."

"I won't, and you shouldn't either." I scooped up our plates. "You can get better."

He shook his head. "I should have died. Isn't me just being here enough?"

"No, it's not," I said without thinking. "I want my husband back. I want you to remember us. I want to feel like we are a family again." I dumped the plates into the sink. "This doctor in Houston works with veterans, and he's had a lot of success. At least talk to him."

James stepped toward me before halting. "Bee, I'm not going to get better. Either accept me as I am or don't." His eyes glistened. "I'll understand if you want a divorce."

"A divorce?" The word ricocheted through me, punching more holes in my already confused brain. The gaps in the once-solid wall surrounding our marriage widened. "Why would I want a divorce?" My voice shook. "I would never do that. Never."

"I'm broken," James said. "This isn't fair to you or the boys." His arms hung heavy at his sides, and he stumbled into me. I caught his dead weight and leaned against the counter for support.

Holding James up had become a habit.

I rubbed large circles across his back. I was trying to calm him as much as myself. James thought I didn't love him. Was I not trying hard enough? What else could I do?

"Don't let a bad couple of months overshadow fourteen good years." Wetness seeped through my shirt where James rested his head, and I blinked back my own tears and tried to calm my pounding heart. "I promised in sickness and in health, and I'm keeping my promise."

"I don't deserve any of you."

"You do, baby. Trust me, you do."

For our anniversary in August, I gifted James a treadmill and organized the garage into a workout room. I had read about running programs for vets and believed it was exactly what James needed—an outlet to channel his PTSD anger. Plus, he had gained weight since the accident, and it was hurting his self-image.

James started running. First it was just little jogs on the treadmill, then around the block, and before long, he started running home from his office every day. It was a brutal route that took him up several steep San Francisco hills, but the emotional and physical results were impressive. He dropped weight fast, and his scowl faded.

New shoes, tracking devices, and running clothes became his obsession. He formed friendships with coworkers who also ran and traded tips with them. At their insistence, he signed up to run a 10K through Golden Gate Park on his thirty-fifth birthday, and he spent most of his free time training.

Neither James nor I recognized the dangerous slope he was on. I only saw that he did everything I asked: going to therapy, exercising, and fathering our boys. In fact, he and Leo had started having weekly dates to Japantown, and I took these changes to mean he was improving, and divorce hadn't been mentioned again.

Over the course of the next two months, James ran every day and posted his progress on Facebook. School parents commented how great he looked, and it seemed as if we had turned a corner. James acted better, but I now understand how sick people become experts at saying what other people want to hear, and that very few people actually look close enough to see what's really going on.

My fear of James blurting or acting inappropriately lessened, and in the middle of September we left the boys with

Molly and Joe to attend my friend Allison's weekend-long wedding in Lake Tahoe. We had reconnected after she moved to San Francisco and met up three mornings a week to have our asses kicked by our personal trainer. Out of all my friends, she was the only one who questioned my public version of life with James.

As we drove into the mountains, I sang along to the radio, trying to get James to laugh. Every once in a while, he'd chuckle and roll his eyes, and I considered it a good start to the weekend. Since he started running, he laughed more and wasn't having as many nightmares.

We deserved a fun weekend after the past ten months.

At the resort, we changed our clothes and, eager to go out without kids, headed to the rehearsal dinner. Allison had more friends than I could count, and the massive party took over the entire restaurant.

"Are you having fun?" James's breath tickled my ear, and I reached my hand around to touch the back of his fuzzy head. He planted a kiss on my collarbone.

"Yes." I turned to face him. "Are you?"

He rattled his old-fashioned and smiled. "I am."

This was how things were supposed to be. James and I were supposed to touch and kiss and flirt. We had always been that couple, and we could be that couple again.

I kissed his cheek, and James rested his hand on my hip. "I'm going to go talk to some of the girls," I said. "Are you okay here, or do you want to come with?"

James didn't know anyone other than Allison, but he'd been welcomed into a group of guys near the bar. "I'm good. Go have fun."

I spent the next couple of hours laughing with friends, and the anxiety I had become used to lessened. Around two in the morning, the bar emptied, and I went looking for James. I found him on the patio with a small group of guys, smoking a cigar, and holding a half-full glass.

"I'm tired." I leaned my head against his arm. "Do you want to go?"

"Not really," James slurred as he bumped into the guy next to him.

"Whoa, buddy. Maybe you've had enough." The guy steadied James.

"I'm good." James set his cigar on a table and dug into his jeans' pocket. He stumbled forward a little, and his drink spilled over the side of the glass. "I'll be up later. Here."

He tossed me the room key.

I caught it. "I think you should come with me."

"Naw. I don't need a babysitter."

I took a deep breath. I often smelled the aftermath of James's drinking sessions, but I had never seen him sloppy drunk—not even when we were in college. I touched his arm. "You should come back with me."

James pushed my hand away and stumbled into the wall.

One of his new friends grabbed his arm. "You need to sleep this off."

Anger twisted James's features. "I'm fucking fine."

I tried taking his arm again. "Baby, c'mon. Don't make a scene."

"Stop telling me what to do!" James stepped toward me and crashed into a high-top.

"Let's go." I linked my arm through his and gave a weak smile to the other guys. "The party's over."

James stared at me with drunk, unfocused eyes. "Fine."

He could barely walk and needed me for support. I led him back to our room and to the bed where he passed out before changing his clothes or taking off his shoes.

I unlaced his boots and shimmied the blanket out from

under him. After I washed my face and changed, I climbed into bed. James reeked of whiskey, and I had to turn my back to him.

In the middle of the night, he woke and fumbled around the room for a minute before opening the closet and peeing all over my suitcase full of clothes.

When I flipped on the light and saw what he was doing, I shouted at him. He just shrugged and went back to bed.

Over breakfast, we laughed about it with our tablemates, but I was livid. I had to send my clothes out to be washed and wore yoga pants and a T-shirt to the daytime wedding festivities. Everyone else thought it was a hilarious story, and that made me feel as if I was being too judgmental. After all, it was a wedding and excessive drinking happened. I needed to loosen up.

At the wedding reception that night, the cycle repeated, only this time I joined James and drank my way through the evening. I hadn't been drunk since college, and I didn't know when to stop. James ordered me back to the room, but not before I signed the wedding book with, "I wish you all the happiness James and I have. Xoxo," and my heart sank. I was not happy, and I was growing afraid of James's erratic behavior.

The next morning, as I hugged the toilet, James scoffed at me. "You're a lightweight. Get dressed. You need something in your stomach."

How was he fine? How did he drink more than me without the slightest hangover?

At breakfast, James had several Bloody Marys and teased me for being weak. Maybe it was my hangover, but I'd never felt more miserable. Where had my kind, compassionate James gone?

8

November 2009

"Hey, Bee." James's smooth voice came heavy through the phone. "It's late, but I wanted to say good night." He was in Europe doing his annual filming while I was home taking care of two sick little boys. It hardly seemed fair.

"I miss you," I whined. "I'm lonely."

"I miss you, too. I'll be home soon." He yawned into the phone. "Hey," he said this time with more energy. "I read your blog post today. I loved the outfit."

"Really?" The week before, I started a blog called Mom Wore This that chronicled my daily outfit and schedule. The boys took pictures of me, and I did a write up to accompany them.

"Yeah. You looked hot."

"Is it too vain?" I asked.

"No. I like it. It's very you. But Jesus, I didn't realize how busy you were every day."

"Mom life," I answered with a laugh.

We bantered back and forth, me filling him in on the minutiae of my life, and him telling me about White Nights in Paris and how he *and his coworker found their way into a bunch of parties. He was now in Rome.*

"I thought this was a work trip?" I teased.

He sighed. "It is, but we have time at night. I can't work twenty-four seven."

"I wish I had a fancy work trip." With a two-year-old, the most exciting thing I ever did was leave the house without a diaper bag.

"Maybe next year you can come with me," he said.

"Really?"

"Yeah. Let's make it happen."

November 2011

November arrived again, which meant James's busy travel season was in full swing. He had hopped on a plane for New York hours after Leo's birthday dinner and had flown home for a few days to coach Ryan's soccer team in their championship game. Unfortunately, James got a call from his boss and suddenly needed to leave for New York that night—he would miss the game.

His schedule had him coming home a few days before Thanksgiving and the anniversary of his accident, and it finished with a two-week trip around Asia. He'd be home just before Christmas. It would be a month of travel, and I worried about his mental health.

Originally, I was going to join him on the European leg again, but my increasingly busy writing schedule wouldn't allow it. My agency had decided to publish my first book for me, and it was coming out December 5th. Plus, I had taken on more ghost-writing jobs, and my agent had sold the foreign rights of my trilogy to a German publisher. They'd already cut my first check, and I needed to turn in a draft of the next book in mid-January. Traveling with James was out of the question.

As I read a story to Tate on our bed, James meticulously packed his luggage. He always traveled light, taking only a carry-on, and needed to fit ten days' worth of clothes in it. He wrapped his running shoes in plastic bags and placed them at the bottom. Then he layered on his running clothes and finished with his suits.

Since returning from New York earlier in the month, James had been spending two to three hours a day pounding the pavement. Admittedly, I resented all his alone time, but if it helped his brain, I couldn't object. He ran because I suggested it.

"I'll miss you," I said as he zipped the suitcase shut. Tate had taken the book from me and flipped back to his favorite part. He was four and couldn't read, but I had read the story to him so many times he had it memorized. He pointed at the words and recited the story.

James studied Tate and me for a moment. "Same." There was no warmth in his voice, just a strange flatness, like he was simply saying what I expected him to say. But when he bent and planted three kisses on my forehead, I felt like I had read too much into his words. James scooped up Tate and hugged him tight. "I'll miss you, buddy."

Tate ran off toward the family room when James set him down.

"You should call the team before you get on the plane," I said. James had never missed a soccer game in his five years of coaching, and the kids were sad he was missing their championship game.

"Good idea. Keep your phone on." He pushed the navy curtains I had sewn aside and peeked out the window. "My cab's here." He stuck his head into the hallway. "I'm leaving!"

The boys and I followed him down the steep staircase to

the porch. I threw my arms around James's neck and kissed him good-bye. He tensed, and I stepped away. Before his accident, James had been the more affectionate of us, always holding my hand when he drove and rubbing my feet while we sat on the sofa at night. I, however, often flinched when he unexpectedly touched me. Since his accident, we had changed places.

Molly joined us on the porch, and she hugged James. He tensed again. *At least it isn't only me.*

"Be good. Be careful. Don't do bad things. I love you!" I called out as James hurried toward the sidewalk.

He dropped his bag into the trunk and slid into the backseat without looking up to see the boys and me waving good-bye.

James called before the soccer game, and I put him on speaker phone so he could give the team a pep talk.

"He's such a great coach," Dara said. Her son had played on James's team since kindergarten. "I love his commitment."

I smiled. "I know. He's heartbroken he can't be here."

Mac, a no-nonsense dad who always intimidated me a bit, nodded. "I don't know how he does it with all his travel."

"He just loves coaching." My heart swelled with pride. James really was a great guy. Everyone could see it.

Through the phone, James told the team to do their best, play hard, and bring home the win. The kids cheered in their huddle around me. When he was done, I placed the phone to my ear as the team ran off to start the game.

"Way to go, Coach! You got them fired up!"

James had already hung up. He hadn't waited to say good-bye to me.

The referee blew the whistle to start the game, and I stared across the bay. It was a beautiful sunny day, and the rough water glistened beneath the Golden Gate Bridge. It captured how I felt: my life looked perfect, but inside, the turmoil was becoming more constant. My hair was falling out, my stomach always hurt, and I struggled to sleep more than two or three hours a night.

James never called to get the result of the game and disappeared into Europe. I only knew he was alive because Owen and I were Facebook friends. When I finally did hear from James after a week of silence, it was a rushed conversation telling me he needed to stay an extra two days in Rome to finish filming—something about reshooting a few executives.

"The company is paying for you to stay longer in Rome? I should have come, too!" I joked.

"It's work," James said sharply. "Don't give me grief about fucking work."

I was taken aback. "I'm sorry. It was a joke. That's all." A now-familiar sick feeling swelled in my stomach. "I just wish I were with you."

"It's not vacation. I'm working." James paused. "I've got to go."

After he hung up, I sat on the edge of the sofa, holding back tears. Our trip to Europe the year before hadn't been ideal, but it had been special. Had James forgotten? Was I asking too much?

Giving Thanks
Sunday, November 20, 2011

My husband is alive.

I say this so often, I suppose it's become my mantra: my husband is alive. He's alive, and I should be thankful.

He's alive even though a truck struck him, dragged his body twenty feet, and pinned him beneath a back wheel. He stayed under the truck, growing colder, until paramedics removed him.

The doctors told me it was a miracle his injuries weren't more extensive or life-threatening. Many people aren't as lucky.

His very existence should be enough.

Perhaps I'm selfish, wanting more than I've been given. But last year—two days before Thanksgiving—this accident robbed me of the gentle laid-back man I married and replaced him with someone fragile and erratic. In addition to two dislocated shoulders; a broken wrist; street burns down to the skin on his knee and ankle; and a deep, long gash requiring numerous stitches, he suffered a front brain injury— similar to football players who have had multiple concussions—and post-traumatic stress disorder. In a few awful seconds, his personality shifted.

No one knows if he'll ever be the same.

Immediately after the accident, he couldn't tie his shoes or get dressed or shower without help. He could barely walk, let alone carry his work gear. Yet he insisted on going on a two-week business trip to Europe just four days after the accident. So, I left our boys at home with family and tagged along on his work trip—first to Europe and later to New York City.

"He needs me," I'd explain to our family and close friends. "He can't be alone. He has nightmares and freaks out when he sees a motorcycle or white truck." I started turning down social invitations. I couldn't leave him with the boys. He was too angry, and I didn't know what he'd say to them.

And while there is truth in that, it isn't the real reason.

His accident scarred me, too. It left me with panic attacks, the inability to sleep, and so, so much fear. Even a year later, the thought of being away from him sends my heart racing and leaves me gasping for breath. Sometimes, I just sit on my bed and cry when he's gone. And he's gone a lot. Weeks at a time.

The truth is, I'm barely functioning. I'm angry I can't make him better. No matter how many times I put the pieces back together, something comes along and knocks them over. Again and again.

We—he and I—put on smiles in public and pretend it isn't happening. We're good like that. A team. That's the one thing that hasn't changed.

But our boys know. Kids are smart that way, seeing what you don't want them to. They watch me flail as I try to figure out how to stop letting this damn accident spill over and hurt everyone. How do I prevent my boys from growing up thinking their dad is a jerk who yells? How do I keep him from saying things he doesn't mean—or even want to say? How do I keep my family from imploding? How do I stop being so angry?

The hardest part is that he looks great—healthier even. He's lost fifty pounds in the past five months. But sometimes I watch his face as he struggles with what he knows he shouldn't say. Swallowing, swallowing, swallowing each word until something less offensive comes out.

And yet, somehow, what he does say still smarts.

He has no short-term memory and often can't recall what he said or did moments earlier. It's frustrating for both of us. Especially when he hurts one of the boys' feelings and doesn't understand what's happened to make our son cry.

My heart breaks watching him struggle. It shatters when I realize I can't fix him.

Yet I am thankful. Because he's here, holding my hand. Telling me we'll get through this. Somehow. The two of us.

My husband is alive. And I am thankful.

My finger hovered over the button. All I had to do was push it, but I hesitated. I'd spent two days writing the blog post commemorating the anniversary of James's accident. It was raw and heartfelt, and exposed everything James and I had been hiding for a year. I should have sent it to him privately, but it was the age of oversharing.

Naively, I believed James would see the post as a testament of my love and my commitment to our marriage.

Still, I hesitated. Did I really want everyone to know? Could I betray James's privacy? Was it wrong to want to tell my story?

The past year had worn me down. My friends commented that I never went out anymore, and my response was always that James was traveling so much that when he was home, I liked to spend time with him.

If I published this, everyone would know I'd been lying, and they would see James differently. Was that fair to him?

Was it fair to expect me to keep hiding the truth? No, it wasn't.

Before I could change my mind, I pushed 'publish,' and a deep sense of relief swelled inside me. The truth was out there, people would know, and maybe we would get support. I linked the post to my Facebook account, knowing James usually checked Facebook during the day, and I waited anxiously for him to call me.

Two hours later, the call came.

"What the fuck?" he growled. "Why did you post that?"

I bristled. "What's wrong with it?"

Since coming home from Europe, James's temper had ratcheted up. He screamed at the boys for no reason, locked himself in our bedroom for hours, and refused to talk to me. Molly and I marked it up to the anniversary of his accident. It was the only thing that made sense.

"You know exactly what's wrong with it."

"No, I don't." I blinked back tears. "Why are you being so mean?"

"Take it down."

"No."

He slammed down the phone, and I gasped in disbelief. Stunned, I opened my laptop and logged into Facebook. My post had over a hundred comments, each one expressing support. I furrowed my brow. Was pissing off James worth it? After all, my point wasn't to upset him, but to show him how loved he was. I had done just that. Hundreds of people had liked my post.

I left it up.

9

November 2011

Thanksgiving weekend, my mom invited the boys to her vacation home, and not wanting to rock our precarious relationship, I agreed. Over the years, James repeatedly pointed out the unhealthy nature of my relationship with my mom, and on several occasions, he had confronted her. It always ended the same: with her crying about how she had done her best and that our perception was unfair.

Her inconsistent attitude about acting like a mother was a pattern I worried about repeating with Ryan, Leo, and Tate. When I was eighteen or so, Mom told me she didn't like me, but she'd always love me. Despite her cutting remark, I clung to the hope that she would at least like me and one day love me as much as she did my siblings. So, it isn't strange that I did not turn to her for help during this time. After all, she told everyone that she liked James better than me, and I had gotten lucky.

James was perfect. I was the one with the problem.

Mom's invitation had been a surprise. Even though she lived only forty minutes south in Silicon Valley, she rarely made time to see the boys and often used my much-younger brothers as a reason for not being able to come visit. James and I debated whether or not the boys should go—he argued for and I against. In the end, my desire to make James happy after the Thanksgiving-from-hell won out.

On Thanksgiving Day, James had refused to interact with anyone, and I spent the day crying while I cooked alone. The only picture we have from that day is of our family plus Molly and Joe lined up in front of our house. James stands behind me with his hands shoved into his pockets, and I smile. It's a nice family picture on the surface, but if you look closer, James's eyes are crazed, the boys aren't smiling, and I am vacant.

Our drive into the mountains was uncomfortably quiet. The boys watched DVDs, and I tried telling James about the great things I wanted to do. He grunted a few responses but didn't say much else.

I had dreams of us sleeping in, grabbing brunch, going to the movies, and having dinner at a non-kid-friendly place. But really, all I wanted was sex and more sex. That was my coping mechanism, and the sadder and more scared I felt, the more I turned to sex to fix things. Since the accident, even if he seemed angry with me, James and I had sex four or five times a week.

At my mom's, James goofed around with my younger brothers and our boys on a tree swing that dangled dangerously over the edge of the mountain. I discussed logistics with my mom and fought the urge to tell everyone to be careful on the swing. When the boys finished their turns, James climbed on.

A few years ago, I found a picture of James on that swing. I don't know who took it, but James's smile is wide as his body flies through space over the mountain edge. When I look at the picture now, knowing everything that came after that moment, I wonder if James felt free or did he pray the rope broke so he could plummet to his death?

I recently showed him the photo, and he doesn't remember

anything about that day. I am not surprised since I heavily edited our stories for him during this time, picking and choosing the best parts, trying to create the history I desired. It's disorienting to have a lifetime of memories with someone who only remembers the bits you tell them, and if this picture didn't exist, James could argue the day hadn't happened.

But with this concrete evidence, James acknowledges that we did drive the boys to my mom's, and after smothering them with good-bye hugs and kisses, we must have started the three-hour drive back to San Francisco.

I didn't tell James about what happened after we left until recently. I held the story back, happy to let it slide away.

Here's my version: in between me prattling on about a movie I wanted to see, I scanned my phone for nearby restaurants. James had given up fast food, and I thought eating on a patio— something we couldn't do in San Francisco—sounded amazing. We had just pulled off an exit in Sacramento when my mom called to say we had forgotten to leave the car seats.

As I spoke, James guided the minivan into a crowded gas station parking lot. He glared at me as he listened to my end of the conversation. When I hung up, I shrugged. "I can't believe we did that!" I winked, trying to be playful. "I guess we were in too much of a hurry to get home."

"This is your fault." James bashed the steering wheel with his fist. "You were so eager to leave that you forgot about the boys."

James, my James—the one that left that rainy November morning—would never act like this. He would have laughed and commented on how we get even more alone time. It would have been a nuisance, not a catastrophe.

"We both forgot," I said. "Mom asked both of us to get the car seats. It's a mistake. No big deal."

"You're the mother," James snapped. "Your only job is to

remember shit like this. Can I even trust you with them when I'm gone?"

His words zeroed in on my newest vulnerable spot: my ever-present belief that I was not a good mother. I knew it, and James knew it, too. Good mothers put their kids before their husbands. Good mothers protected their children. I was doing neither.

After Leo was born, my girlfriends and I would gather at the park for playdates. All of them had been career women before stepping out of the workforce, and I was the youngest of the group by eight years. As stay-at-home moms, we organized preschool fundraisers and enrichment activities.

One afternoon, between handing out snacks and mediating playground conflicts, we had a lively discussion about Lisa Belkin's controversial *New York Times Magazine* piece, "The Opt-Out Revolution." The older women in my group believed they could slide back into the workforce once their kids attended full-time school, while the younger women felt raising kids was a fulfilling life passion. The consensus was that child-rearing was a higher calling than work, but work shouldn't be removed from our list of options. Husbands came after everything else.

"I disagree," I had said, digging my toes into the playground sand. We had been sitting in a loose circle at the edge of the play structure. "James will always come first, because if we don't have a strong marriage, we can't provide Leo and Ryan with the love and attention they need."

Stephanie had shaken her head. "You're wrong. Marriages end all the time. Kids are forever."

"She's right," Lisa had added. "You should make the kids the center of your life, not your husband. And keep your job skills sharp." She had handed a string cheese stick to her preschooler. "Even the most content wife needs an escape plan."

"Why would I need an escape plan? You've met James. He's the most loyal, devoted husband ever." I had adjusted Leo in my lap and scanned the playground to find Ryan on the monkey bars.

"You should always be prepared," Stephanie had said.

That night, I had recounted the conversation to James. He told me I was right, and I too came first for him. He promised to always take care of me. There was no need to worry about my job skills unless I wanted, and I never needed to worry about divorce—I was his everything.

As we drove back to my mom's, I wondered if I had been wrong all those years earlier. I spent so much time trying to fix James—and by extension, our marriage—that I neglected the boys. I knew this but had comforted myself with the fact that the boys had Molly and Joe to fill in for me emotionally and physically.

James was right. I was their mother. I needed to do better. Did that mean I needed to give up on him? And if I did, wouldn't that cause more damage to the boys? After all, my parents' divorce had long-reaching tentacles that still whipped at me and stung.

As we drove, James's steely forward-facing gaze chilled me, and I fought against the nasty words sitting in my throat. PTSD couldn't be argued or reasoned with, and that's all this was. But even in my distressed state, I knew his behavior had grown worse. Something had changed when he returned from Europe. Maybe he had stopped taking his antidepressants? Or maybe that trip and the time of year was triggering memories of his accident from the year before?

Whatever it was, I needed to support James through it, repair my marriage, and give the boys a stable, loving family again.

"I'm sorry." I touched James's arm, and he yanked it away. "Why are you so angry with me?" I asked. "It's just a few extra hours. You love car rides, and we get to spend it together."

"You're what's wrong." He kept his eyes on the road as he

sped up the side of the mountain. "You. All you do is take take take. Want want want. Try being a giver for once. How about that? Can you just try being a giver?"

My eyes stung. Did James not see everything I did for him? The way I ran in front of him, clearing the way of anything that might cause him pain? Did he not see how I wanted nothing more than to help him remember our life together and for him to be the dad he once was?

I pressed my head against the air conditioned-cool window. The distance between James and me had become tangible, and his silence felt cruel, like he had cut me out of his life.

When we arrived home, we were both starving since we never stopped for dinner, but James retreated to the bedroom and slammed the door. I stared in confusion at the barrier separating us. The entire ride home, I had sat silently mulling over his words. Maybe I was a taker. Maybe this was my fault. He had been through a horrific accident and forgotten large pieces of his life. Who wouldn't be upset and angry about that?

I knocked softly on the bedroom door. "Do you want dinner? I'm hungry."

James flung the door open. His once-gentle eyes flashed in anger. "Yes, I want to eat, but I don't know if I want to do it with you."

"What's wrong?" PTSD or not, I'd had enough. "You're being an asshole. This is supposed to be a nice weekend for us, but you're making it miserable." In frustration, I shoved him on the chest, and he took a step backward, bumping into the wall.

The narrow hallway was only three feet wide and opened

onto a steep, curving staircase. Our bedroom door sat five feet from the top of the stairs, and I stood on the small landing facing an enraged James.

He grabbed my wrists and shook me. Stunned, I froze. In our thirteen years of marriage, he'd only recently started raising his voice and had never been physical with me. The one time he had accidentally hurt me, he hit me in the head with a football. For days afterward, he doted on me, worried he'd given me a concussion.

"Let me go." I pulled back hard just as he released me. I lost my footing and tumbled down the first set of stairs and into the upper landing wall. I fell hard on my wrist, and pain shot up my arm.

"Oh my God. I'm so sorry, Bee. I'm so, so sorry." James raced to me and scooped me into his arms. "Are you hurt?"

I was too scared to cry and pressed against the wall. All I wanted was a nice weekend, and I had ruined it. I should have turned away and made dinner, not confronted him.

"Bee?" James's voice softened. "Sweetheart? Are you okay?"

Relief filled me. This was my James, not the angry, yelling one. I grasped my lower arm. "I think I hurt my wrist."

He touched me gently, and I winced. "Here?"

"Yeah."

"Can you move it?"

I bent my wrist and flinched in pain. "It hurts."

"But you're moving it. That's good. Let's get you some ice." James carried me to the couch and grabbed a bag of peas. "I'll make a dinner reservation, okay? Would you like that?"

"Yeah." My wrist had started to swell and throb, but I didn't want to tell James. I didn't want to worry him.

James placed frozen peas on my wrist. "I'll be right back."

I tried tapping my fingers together, but pain shot up my arm. Panic overwhelmed me. If I broke my wrist, I wouldn't be able to type, and if I couldn't type, I'd miss my deadline. My first novel's debut was two weeks away, and I had dozens of blog interviews that needed written answers for my upcoming tour. My job, and sanity, depended on me being able to type.

I kept making a half-fist, hoping that if I stretched it, the pain would stop. After ten minutes of waiting for James, I walked down the hallway to our bedroom. He sat on the edge of the bed with his head between his hands, and his body shook as he sobbed. "I should have died. I should have died. I shouldn't be here."

Even though my wrist ached, I wrapped my arms around him and rocked him back and forth like I did when soothing one of the boys. "I love you," I said softly. "I love you, and I need you. I would be lost without you."

"Stop saying you love me!" James shoved me away and fell back onto the bed. "I don't deserve it."

In that moment, I realized how far in over our heads we were. Nothing was helping. Not the antidepressants, not therapy, not my love. Nothing.

"I love you, and you do deserve it."

James twisted his face into a scowl. Over the next few months, he'd capture that look on Facebook with his daily self-ies. It was a look that made everyone ask if he was okay. I'd shrug, and say, "James needs to work on his selfie game."

December 2010

"*You wrap like a drunk elf.*" *James balled up a piece of gift wrap and threw it at me.*

After the boys were asleep, tucked into their beds dreaming of what Santa would bring them, we had hauled their presents from the basement to our third-floor flat. This was our tradition: wrap everything on Christmas Eve while eating cookies. We'd already celebrated with our family over a big meal, and the house still smelled like ham and sweets.

I frowned at the misshapen gift on my lap. "It's a hexagon box. How do you wrap a hexagon box?"

James chuckled. "I have no idea, but that doesn't mean I can't harass you."

Piles of presents covered the small area between the couch and fireplace. James had organized everything into presents for Ryan, presents for Leo, and presents for Tate. The unwrapped ones sat on his left; the finished ones were neatly grouped to his right. Each boy had their own wrapping paper, another of James's ideas.

I had never met anyone who loved Christmas as much as James. His face would light up as he watched the boys open their gifts, one at a time, and he always insisted on doing the holiday shopping, often leaving me surprised by what he bought. This year, despite his accident and travel schedule, he had outdone himself with the presents.

Eventually, I grew tired of wrapping. "I'll write the Santa letter."

James reached out and touched my leg. "Wait a minute." He disappeared down the hallway and reemerged with a wrapped medium-sized rectangular box.

"What's that?" I asked, raising my eyebrows. Every year, we agreed to not buy presents for each other, and every year, he got me something.

He held it out.

I side-eyed him. "I thought we said no presents?"

"Take it."

When I didn't hold out my hands, he placed it on my lap, and the weight caught me by surprise. I cautiously ripped the paper's edge, revealing a familiar logo.

"Are you serious?" My voice ticked up in excitement. I tore off the rest of the paper, tossing it haphazardly on the floor.

"Do you like it?"

I stroked the MacBook Pro box. Even the packaging was beautiful. "It's too much."

"Your laptop is dying, and you've been eying this forever." He leaned over and kissed my head. "Now you can write all your stories without worrying about your computer crashing."

My novel had been on submission for months, and my agent wanted me to keep working on new projects. I hadn't done much writing since James's accident even though he insisted on giving me time to work when he was home.

"I'm going to write a bestseller," I said. "I'm going to make you proud."

"You already do."

December 2011

James didn't send flowers or call the day my first novel debuted, and I was devastated. I kept my phone on me, just in case he did call from Asia, and stayed up all night. I waited. And waited. And waited. He didn't return my calls or texts, and I fought images of James injured somewhere in a foreign country.

Two days later, when the call came, it was a relief.

"Hey! I was beginning to worry." I kept my voice upbeat even though I was upset that he hadn't acknowledged my book release. "I miss you!"

"Can you deposit your book advance money into our joint account?"

A few weeks earlier, despite not being able to find a US publisher, my first book sold at auction in Germany, and I had received part of the sizable advance a few days before James left for Asia.

"Why?"

"My American Express card doesn't work in China."

"You have no money?" I fidgeted with the Velcro strap on my wrist brace. I had a microscopic fracture that didn't require a cast, but I needed to keep my wrist wrapped for a month.

"Not enough for the rest of the trip." He breathed heavily.

Even in our new reality, it was odd that he didn't ask about the boys or mention my book. "Everyone is doing great here! We miss you."

"Can I have the money?"

I sighed. "I'll go to the bank now. How much?"

"Five thousand."

I gasped. "That's almost all of it. I wanted to save it for—"

"I'll pay you back when I get reimbursed."

I pressed my lips together. I had no choice; I couldn't leave James stranded in China. "Okay."

"Thanks." He hung up.

I fought my disappointment while I gathered Tate for the thirty-mile drive to our credit union. First, I had to stop by my local bank to get a cashier's check for five thousand dollars. It was money I had planned on using when we bought our Russian River retreat.

As I handed the cashier's check to the credit union teller, my chest tightened. Why would his firm give him an American Express card if it didn't work in China? James had promised to pay me back once he got his expense check, so why was I concerned? China was known for blocking foreign sites, so maybe they did it with credit cards, too? And besides, it was our money, just like his paychecks belonged to both of us.

Once I deposited the check, I phoned James. My call rang and rang. Finally, he picked up, sleepy sounding.

"Tired?" I asked.

"Yeah. I was taking a nap."

"The money is in the account," I said. "You won't be stuck in China." A low voice mumbled in the background. "James?"

"Yeah?"

"Is someone with you?" I drew my brows together and pressed the phone harder to my ear.

"It's the TV," he answered briskly. "I'm in my room."

"Ah. Right." I waited for him to acknowledge my book, but again, he didn't. "Well, I miss you," I said in my most upbeat voice. "I can't wait until you get home. The boys—"

"I have to go. I'm late. Owen's waiting."

"Okay. I love—"

He hung up before I could finish.

"Ryan, can you put the jelly cookies on the tray next to the kiss ones?" I surveyed the family room. The boys and I had tidied up, decorated the Christmas tree, and made dozens of cookies. "When you're done, put the tray on the table where Dad can see it right away."

"Okay."

Next to me, Tate licked a spatula, and Leo gingerly shook sprinkles on the sugar cookies. We had a fire roaring and the house smelled delicious.

The front door swung open, and James's boots clomped up the stairs.

"Wait until he gets all the way up," I said to the boys. They jumped up and down in anticipation. James had been gone more than two weeks, and like me, the boys couldn't wait to see him.

When James appeared at the top of the stairs, I whispered, "Okay," and the boys flew down the hall to greet him. He stared over their heads at me, didn't say a word, and disappeared into our bedroom.

The boys looked at me in confusion.

"Come on," I said forcing a smile. "Give him a minute."

We waited for James to come back, thinking he was going to give them their souvenirs. Instead, he returned with a sour expression.

"You made cookies?" He narrowed his eyes.

"Mom made most of them," Leo said. "But we helped."

James glared at me. "You didn't make enough jelly ones."

"We can make more, Daddy." Leo turned toward me. "Can't we?" Like me, Leo constantly told James how much he loved him, and like me, James pushed him away. But Leo had inherited my stubborn streak and refused to give up, something I worried about given how terrible loving James made me feel.

"Of course we can make more cookies!" In my socks, I slid across the hardwood floor toward the kitchen area. "We can do it now, and Daddy can help if he wants." Usually, we made cookies as a family, and James always insisted on being in charge of the Hershey Kisses, and he always ate more than he put on the cookies.

But on this day, he scowled. "I have to work."

"You just got home. I think you can take the afternoon off."

"I have work."

I leaned against the kitchen counter. "You've been gone for nearly a month, and I can tell you're exhausted. You should nap. That flight is hell."

James sour-lemon lips appeared. "Someone in this family needs to earn money, and it's not you."

I drew a sharp breath, paused, and collected myself. "Boys, why don't you go see Grandma and Grandpa?"

The boys, probably sensing the tension rolling off James, ran off, leaving the two of us staring at each other.

"What's wrong?" I asked. "You're acting weird."

James collapsed onto the couch. "I'm just tired."

Between his awful attitude and not asking about my book, I was annoyed. The boys and I had a pleasant rhythm when James traveled, and his return threatened it. I sat and faced him. "I know traveling like this is tough on you, it always is, maybe even more now than before, but you can't behave like this toward the boys."

"Sorry." James ran his hand through his hair and stared past me, out the window at the dull, gray fog swirling outside.

After a few uncomfortable minutes, I said, "My book is selling really well."

James blinked. "Oh. Right. Khalie said it's really good."

"Who's Khalie?"

"The coms contractor I work with. She read it and liked it." James smiled at me, and I relaxed. He hadn't forgotten after all, and in fact, had told people to read it.

"Now I'm embarrassed." I giggled. "It's weird thinking about people I don't know reading my book."

James gave a half-laugh. "Get used to it. I have a feeling this writing thing is going to be your career since you're apparently good at it."

It was a Christmas miracle.

James disappointed all of us during Christmas break. Normally, he took the week between the holidays off, but that year he went into the office on the 26th and worked straight through. I spent the time taking the boys ice skating and to nature parks, and I snapped pictures for Facebook to prove what a wonderful time we were having.

It felt like the boys and I were the only ones who saw the changes in James. Was I crazy or expecting too much from him? After all, Molly and Joe never mentioned his behavior to me, and if they spoke to him, I was unaware. And even though I had received great virtual support on my "Giving Thanks" blog post, only Julie and Allison asked me about James, and I lied to them. Aside from comments about his daily selfies, no one mentioned the differences they saw in him—if they saw any at all.

Looking back, it's possible that the false narrative I was actively creating about our lives and James's recovery through curated pictures and blog posts was easier for others to believe than the reality that something was wrong.

James's office was closed on New Year's Day, so he was forced to be home. Since it was a beautiful mid-60's winter day, I suggested we take the boys and Ryan's best friend to Tomales Bay for a beach day. James wanted to stay home, but I swayed him with a stop at Cowgirl Creamery for a picnic lunch.

We drove along serpentine roads toward the coast, past the black-and-white cows dotting the Marin Headlands. We'd all learned not to speak too loudly around James, and the boys sat silently in the back of the minivan, but this silence was different. It wasn't so much silence as a screaming void of tension. Since James had come back from Asia, his temper and mood swings had grown worse, and I worried constantly about the boys doing or saying something to upset him.

I didn't know what to do about the growing unbridgeable distance between James and the rest of us. The harder I tried to reach him, the farther he retreated. Mostly, though, my heart broke every time James shunned Leo. All our son wanted was his dad back, and James couldn't do it. He couldn't release himself from his misery cloud long enough to tell Leo he loved him.

At the beach, James and I found a dune away from the water and let the boys run wild. I never let them get close to the ocean because the Northern California coast was notorious for sneaker waves that could sweep you away with no notice.

Had a sneaker wave washed over my family?

I established the boys' boundaries and settled into the sand next to James. I had a strong urge to hold James's hand, desperate for any kind of connection, but I worried he'd snatch it away. After a week of sleeping on the couch, my heart couldn't take any more rejection.

As we sat there, not talking, I watched the boys run and laugh. This was my family, and I had to protect it. I had promised to love James through sickness and health, and I had to keep the boys safe. In that moment, those two things seemed irreconcilable. James was the only thing in the boys' lives that caused them pain.

After a while, James stood and went down to help the boys build a sandcastle. Tate's little giggle drifted back to me, and Leo smiled widely when James let him cover his legs with sand. Maybe I had been wrong? Maybe the problem wasn't James, but me, and I needed to have more patience. It was clear the lawsuit and testing along with a month of solid travel had worn James down. He needed time to regroup, and I needed to support him and give him the space to do it. I owed it to the boys.

When James returned, he sat about two feet away from me.

I swished my hand over the sand. "You looked happy."

He shrugged. "I guess."

Not knowing what to talk about, I said, "Julie sent over a bunch of stuff about summer camps. Registration for a few starts on the fifteenth." James didn't respond. "We should probably make our summer plans. We need to figure out when we're going to Michigan, and Ryan has travel lacrosse. There are a lot of moving pieces this year." Michigan seemed like a safe topic. James often said it was the most relaxing place on earth, and he loved it there.

Instead of answering me, James stared at the ocean crashing against the shoreline. Seabirds scuttled along the coast, flying away when the boys got too close, and a soft breeze rustled the tall dune grass next to us.

"So, what do you think?" I took out my phone and pulled up the calendar. "We always go to Michigan in August, and the boys don't start back until late this year, so maybe from the fifth to the twentieth?"

"I can't make plans with you."

His words froze me, and my phone fell onto the sand. "What?"

"We don't have a future, and I can't make plans with you."

There was no air. No sound. No sense of up or down. I was floating away, untethered.

"Do you want a divorce?" I whispered.

He refused to look at me.

"Do. You. Want. A. Divorce?" I hit his arm. "Answer me."

"I don't know."

I leaped to my feet and ran barefoot across the dunes until I found a small opening in the dune grass where I collapsed. I expected James to chase after me, or to at least try to find me, but he didn't.

What had I done wrong? How had this happened? I knew things were bad, but did James really not see a future for us? Was I going to be a middle-aged mother of three who had been cast off by her husband? I folded in on myself. Did I push too hard? Was I overbearing? I was trying to be more of a giver.

The roar of the ocean drowned out my screams.

"What am I supposed to do?" I yelled. "What?"

I threw fistfuls of sand, but what I really wanted to do was find the driver of the white truck and hurt them. I wanted them to see what they had done to my family, and I wanted to make them sit with the guilt of destroying our lives.

After a while, James and the boys stomped past my hiding spot toward the parking lot. I wiped my face with my fleece jacket and followed them. My red, swollen eyes were hidden behind sunglasses, and no one asked where I had gone. We drove home in silence.

I jumped out of the car before James could pull into the garage and ran upstairs where I flung myself on our bed. It felt as if my skin had been turned inside out, leaving all my nerves and innards exposed and raw.

James followed me, and he lay down next to me and wrapped me in his arms. It was the first time he had willingly touched me in weeks. "I don't want to hurt you."

His words and differing actions made no sense.

"How am I supposed to live without you?" I sobbed. "I can't. I can't. I can't." The day of his accident, when I thought he had died, was the worst day of my life, but until this moment, I didn't understand how those six hours of not knowing where he was had impacted me. Images of him lying on the hospital table, pale and lifeless, flashed through my mind. I couldn't let someone else's careless mistake ruin my family.

Aside from my father, every relationship in my life ended with me feeling abandoned or betrayed. For fourteen years, James had been my world, and I believed him incapable of hurting me. He was a doting father, a supportive husband, and an ambitious employee in his career. He, in my mind, had been perfect, and I could not reconcile the wildly divergent Before-Accident James with the Post-Accident James.

"Give me six weeks. I need to figure things out." He nuzzled my hair as I cried. I longed for his touch and rolled over so that our faces were inches apart. The boys were downstairs with Molly and Joe, and I took the opportunity to kiss James. He didn't pull away, and instead, ran his hand over my hip, under my shirt, and higher until his fingers danced across my stomach.

I didn't hesitate when James undressed me. Sex was how I showed James I loved him. Before the accident, I sometimes teased James that he didn't love me enough, but really, I believed he loved me more than I loved him, and I lived in fear he would one day discover this perceived inequity and leave me.

His revelation on the beach was evidence that he was beginning to see it.

"How can I make you love me," I whispered. "How?"

Despite his tenderness moments earlier, James ignored me.

"James," I cried. "How do I make you love me again? What can I do?"

Tears glistened in his eyes, and he sniffed. "I don't know."

"Do you want to love me?" My voice hitched, exposing the jumble of pain, horror, and nausea consuming me.

James shrugged. He gathered his clothes and left.

One of the delicate strings holding us together had been cut.

On January 2nd, James fled to New York again. I tamped down my confusion over his confession and focused on the boys. We packed away the Christmas ornaments, took walks through the Presidio, and didn't mention James, who never called. His daily Facebook posts angered me, and I left snippy comments. He was out at restaurants, having fun, while I cleaned up after him.

When James did come home three days later, he went straight to the office. He called me late in the morning, his voice rough, and begged me to come get him. I packed Tate in the car and drove downtown. James paced outside his building, head down, fingers clenched against his chest, and when he climbed into the car without a hello, he wrapped his arms tightly around himself. I held back my biting comment only because I didn't want James melting down in front of Tate. As I wound my way through heavy downtown traffic, I cranked up the radio so I didn't have to listen to James's silent anger.

At home, he ran ahead of me, toward our in-law unit where

I'd set up my office. Puzzled, I helped Tate out of his booster seat and followed James. He had locked himself inside.

My anger gave way to dread, and I sent Tate to Molly's before heading back downstairs.

"James." I knocked on the door. "Can you let me in?"

No answer.

"James?" I banged harder. "Are you okay?" I pressed my ear to the door and heard nothing.

The worn doorknob required an old key. That was the problem with our home: it was over 100 years old, and there were a lot of old keys lying around. It wasn't unusual for me to find a ring of them during one of my frequent purging sessions, and when I asked what they belonged to, Molly and I would spend an afternoon trying to figure it out. Most of the time they went to nothing, and we'd throw them away.

I banged louder and my franticness grew. "Let me in," I yelled. "James, open the door."

"Is everything okay?" Molly called from the garage entryway.

"He's locked himself inside, and I can't open the door."

Molly walked calmly into the garage, toward the one window that we kept permanently propped open, and ran her hand along a splintered dust-covered ledge. She lifted a heavy metal ring with several keys dangling off it. "Try these."

The first key I tried worked, and I shoved the door open. James had smashed himself into a ball on the tiny, gray loveseat. His knees were pulled to his chest, and his arms covered his head.

I knelt next to him. "James?"

"Go away."

"Please. What's going on?" I asked.

Molly waited in the doorway. When James didn't answer, I turned to her. "What should I do?"

For the first time, she looked lost. "I don't know."

I crouched next to James and pried his hands from his face. His deep-brown eyes met mine, and it wasn't the typical disdain I saw, but pain so deep it stole my breath. "I'll take care of him," I promised Molly. "Can you watch the boys? I don't want them to see this."

"Of course."

In that moment, she took over raising my sons, so that I could care for hers.

When Molly was gone, I shut the office door and made James sit up. He had lost nearly fifty pounds since he had started running, and there was plenty of room for both of us. I snuggled in next to him on the loveseat and held his hands in mine. "What happened?"

There was a shift in him, a breakthrough. "I can't work. I can't remember shit. I can't concentrate."

It wasn't the first time he had told me this, but he was more distressed than before.

"What can I do?"

He shrugged. "There's nothing anyone can do. I'm broken."

Before the accident, I marveled at James's ability to do complex mental math. He never forgot a name or face. He was laser sharp. Since the accident, I had watched him struggle through basic memory tasks.

"Broken things can be fixed," I said.

"Not if they are ruined beyond repair."

"Nothing is ever that broken." I clasped his hand tightly in mine and rubbed his still-naked ring finger with my thumb. When James didn't pull away, I thought it was a good sign. "Our life may look different, but it's not ruined."

James exhaled as if a thousand pent-up things had rushed out of him. "Do you know what it's like to have someone constantly tell you they love you when you don't remember marrying them?" He stared at me, daring a reaction from me. I gave him nothing even though my heart trembled. "It sucks." He clenched his jaw and huffed. "You love me so much, but why? Why do you love this?"

I wanted to wail. I wanted to lash out at him for constantly breaking my heart, but I couldn't. He was injured more than I had realized. "Because I promised to always love you, and I do. We're a team. We'll get through this."

He hung his dark head. "How? How are we supposed to fix this?"

My breath grew unsteady as I realized what he was trying to say. He didn't need six weeks; he had already made his decision. "You don't love me, do you?"

"I don't know." He squeezed my hand. "I want to. I do."

"Then do it. Why can't you?"

He stared into the corner of the cozy room. "I don't love myself, how am I supposed to love you?"

Condensation from the ever-present fog ran down the window. "I have enough love for both of us."

He turned toward me, and his chin quivered. "Are you sure?"

"Yes." I meant it. I would pull us through this nightmare. I'd fix everything: James, our marriage, our family. "We were happy. Always so damn happy," I said. "You need to know that."

James sniffed. "I want to remember, Bee. I really do."

August 2009
Lady Gaga's "Paparazzi" blasted as James and I flew up the gravel road, dust kicking up behind us. The earthy smell of farmland wafted in through the window, and I stuck my hand out, letting air rush between my fingers. In the backseat, the boys sang the chorus loudly.

"I bet you have a winner," James said with a laugh.

One of our Michigan vacation traditions was to buy lottery scratchers and novelty candy from the country store. We never won, but it didn't stop us from buying tickets. On that day, I had picked a crossword game while James selected bingo. When we got back to my dad's, we'd spread them over the picnic table, let the boys scratch a few, and spend at least an hour bemoaning our lack of winnings.

"I bet you do." I pulled my hand inside and rolled up the window. James was the luckiest guy I knew. Nothing ever went wrong for him, and most of the time it felt like I lived under his protective umbrella.

He kept his eyes on the road, but grinned. "I'm already a winner. I have you."

I giggled and hit his arm. "Stop it."

"I'm serious. I'm a lucky guy." He reached over and squeezed my hand. *"I get to hang out with my best friend all the time."*

"Is Dad your best friend?" seven-year-old Ryan asked from the backseat.

I smiled and turned around. Ryan's lips were ringed with chocolate. "Daddy's my best friend forever."

February 2012

James's six-week deadline fell on Valentine's Day. He missed it because he was in New York again, and I breathed a sigh of relief that he hadn't left me yet, but I had noticed my stomach hurt less when he was gone, and I slept better. A sense of calm enveloped the house when it was just the boys and me, and we had a rhythm James's anger disrupted.

He had missed Tate's fifth birthday and flew home the next day—the day before my birthday. An ever-present scowl lined his face, and he didn't say hello to any of us, even though he'd been gone for a week. Instead, he locked himself in our room and refused to come out. All the progress I had hoped we made before he'd left, vanished.

"Why doesn't Dad like us anymore?" Leo asked, looking up from his Lego creation.

I patted the spot next to me on the couch, and he climbed next to me. Ryan and Tate kept playing. "He loves you, buddy. All of you. It's just that Dad's brain is a little broken."

"He should fix it," Leo said. "He isn't nice to you anymore."

I exhaled. I had hoped the boys hadn't noticed the tension between James and me. "Daddy just needs help. And love. We need to give him all our love to help him get better."

"Okay." Leo wrapped his little arms around me and hugged tightly. "Make him better."

I held back the tears stinging my eyes. "I'm trying, baby. I promise, I'm trying."

That night, as I lay awake on the couch, my resolve to fix things grew. Our boys deserved parents who loved each other, a mom who didn't cry all the time, and a dad who engaged. If James didn't put in more effort, we would need to make changes —changes I wasn't sure I was ready to make—but at some point, I had to put the boys before James.

The next day, on my birthday, Leo attempted to bake me a cake. He found a recipe, gathered the ingredients, and was carefully measuring flour when I walked into the kitchen. His face lit up when he saw me.

"Whatchya doing, buddy?" I smiled. Like me, Leo enjoyed being in the kitchen.

"I'm making a chocolate cake with chocolate frosting." He jumped off the stool and left flour handprints all over my shirt when he hugged me. "It's for your birthday."

"Oh, honey, thank you! I bet it's going to be delicious!"

"What's going on?" James boomed from behind me.

Leo cowered against the counter, and I spun around. "Leo's making a cake."

"He's making a fucking mess." Flour dusted the countertop and sugar had spilled onto the floor, but it was nothing major. "He's too little to cook."

Leo burst into tears.

"Are you crying?" James snapped. "Really?"

I tried to shield Leo from James's view. "What's wrong with you?" I snapped. "Why are you being a dick?"

"What's wrong with me?" James said, his nostrils flaring. "Are you seriously asking what's wrong with me?"

"Yes." In that moment, leaving James was no longer a question. The boys couldn't be around this chaos anymore, and I needed to put them first.

James stormed down the hallway. "Get dressed," he bellowed at the kids. "Ryan, you have a lacrosse game in half an hour."

"Go get dressed." I dabbed Leo's cheeks with my T-shirt. "We can work on the cake when we get home."

His big, brown eyes met mine. "Dad's mean."

I inhaled and let the air rush between my lips. "I know."

While I dressed, James sat on our bed with his face twisted into a grimace. He typed away on his phone, ignoring me. Part of me wanted to bring up his behavior toward Leo, but the other, bigger part of me didn't want to spoil the day even further.

I pulled on a dress, tights, and boots before wrapping a scarf around my neck. I studied myself in the mirror. Thirty-six didn't look much different than thirty-five aside from the sadness in my eyes.

"You look fine," James barked. "Let's go."

"It's my birthday." I walked to the end of the bed. "Did you forget?"

"What?"

"It's my birthday. That's why Leo was making a cake."

James's eyes grew wide as his error became obvious. He tried to cover it. "I know. I made dinner plans."

"Oh? Where?"

"It's a surprise."

I snorted. There were no dinner plans. He'd completely forgotten my birthday, but I had become so afraid of upsetting James that I swallowed my anger.

The din of conversations and plates clanging hung over the small, crowded bistro. Our table was along the wall, and I sat across from James, facing the center of the room. He had ordered a bottle of red wine for us even though I only wanted a Coke.

"You're more fun when you're drunk," James said as he sipped from his glass. Over the past few months, he'd developed a love of wine and read various wine publications. I neither understood nor cared about any of it.

"Gee, thanks."

"You're not as uptight." James set his half-drunk glass wine down and peered at me with a stony face. "You know that, right? That you're wound really tight."

I clenched my jaw. He had asked me for six weeks, and I gave it to him. I hadn't badgered him; I gave him space to think; I didn't really bring it up because I didn't want the answer I knew was coming. But I was done. Done with his mood swings and misplaced anger. I refused to put my children in harm's way any longer.

Before coming to dinner, Molly and I had had a long talk. I shared everything with her, and she sat slack-jawed for a long moment before saying, "We love you, and you will always have a home here. Whatever James is going through, he needs to fix it, but you're right, we can't keep exposing the boys to this. You need to protect the boys, and even if that means James needs to leave. We'll support you."

Knowing this, I said the words I'd practiced all afternoon. "I want a divorce."

James flinched. "What?"

"I can't do this anymore. It needs to stop." I crossed my arms, kept my chin up, and my gaze even. I wanted James to understand I was serious.

"You can't," he sputtered.

"Yes, I can. I have the paperwork." After returning from Ryan's game, I took advantage of James hiding in the bedroom to print off California's divorce paperwork and researched everything I needed to do to file. Logistically, I was prepared, even if I wasn't emotionally.

The waiter placed our food before us, but I had no appetite and pushed the steak frites away. "You need to move out," I ordered. "Your parents support my decision."

James's mouth dropped open. "No. Just no. You need to give me a chance." He no longer called me Bee, and my given name was often spat in disgust. "You don't know what you're doing."

Despite my determination to stay strong, I wavered. All I wanted was for James to show he still cared, and when he reached for my hand, his touch caused the tears I'd been holding back to flow.

"I want a divorce," I repeated softly. I didn't feel steady or strong. Or even resolved. I felt like I was moving through the motions of something I didn't want to do but had to. "You need to go."

"You're not kidding?" A light flicked on as he realized how serious the situation had become.

"I'm not kidding." My napkin fell to the ground when I stood.

"Where are you going?"

The small room suffocated me, and I needed to get fresh air and away from James.

"I don't know." I pushed between the neighboring tables and ran for the exit. When I was outside, I turned down an alleyway and began walking toward Allison's house. I wasn't sure if she was in town, but she lived close by, and I could hide from James there. I'd call Molly later and explain the situation to her.

In a daze, I walked a few blocks with snot and tears pouring down my face. I'd left my purse at the restaurant and had no money for a cab or Muni. As I walked, each step taking me away from James, I settled my emotions. I would not let him treat me or the boys like this anymore. I would not continue to make excuses for his behavior. I would be strong and walk away from this disaster.

James pulled up next to me. "Get in the car."

I kept walking.

"Please. Come home with me. We need to talk."

My high heels pinched my toes. Realistically, I couldn't walk much farther. I yanked the car door open and reluctantly climbed in. James tried talking to me on the ride home, but I was done talking and ignored him.

That night, after trying to force me into a conversation I refused to have, James walked to his lifelong church three blocks away. While we weren't the best Catholics, we were involved in our church community, and it was logical for James to seek help from our clergy. He called near midnight to tell me where he was and to ask if he could come home. He'd spoken to our priest and realized he needed to make changes. He wanted to work things out with me.

Despite not fully believing him, it was a relief. Deep down, I didn't want a divorce. I wanted my old marriage and my old husband back. I wanted a loving father for the boys. I wanted stability and peace and a future we could both see, and I wanted it with James.

If he was willing to try, really try, then so was I.

That night rocked James, and for a month, things got better with me and the boys. He no longer yelled, and his travel schedule wound down. He rarely reeked of whiskey, and he engaged more with the boys. I clung to these small improvements as signs that he really did want to save our marriage and his relationships with our sons.

For spring break, he surprised me when he said he'd booked a trip for us to see my parents in Michigan. He thought it would be good for all of us to get away, and I agreed.

The day after Easter, as my stepmom and I cleaned up after lunch, I stared out the dining room sliding door. James had been playing baseball with the boys on the field in front of the house, but now he paced along the gravel road, phone pressed to his ear. He kept his back to the boys.

"Is everything okay?" Ma asked. "The two of you seem off."

"Work and the lawsuit," I answered. "He's stressed." I didn't want my parents to know how bad James was. I needed them, like everyone else, to believe in the James Miraculous Recovery Myth.

Suddenly, James stormed toward the house with a beer can in one hand and his phone in the other. Normally, he only drank in the evening while sitting at the firepit with Dad where they'd talk about random things. But on this trip, James had barely spoken to anyone except his phone. Mostly, he pounded beer after beer until passing out.

Ma sighed. "Maybe he should go with you to Chicago. Daddy and I will watch the boys." The next morning, I was supposed to drive to the Romantic Times conference, and James was supposed to stay behind with the boys. When he planned our surprise trip, he made sure to work around my conference schedule.

"You will?" The thought of a few days alone with James made me nervous. We hadn't had any time alone since our disastrous Thanksgiving weekend.

"Yeah. Daddy and I already discussed it. It'll be fine."

James burst into the house, nostrils flaring, and jaw set hard. He paused when he saw Ma, and I braced for the storm, but he glanced at us and darted around the kitchen table toward our bedroom.

"Do you want to come to Chicago with me?" I blurted. "Ma suggested it. She and Dad will watch the boys."

James turned around, and discomfort flashed across his face. He didn't want to go. After all the promises he had made over the past month, he didn't want to be alone with me.

I balled my fists. It was one thing for him to reject me when we were alone, but another for him to not play the devoted husband in public.

"Really, James, it's fine. Go," Ma said. If she sensed the tension between us, she ignored it. "You two have fun."

The pressure building in my chest released a little. James couldn't refuse my parents. "Please?" I begged. "I already have a room. It won't cost anything extra."

He huffed. "Fine."

We decided to drive to Chicago after making plans to meet my parents and the boys in Grand Rapids after the conference. As James and I skirted the shores of Lake Michigan, I sung loudly and made silly faces to break the tension between us. In the past, James always laughed when I did that, but he wasn't laughing now. He kept his eyes trained on the road and ignored me.

"You didn't have to come." I sank against my seat. "I know you don't want to be here."

"You ambushed me," he growled. "I had no choice." But then he surprised me by reaching for my hand and squeezing it. The nervous energy I had been holding onto lessened, and I tried not to get too excited. James rarely touched me anymore.

Maybe Ma was right. Maybe we just needed some alone time.

We arrived at the hotel near midnight. There had been road construction, and the drive took us four hours longer than expected. James was livid, but at the check-in counter, he upgraded our room to Club Level so I could have unlimited access to free drinks and snacks throughout the day. "Conferences are tiring," he said. "You'll want this. Trust me."

It was the most thoughtful thing he'd done in ages, and I hugged him. He didn't stiffen, so I kissed his cheek. "Thank you."

After dropping off our bags, we grabbed a quick bite at the hotel bar and planned out our time in Chicago. I'd attend the conference during the day while he explored the city. A Chicago company had recently approached James about a new job, and he wanted to see if he liked the city before engaging in a deeper conversation with them. I didn't want to move, but I was willing to entertain the idea if it would help our family.

"You should look at the neighborhoods in the north part of town," I said. "I think that's where Beth said the good schools are." I had several writer friends living in Chicago and had made some inquiries.

James nodded. "Yeah. I'll do that. I think those schools have lacrosse programs, too."

I rolled my eyes. James was obsessed with Ryan and Leo playing lacrosse. "Schools and safety and walkability," I said with a wag of my finger. "Those are the priorities, not lacrosse."

"Yes, ma'am." He grinned, and I grinned back. How was it,

after the horribleness of the past year, that James's smile still made me weak?

On the way back to our room, James stopped suddenly. "This has been nice," he said, pecking me on the forehead. "Ma was right."

I wrapped my arms around his torso, savoring his closeness. This was the James I had always loved. "I'm happy you came."

I had high hopes while I brushed my teeth and changed for bed. James seemed relaxed and like his old self, and in a fit of bravery, I left my clothes on the counter and walked out naked. The lights were off, and James lay on the bed. I slipped in next to him and placed my hand on his back. He was bundled in a shirt and sweatpants.

"James?"

No response.

"Are you sleeping?"

Silence.

Disappointed and a little embarrassed that I read the situation wrong, I flipped over onto my back and stared up at the ceiling. Light streamed in through a crack in the curtain and across James's body. He reached out and grabbed his phone off the side table.

"You're awake?" I asked, moving closer to him.

"Barely." He flipped the phone over face down. "Go to sleep. You have an early day tomorrow." Within minutes his soft snores filled the room. With a frustrated exhale, I turned to my side and drifted off.

The next morning, as I showered, James packed his suitcase. We had not even been at the hotel for twelve hours.

"What are you doing?" I asked when I emerged from the bathroom.

"I need to go to New York. Work crisis." He kept his back turned while he typed on his phone.

I pressed my lips together. James's mood swings were dizzying.

"What about our plans?" I pulled the towel tighter around me, and my wet hair dripped over my shoulders. "And what about the boys?"

"I got you a plane ticket to Grand Rapids. I'll drop the car off at the O'Hare."

"You're serious?" I stepped around him so that I could see his face. I was being robbed of our few days together. "You can't tell work to fuck off for once?"

"No, I can't tell work to fuck off. What's wrong with you?"

All James did was work. He had gotten a promotion right before his accident and repeatedly told me that he needed to earn his battle pay, but this was getting ridiculous.

He shoved his phone in his pocket and refused to look at me as he busied himself with repacking the clothes he'd hung in the closet the night before.

"When are you leaving?"

"Now. My flight's at ten."

I tossed up my hands. "Awesome."

James zipped his bag shut. "I'll see you when I get home."

His hasty exit cemented what I already knew: James didn't want to be married, but like me, he didn't know how to not be married.

I sat at a long, high-top table in the hotel bar with my friends. We had dumped the contents of our swag bags into the middle and were taking turns reading the raunchiest passages of the free novels out loud.

Even with James's abrupt departure, I was having a great

time. The next morning was my first book signing as a published author, and I was equally nervous and excited.

As Deb read aloud about three-way leprechaun-gnome sex, my friends and I shrieked with laughter. I was two vodka cranberries into the night and laughing came easily. Knowing the boys were safe with my parents, and that James and his barbed-wire tongue were hundreds of miles away, helped.

My phone screen lit up.

"Hello?"

"It's Molly. I hate to bother you, but James isn't answering his phone. Is he home?"

"He's in New York," I said. "Why?"

"Joe and I hear someone walking around upstairs."

"Oh." I paused. "I guess you should call the police?"

"Can you call James? We didn't see him come home, but it may be him." Molly's voice shook.

"Okay." I hung up and excused myself from the table. I dialed James and pressed my finger into my ear so that I could hear better in the noisy bar.

"Hello?" James's scratchy voice sounded distant.

"Are you home? Your mom said she hears someone walking around upstairs."

"Yeah."

I pursed my lips. "I thought you had a work crisis?"

"I fixed it."

"Oh."

"Bee?"

"Yeah?"

"I don't want to live anymore. I can't do this."

I glanced back at my laughing friends. For a brief moment, I was one of them, and it was amazing, but now I was hurtled back into reality. "Are you going to hurt yourself?"

"I don't know."

The persistent, sick feeling that I had shaken for a few hours returned. "I'm coming home."

"No. You need to do your signing."

"James, I'm scared." I leaned against the wall to hold myself upright. "I'm going to call your mom." He was quiet. "James?"

"Okay."

When Molly found him, James was barricaded in our bedroom, sobbing and insisting that he wanted to die.

"I'll stay with him until you get home." Her voice trembled. "He'll be okay. Don't worry about anything."

Despite Molly's reassurance, I didn't believe James would be okay. What would happen if we did leave him alone? And how was I supposed to drag my husband away from his suicidal thoughts when he wouldn't share any of his medical information with me?

With those thoughts running through my head, I posed for pictures and smiled at my signing the next day, but inside I was a frantic mess. I left my table at one point and threw up, and I kept my phone on the table next to me and checked it frequently. I couldn't get home fast enough.

When the boys and I arrived home, Molly was a wreck. She hadn't slept in two days, and dark bags lined her eyes.

"I think he's through the worst of it." She hugged me tightly, and I pressed my lips together, trying to convince myself I could handle the current situation.

"He's in our room?" I asked.

"Yes." Molly's squeezed my hand. "I took everything dangerous out of there."

"Good." I had left the boys downstairs with Joe to give me time to assess the situation. "I'll take it from here."

I climbed the steps to our flat, sorting out the circumstances. Every time James came home from travel, he fell apart, so clearly, he needed to stop traveling and give his mind a break.

MIA HAYES

My heart sank when I found James lying curled on our bed with a pillow over his head. His phone dinged endlessly, and I picked it up to turn it off. He didn't need to deal with work.

Even though he seemingly hated me, I stretched out next to him and peered under the pillow. "Do you want to talk?"

James shook his head. "I'm okay, now."

"Are you sure? I think I should call your therapist. What's their name?" James, at Emily's prompting, had switched to a therapist her law firm had recommended.

"Nothing is going to help me."

"Let's at least try."

James tossed the pillow across the room. "Stop trying to fix me! Stop!"

Not knowing what else to do, I left him alone. My approach wasn't working, and even though I could quote endless facts about PTSD and TBIs, I didn't know how to save James from himself.

April 2012

A few days later, as James sat on the couch staring blankly at the wall, I straddled his lap and kissed his neck. He hadn't touched me since our trip to Chicago, and the only way I seemed to be able to reach him was through sex.

"Let me love you." I stroked James's rough facial scruff. His mood had improved over the past several days, and he didn't seem suicidal, because he engaged more with everyone but me. "Please let me love you."

It was a ridiculous plea. Even with James's hot-cold behavior, I still believed I could make him see how much I loved him. I had stopped my threats of divorce, ignored my hair falling out in clumps, shrugged off my jumpiness, and marked my upset stomach to too much gluten. All I wanted was for James to love me again, and I ignored the physical symptoms that signaled that maybe I wasn't okay either. Instead, I thought acknowledging my strange health symptoms would damage James even more if he knew about them.

His hands lingered on my hips, and I leaned over him, my lips longing for his. James lifted his face like he was going to kiss me, but he ripped me off his lap and shoved me aside. "I don't deserve your love."

The scowl marks between his eyes had deepened since his breakdown. Despite my encyclopedic knowledge of PTSD and TBIs, nothing I did was right. I couldn't fix James, and he seemingly had no interest in fixing himself.

"Did you take your meds?"

"They don't work."

The bottle of antidepressants had disappeared from the bathroom counter shortly after my return from Chicago. I assumed James had taken them to work and that's what had brought about his temporary, more stable mood, but now I wondered. "Do you take them at all?"

He was silent, and his gaze slid left like he was choosing his words carefully. "I took them."

"Okay." I didn't press. I didn't want to make him angry.

His teary gaze settled on me. "I just want to feel normal again. That's all I want."

It was a rare moment of vulnerability, and I threw my arms around his neck, hugging him tightly. "We'll get through this." The crack in his stone-like façade gave me hope. "We can get through this. You just need the right help."

His body fell limp against mine until his head rested in my lap. I played with his hair until a soft snore rumbled out of him. Afraid to wake him, I reached for my phone and called Molly. She agreed to keep the boys.

I sat like that for hours, watching my husband sleep and comforting him when his demons thrashed through his dreams. The fact that he sought me out as his safe place meant he trusted me. It reinforced what I already knew: that despite our increasingly tense relationship and how he treated me, I could never turn my back on him. Not when he needed me most.

In mid-May, Emily asked me to consider filing a separate loss of consortium claim. I wasn't sure. If I moved forward, I'd be deposed about the deterioration of James and my relationship, and while I had written the blog post back in November, I had since reverted to my old ways publicly, repeating the James Miraculous Recovery Myth and us as a perfect, happy couple.

After Emily explained how the new claim would strengthen our existing case, James pressed me to do it, and I gave in.

Emily set the deposition for the end of May—nearly fifteen months since we began legal proceedings—and gave me several lengthy documents to complete. One required me to submit pictures of James from before and after the accident, and I spent several days crying as I searched through piles of photos. There was one of us on the beach, another of our family standing next to our Christmas tree, and even more of us laughing in Michigan. The most devastating pictures, however, weren't the happy ones; instead, they were the pictures James had posted of his angry face on Facebook during the previous nine months. As I pulled them up to print, a clearer image of James's steady downhill slide formed.

Every day, James posted a picture, and every day, without fail, someone would joke about his "Blue Steel" look. Despite his obvious cry for help, James never responded. He simply continued posting his daily photo, and his transition from a happy, devoted father and husband to a possibly suicidal man was on display for everyone to see.

It became clear I had been too in the trenches to accurately see how bad he was. Since James had never given me his therapists' names and the bottles of medicine had disappeared, I had no way of knowing who to call without asking James. Since

December, he had refused to share anything about his tests or treatment with me.

As I sat on our bedroom floor sorting through photographs, James came in with his suitcase. He stepped over the pictures I had scattered across the floor, ignoring me and my tears, and dug around in his closet. He had a quick two-day trip to Los Angeles, and I watched him pack. He dropped a pair of swim trunks with tags attached into his carry-on.

"When'd you get those?" I asked. The day before, he had yelled at me about the grocery bill, but he had money to buy swim trunks?

"I don't know." He closed the suitcase.

"You don't know?"

"They were on sale, so don't give me grief." He glared at me. "Plus, I've lost a lot of weight, and my old trunks don't fit." He now looked almost skeletal, and his face was full of sharp angles that matched his new, prickly personality.

"Why do you need swim trunks on a business trip?"

He threw a T-shirt on top of the trunks. "My hotel has a rooftop pool. I may go up there at night."

"What hotel?"

James rattled off the name, and feeling uneasy, I tucked the info into my memory. When he was done packing, James called a cab. I waited until he was gone to look up the hotel phone number and save it to my phone.

James wasn't staying at that hotel. I called the front desk, and they had no record of him despite his call to tell me he'd checked in and would be in meetings the rest of the day. I debated whether or not to call his cellphone, but honestly, I didn't want the confrontation. Instead, I finished out my day with a growing pit of doom in my stomach.

James had lied.

Unable to sleep, I crept down the hallway from the family room to my bedroom knowing that Molly and Joe could hear my footsteps. When I reached my closet, I dug into the pocket of a dress and found a baggie. A friend—someone who meant well —had given me a bunch of Valium after I confessed I struggled to sleep. I hadn't been brave enough to take any yet, but in that moment something changed, and I dry swallowed one.

Nothing happened. I didn't know what I expected, but I felt nothing.

Desperate to stop the thoughts banging around my brain, I dressed and left the house. The boys were sound asleep, and if anything happened, Molly and Joe were downstairs. It would be fine. I locked the door and ran down the front stairs to the side-walk, ducking under my in-laws' windows.

I stood in front of my house near the garage with my back pressed against the orange bricks and considered my options. I never went anywhere alone—especially not after seven at night.

Shouts from down the street caught my attention. A dark, dank bar sat on the corner, and a few rowdy patrons stood out front, smoking. Not knowing what else to do, I headed there.

I hadn't been in a real bar in years, and I wasn't sure what to do. A few customers sat at the counter, nursing drinks and talk-ing. I lingered in the doorway surveying the dimly lit room until the bartender waved to me. "Come in," he said. "Join the fun."

Yes. What I needed was fun.

"What can I get you?"

I studied the wall of liquor. James drank whiskey, and when I did occasionally drink, it was a vodka cranberry or wine, but neither seemed right. With an increasingly foggy brain, I scanned the shelf before zeroing in on a tequila bottle. I pointed. "A shot."

Next to me, an elderly man whistled. "That kind of night, huh?"

"It's a Monday. The worst day of the week," I answered, and everyone laughed.

The man next to me held up his beer glass, and I clinked it with my tequila shot. The liquor burned all the way down, but I didn't mind. I asked for another, and the bartender refilled my glass.

The anger at James's lie paused, and I propped myself against the bar. James was right, I was more fun when drunk. I climbed onto a barstool and made small talk with the bartender and the elderly man.

After my third shot, the bartender took my glass and informed me I was done. I slipped off the stool, pulled my sweater tighter across my body, and tried walking to the door. The floor pitched, and I couldn't find my footing. I stumbled into the doorjamb.

"Call you a cab?" the bartender asked.

I shook my head. "I live up the block. I'll walk."

Outside, I stood on the busy corner, watching the whizzing lights of cars zip up Geary Boulevard. It was after midnight, and the traffic kept coming and coming. Where was everyone going at this time of night?

I fumbled in my purse for my phone and rang James. It went to voicemail. I rang again, and he answered.

"What's wrong?" he asked in alarm. "Is everything okay?"

"Where are you?" I slurred and pounded the crosswalk button. I wanted to go for a walk.

"What? I can't understand you."

"What hotel are you at?" Speaking clearly was an effort.

"Go to bed. I'll call in the morning." James hung up.

Speeding cars roared by. I waited for a break in the traffic and stumbled across the intersection until I reached the medium. I could step in front of a car. I could do it. And if I did, it would be a drunken accident. No one would be to blame, and the pain I was beginning to acknowledge would vanish.

Someone grabbed my shoulders. "Where do you live? I'll take you home."

It was the elderly man. I pointed in the opposite direction, toward my house.

I don't remember going home, but when Molly found me in the morning, I was sprawled on the bathroom floor with puke covering my hands and crusted in my hair. She cleaned me up and put me to bed where I stayed for the next two days.

THE AFFAIR

During my parents' custody battle, my mom dumped a box of kittens at my grandpa's, where I was living. Delighted, my sister and I quickly picked out our favorites and ran into the cyclone-fenced yard. Next door, a Doberman Pinscher paced back and forth. I loved animals and had pet him many times.

I was five.

I stuck the kitten through the hole in the fence so the dog could see it.

He snapped the head off.

Our screams brought my dad running. As the kitten's body convulsed on the ground, my sister wouldn't stop screaming, but I went into fix-it mode, wanting to stitch the kitten back together. I lifted the writhing body and smashed the head to it. Blood covered my hands, and my dad tore the pieces from me.

"Some things can't be put back together," my dad said later as he balanced me on his lap. My dad always wore work boots and jeans—even in the summer heat. He had a strawberry-blond mustache and long hair that tickled when he'd kiss me. "You can't fix what happened. You need to forget about it."

Maybe that's when I learned to push unpleasant events from my mind and explain away my pain. The next day, I gave the dog a treat.

I forgave the dog, but not myself.

May 2012

Emily spent an hour going over what to expect during the deposition. I was to answer "I don't recall" to anything I didn't positively know, I was not to speculate or guess, and if I was unsure of how to answer, I was to consult with her privately.

A thin man with a graying handlebar mustache and beard sat across from me. All he needed was a ten-gallon hat to look at home in a Spaghetti Western. He dropped a soft, leather briefcase on the table, exchanged pleasantries with Emily and the other side's attorney, and poured a glass of water without acknowledging me.

My palms sweated, and I dragged them across my skirt.

"Are you okay?" Emily asked.

I lied. "Just thirsty."

"Try this." She handed me a glass of water. "Are you ready?" she asked in a hushed tone as I guzzled the water. "It may take all day. You need to stay calm."

"I know." Emily had explained during our practice run that the deposition could take six hours or more. I didn't understand why. After all, how hard was it to understand that my husband had gone from being a devout and loving family man to a crazed and withdrawn man prone to angry outbursts. I had Facebook posts, pictures, and medical records to back me up—it would be simple.

Outside the fourteenth-floor windows, the bay glistened. It was unusually sunny for a late-May day, and Emily lowered the shades.

"Are we ready?" she asked, taking the seat next to me.

"I am." I wanted to get it over with. My deposition marked the start of the nightmare ending, and once I did it, we'd move into mediation with both insurance companies. Everything would be wrapped up by July.

Handlebar Mustache cleared his throat. He asked me basic questions about my name, birthdate, place of residence, and education. I answered those questions easily and felt relatively calm.

He pulled a stack of paper from his briefcase, and I immediately recognized it as the written questions I had to answer the week before. The lengthy questionnaire probed into the most private parts of mine and James's life. The attorney reached into his bag and dropped another stack of papers next to the first. They were the pictures of James and our family.

He leafed through my answers before tapping on the table. "Ms. Hayes, how many times a week did you have sex before your husband's accident?"

I paused. Emily had explained this type of question would be coming, but I wasn't fully prepared. I glanced at her, and she nodded.

"At least three times," I said.

"Even with small children?"

"Yes." I wanted to explain, but Emily had told me to be curt.

"How is that possible?"

"My in-laws live downstairs. We have plenty of alone time, and the boys go to bed at seven thirty."

All the attorneys made notes, and I held my breath. Had I answered wrong?

"And now?" Handlebar Mustache asked. "How often are you intimate?"

"Never." Since coming back from Europe the previous November, James had refused most of my attempts at intimacy until we stopped having sex altogether. This was the real reason I believed Emily was correct with her insistence of a loss of consortium claim.

"Never?" He stared at me over the top of his glasses.

"That's correct."

"How long ago did relations cease?"

I frowned, trying to remember. "I'm not sure."

"Can you give a general idea?"

"March?"

Emily leaned in to me and whispered, "Don't give answers if you're unsure."

We took a short recess after two hours. Drained from the questioning, I sat in a stairwell and sobbed. I now understood why James felt exhausted after therapy and his depositions. Reliving the past year and a half had broken me.

When I returned to the conference room, Emily studied me for a moment before rushing to my side. "Are you okay? You look like you were crying."

"I was, but I'm fine."

"Do you need more time?"

I shook my head.

For two more hours, I fielded questions about our life, and each answer made James sound more and more like a monster. There was no way around it. He had done awful things, and the enormity of it hit me hard.

I left the deposition sick to my stomach. As I walked out of the building, Allison texted and wanted to meet for dinner. James wasn't expecting me for a few more hours, so I jumped into a cab and headed across town, eager to push the deposition from my mind.

Allison was already at the table with a cocktail when I arrived. "I'm so happy you could come!"

After her wedding, Allison and I had seen less and less of each other. Partly from her busy travel schedule, but mostly because I avoided all my friends out of fear they'd see I wasn't okay.

"What have you been up to?" Allison asked. She was, as always, impeccably dressed and her glossy, dark hair fell softly over her shoulders. Even though I had dressed up for the deposition, I felt frumpy next to her.

I couldn't tell her anything about my day or the deposition. I was too afraid of breaking down in public, so I forced a laugh. "Just kids and the normal. Nothing exciting like you, Miss Globetrotter."

"Work travel sucks."

"That's what James says." Just the mention of his name made my heart sink.

Allison studied me for a moment. "You okay?"

I lifted my chin. "Yeah. I'm just exhausted."

Allison frowned, but didn't press me, and I was thankful. I had already aired enough dirty laundry for the day.

We ordered several appetizers and a bottle of red wine. I picked at the food but pounded glass after glass of wine. For two hours, I escaped the reality of my life, and it was a much-needed reprieve.

When Allison put me in a cab, I was drunk and laughing. As the cab sped through my Richmond District neighborhood, I thought, *Maybe James is right. Maybe I'm only fun when I drink.*

But then I arrived home, and sobriety snuck up on me. I couldn't escape reality, and the deposition had highlighted how awful our marriage had become.

On June 8th, we received our first settlement from the defendant's insurance company. His employer's insurance company, however, insisted on going forward with the mid-July mediation date. James phoned and asked me to pick up the check from Emily's office and deposit it into our joint account immediately.

Even after Emily's cut of the settlement, it was the largest check I'd ever seen, and I anxiously drove to my credit union. On the way, James texted and told me to transfer $10,000 into my personal account. When I inquired why, he responded, "You've earned it."

I had no idea what to do with that much money. The summer before, James and I had discussed buying a property along the Russian River, and while that was still my dream, I also felt the need to hoard the money. Having it in an account that belonged just to me felt reassuring.

The next day, I convinced James to celebrate by taking a family trip to Johnson's Beach. As we wound our way along US 101, an unfamiliar calmness settled over me. In the two weeks since my deposition, James had evened out. It was like I had verbally purged our darkest secrets, and he'd been exorcised.

We were happy. Or, at least, as happy as we could be.

As the boys swam, James and I huddled under an umbrella. I sat in a low-slung beach chair, and he lay at my feet, his arm wrapped around my ankle, and kissed my shin.

"You're being silly." A rush of heat raced through me. James was willingly touching me.

"Can't I be?" James answered and licked my leg.

This sent me into a peal of laughter, and calmness enveloped me. If I could keep James like this, we could get better. We would survive this ordeal.

"Can I get an ice cream, Dad?" Leo asked. Water dripped from his shaggy, copper hair and sun-kissed shoulders. Like James, he tanned easily.

James pulled a five dollar bill from his wallet. "Bring back the change."

As Leo ran off toward the snack shack, James adjusted himself so that his back pressed against my legs.

"Thanks for planning this," James said, stretching. "It's nice."

My skin burned where our bodies touched, and I leaned over to run my hand through his messy hair. James smiled up at me—not a scowl, but a smile. Hope grew in my chest. He was coming back to us. All he had needed was for us to finish mediation.

He lay on his side and closed his eyes. After a few minutes, his chest expanded and contracted in a steady rhythm. I scanned the river, looking for the other boys, and found them in a canoe a few feet offshore. Tate waved at me, and I blew him a kiss.

"Mom?" Leo stood next to me, holding a fist full of cash in one hand and an ice cream sandwich in the other. "What should I do with this?"

"Give it to me."

Leo dropped the quarter and bills into my hand. He found a sliver of shade next to James's head and took a bite from his treat.

"Don't wake Daddy," I said softly even though kids shrieked and ran wild around us. "He needs sleep."

Leo nodded. Other than me, he'd taken the brunt of James's anger. Nothing Leo did was right, and yet the boy refused to stop trying. He constantly hugged James and told him he loved him. James either ignored him or pushed him away. But like me, Leo believed our love could fix James, and he refused to stop trying.

James's wallet poked out from his swim trunk pocket, and I

gently removed it. It was weird holding his wallet. James never went in my purse, and I never looked at his things. There was no reason.

I opened the bifold, and a piece of folded paper fell into my lap. It looked like a note a middle schooler would pass. I shoved the bills inside before picking up the paper. I don't know why, but I pulled a corner away. James's handwriting lined the page.

"I love you beyond belief."

My heart pounded, and I opened the note a little more. Had he written me something sweet? Was this how he really felt?

I glanced at his sleeping figure and unfurled the letter.

"Khalie—" Khalie?

The noise around me faded. There was no air. None. When I could draw a breath, I trembled. Who was Khalie, and why did my husband love her?

I know this is asking a lot of you, but it will be worth it. I just need more time. Once the divorce is final, we will be together. I promise.

I love you beyond belief.

James

I sat stunned for a moment. Divorce? Khalie? He loved her? What?

I slammed my foot into James's back. "Wake up."

Leo dropped his ice cream and stared at me. Everything I had believed was suddenly turned inside out, and I shook. "Go play with your brothers." When Leo didn't move, I snapped, "Now."

James rolled over. "What's wrong?" I waved the paper, and he jumped to his feet. "Give me that."

"What is it?" I demanded, trying to keep my voice down, but people stared already.

"It's . . . just give it to me." He lunged for the paper.

141

I balled it into my hand and sprinted shoeless toward the gravel parking lot. When I reached the edge, I followed a small, dusty path into the trees that separated the street from the beach.

James caught up to me and grabbed my arm. I yanked away. "Do not touch me."

"Bee, it's a therapy exercise. That's all." Desperation oozed from his words. "My therapist wanted me to write a note to someone. Just to see if I could feel something."

"To Khalie?" My mind spun trying to think of anyone he knew named Khalie. "Why not me? Don't you love me?"

He reached for me again, but I jumped back, into a wood railing. My foot slipped off the edge. I winced in pain and fell to my knees, overcome with pain and emotions.

"Is it the Khalie the contractor? The one you hired in New York last year?" My voice shook, and I struggled to draw a breath.

"Nothing has happened between us. She doesn't even know about this."

"But you love her?" I shrieked. "How the hell does that work?"

"I . . ."

"Go back to the boys," I ordered, shoving his chest. "I can't see you right now."

He lifted his hand to grab my arms, but I shoved past him. He veered right, and I dodged around him.

Khalie. What the fuck?

After James left, I stood shoeless in the dusty parking lot, under the beating sun, as happy beachgoers unpacked their cars and laughed.

It was a therapy exercise, I insisted despite the suspicion and doubt swirling in my mind. Nothing had happened. She didn't even know.

It wasn't an affair. Just the ramblings of a mentally ill man.

That's all it was. Why would James lie? If he were in love with Khalie, and she returned his feelings, then me finding out would be a good thing for them because James would be able to divorce me.

It had to be a misguided therapy exercise.

So why didn't I believe James?

"Mom?" Ryan stood behind me.

I steadied my breath before turning around. Ryan held my phone and eyed me cautiously. "I thought you might need this?"

Composure. I needed composure. "Thank you." I took my phone. "Why don't you go back down to the beach. Dad's there."

I wandered away from my son, farther along the parking lot, and sat down on a redwood stump. Splinters poked at my bikini-clad butt, but I didn't care. It was hardly any pain at all.

The letter was nothing. James was confused, that's all, and I needed to help get him back on track.

Not knowing what to do, I called Julie. After I sobbed my way through the situation, she told me to bring the boys to her house. She would watch them.

"But what should I do?" I cried. "What am I supposed to do? How do I fix this?"

"Transfer all the money and hire an attorney."

"Why?"

"He's having an affair."

I hung up. James wouldn't do that. He wouldn't have an affair. He had a brain injury. And this was a therapy exercise.

I clung to my self-deception despite the voice shouting the truth in my mind.

To this day, I hate Carly Rae Jepsen's "Call Me Maybe." James played it on repeat as we tore down the highway toward San Francisco. The boys sat quietly in the back of the minivan, and I think they knew. For nine months, they'd witnessed the growing tension between James and me, but this was different.

I didn't cry. I didn't rage. I simply folded up on myself.

After dropping the boys at Julie's, James drove us home. Every single tear erupted from me, and I tossed myself on our bed.

"Bee, I'm sorry."

"About what? A therapy exercise? Why are you sorry about that?" I choked out the words between sobs.

"I don't know." James hung his head.

"You do know! You're sorry because it's not a therapy exercise!" I tested out Julie's theory, hoping James would refute it, but he stared at the ground. "Does she know?"

"No. It's one-sided." James avoided my gaze. "She has a husband. This is all me."

I needed to be bigger than this moment. "Whatever it is needs to stop." I shifted into fix-it mode. "You cannot be alone with her. You cannot talk about personal things with her. You cannot talk to her about anything other than her job. Do you understand?"

James closed his eyes. "Yes."

"Good." Somewhere in my mind, I knew his explanation didn't make sense, but I wanted it to. I needed it to.

It was a therapy exercise. That was all.

He moved so our knees touched. "I'm sorry I've hurt you. Maybe a trip to Palm Springs would be good for you? You and the boys could go down tomorrow. Why don't you see if Deb can drive out and meet you?"

I gaped at him. "You want me to leave?"

"No," he said slowly. "I just think, well, maybe you need some time to calm down. I'll fly down on Friday."

"We can't fix this if we're not together."

He frowned. "I have to work."

"Will Khalie be there? I don't want you working with her." I spied the beach bag on the ground near the door where I had dropped it. Like a siren, the letter called to me, and I wanted to reread it, if only to find clues.

"I have to. It's my job." James took my hand and rub the back of it. "She's based in New York."

"What do you love about her?" I asked. I needed to know where I fell short and the areas where I could improve.

"I don't love her," James said firmly. "Believe me, I don't."

"But you don't love me?"

"There are glimmers. Sparks." He stared at the corner of the room. "I'm trying."

I latched onto his words. There was hope. We weren't doomed.

After much prodding, James persuaded me to take the boys to the desert. I spent the entire time drinking margaritas and neglecting my young children. At one point, Tate slipped off the pool step, and I didn't notice. Thankfully, a man was next to him and pulled him up.

That wasn't enough to stop my drinking.

Thankfully, my friend Deb joined me on the second day, and she took over caring for the boys. When James arrived on Saturday morning, angry and fuming over his flight delays, she hustled all our children to the pool so I could calm him.

But even happy-go-lucky Deb couldn't take James's bad attitude, and she left shortly after his arrival. I tried to salvage the trip, but James grew angrier and more withdrawn, and I grew more suspicious. When he joined the boys in the pool, I grabbed his phone off the cabana table and tried to go through it, but he had changed his password.

I crouched down behind a lounge chair, his phone clasped in my hand, and tried every password I knew of his. Nothing worked.

Why would he change his password? Was he hiding something?

"Did you change your password?" I asked when he returned to the cabana.

"What?" He dried off with a towel.

"Your phone password. Why did you change it?"

He dropped the towel on a chair. "Work made me."

"That's convenient." I trembled and tossed his phone at him. "Open it."

"Bee . . ." He stared at the phone before shoving it into his trunks' pocket.

"The boys and I are leaving," I said. "You can stay or come with us. Your choice, but I'm not staying here with a liar."

"I'm not a liar, and I'm coming with you." He scooped up the pool bag.

On the long drive home, I made sure the boys kept their headphones on and watched DVDs. James curled up in the passenger seat, knees to chest, and alternated between crying and muttering that he should have died.

My anger and confusion lost out to sympathy. James had been through a horrific trauma, but I couldn't stop the voice in my mind telling me he was lying.

14

June 19th, 2012

After we returned from Palm Springs, James touched me constantly. While it felt strange at first, I craved his affection and lapped up his new attention. I wanted to push my unpleasant suspicions aside, and I almost did because James, while still secretive, was sweeter and kinder toward me and the boys.

The letter, however, sat at the front of my mind. No matter how fervently James insisted that Khalie was just a woman he worked with, and that he had written the letter months ago after I said I wanted a divorce, I couldn't free myself of the thought that his explanations were nonsensical.

Well after midnight, we had fallen asleep with our arms and legs twisted together, like a tangled knot. James's arm still rested across my torso, keeping me pinned against him, and I tried to savor the moment, but my mind would not turn off.

Khalie. What was it about Khalie that James had fixated on? How was she different than me?

Street light filtered through the slits in the navy curtains. I squinted at the clock. It was only five, and since school was out, I didn't need to wake up for two more hours, but I couldn't relax. I had barely eaten since finding the letter, and sleep had become elusive, giving me more time to obsess over Khalie.

I imagined her to be tall, blonde, and perky. She had to be stunning with a large, warm laugh and sophisticated style. If James were going to cheat on me, he'd trade up, not down.

The bed shook. My obsessive thoughts paused as I tried to decide if it was an earthquake or a truck rumbling up the street.

It shook again, and I realized James's phone was buzzing. Not wanting it to wake him, I gently pulled away from him and rolled off the platform bed. His phone laid on the bed's platform ledge, and it vibrated angrily.

In the dim light, I grabbed it. My first thought was to turn it off and go back to sleep, but something in my gut told me to go through his phone. The day before, I had stealthily watched him punch in his new password so Tate could play a game, and I had filed the number away.

I crept past Leo and Tate's room to the bathroom. As I waited for my eyes to adjust, I sat down on the toilet seat. The phone lay heavy in my hand, and a sense of wrongness hit me. I should trust James. I should.

But I didn't.

With a shaking hand, I punched in the password. His email box brimmed with messages.

The possibility of what I may find struck me, and I considered returning the phone without snooping. Things were getting better. James touched me. He held me. He told me he loved me. Three months earlier, when I wanted a divorce, he did none of those things.

Did I want to upend our progress?

I hit the mail icon. Three different accounts popped up: work, his old Yahoo account, and one I didn't recognize. I tapped that first.

Every message was from Khalie.

"Why aren't you answering me? Is everything okay? You didn't call. Where are you?"

I blinked. Had James missed a meeting? I looked at the time stamp. Nine thirty at night. James said Khalie lived in New York, which put her time after midnight when she sent the message.

It wasn't a meeting.

Vomit burned my throat, but I tapped the next message. A chain between James and Khalie popped up.

The latest read: "I'm going to leave her, I promise. I just need to get through this lawsuit. Once it's done, we can be together. I can't wait to hold you in my arms again."

"I love you," she responded. "Our faith will carry us through."

What the fuck?

I slid off the toilet and leaned against the wall. My shock kept me reading.

Message after message professed their love for each other and James's plans to leave me and the boys once the lawsuit was settled. A horrible realization hit me: he gave me the $10,000 as a consolation gift. He was preparing me for when he left.

Did Khalie and James laugh over my naivety?

For months, I had run around behind him, excusing and explaining away his horrible behavior, and losing parts of myself in the process. I stood and caught a glimpse of myself in the mirror. My hair stuck out at weird angles, but my ash-white face was stone cold.

I had been an idiot.

I flung the bathroom door open and stormed down the hall. James snored peacefully. He wasn't living my nightmare, but he was about to.

I flicked on the overhead light and screamed, "Wake up!"

James startled and bolted upright. He couldn't see without

his glasses, so I waved his phone in his face. "Guess what? Khalie misses you. And don't worry, you're going to get your divorce."

"What?" He tried to swipe the phone from me as I jumped backward. "Give it to me," he stammered.

I threw the phone at the wall, cracking it. "You don't get to tell me what to do anymore! No more."

James lunged at me and pinned my arms to my side.

I struggled against him. "Let me go."

"No."

I gritted my teeth. "You will let me go, or I will knee you so hard in the balls you'll never be able to have sex with Khalie again."

James dropped his hands, and I ran to the other side of the room, near the windows. He paced back and forth near the door with his hands clenching his head. "It's not what you think."

"Do not try to make me think I'm crazy. You've done that enough." I kept my voice cold and flat despite wanting to crumble into a heap.

"Just let me explain." James stepped toward me, and I held up my hand, halting him.

A million questions raced through my mind, but I picked the most pressing one. "Do you love her?"

James paled. "It's not like that."

"Then what? You used her for sex because you refused to sleep with me?" I stormed at him and shoved his chest. "Because that's a problem of your own making."

He collapsed to his knees. "Please, Bee. Please. I'm sorry. I'm so sorry. You have to believe me."

I folded my arms and loomed over him. "How many times?"

James's gaze darted wildly around the room. "Three times, and it hasn't happened in a while. I was drunk. That's all."

"That's three times too many," I snapped. Every noise was amplified; every word we said permanently etched itself into my brain. "Why should I believe you? You've been lying to me for weeks? Months?"

"Please." James reached up for me. When I pushed him away, he sobbed.

"Stop groveling. It's pathetic." I picked up the cracked phone. It was close to six. "Go downstairs and tell your parents what you've done. Go explain to them why you've been an asshole to all of us. Go on." I yanked him to his feet and pushed him toward the door. "Go be a man for once and own it."

James ran out of the room. As his footsteps thundered down the stairs, I opened his email again and began searching the phone for anything related to Khalie. Dozens of pictures popped up as did emails from the previous nine months. I sat down, unprepared for the betrayal I was about to uncover, and began reading.

When James returned, his eyes were red and his face was blotchy.

I ignored him and kept going through his phone.

"I told my mom. Dad already left for work." James sat on his side of the bed, the side closer to the door.

"And?"

"She's upset." Another sob tumbled out of James "I let everyone down."

"I really don't care about your feelings right now." I glanced at the clock. "The boys need to get up for summer camp."

James nodded. "I'll do it. I'll get them ready and take them."

"Says the man on the verge of losing his family." I sneered at him. "You're disgusting."

He didn't reply as he shuffled out of the room with his head down.

After dropping the boys off, James stalked me. He badgered me. He pleaded with me.

"Go to work. Or see your therapist. Or both." I gnashed my

teeth. The anger I had held back for months had erupted. "I don't care, but I don't want to see you."

When James left, I rolled into a ball on my bed and let my emotions roar through me. I sobbed until my dry eyes itched.

My phone rang. It was Allison.

"Are you okay? I saw James's Facebook post," she said.

"What post?" I grabbed my laptop from the floor and yanked the top open.

Allison blew into the phone. "He wrote a long apology post for the affair he's been having."

The world spun, and I gasped. "He told everyone?" I whispered. "He put it on Facebook?"

"Yes." Allison sighed. "Do you need to talk? I can come over."

I opened Facebook, and James's post appeared at the top of my feed. "Oh my God." I whispered. James laid it all out. His affair, his betrayal, his love for me and the boys, and how we deserved better. "He told everyone."

"I'm on my way over," Allison said. "You can't be alone right now."

I stared at the screen in disbelief as our friends and family responded. The lump in my throat throbbed, and humiliation hit me hard. I absolutely could not see anyone.

"Don't come," I said. "I have a few things to do."

"Are you sure?"

I tried to sound in control. "I'll call you later."

The Facebook comments kept coming: some demanding James remove the post, and others clearly enjoying the train wreck. How would I ever show my face in the schoolyard again? How was I breathing? How was any of this possible?

I called James.

"Bee?"

"You asshole! You motherfucking asshole!" I screamed. "You really want to ruin my life, don't you?"

"I—"

Click. I couldn't listen to him anymore, and I refused to let him control the situation. I had to do something to knock him sideways.

He needed to hurt as much as me.

It was clear I couldn't stay in San Francisco, not with everyone knowing.

I steadied my breath and focused. I had money. A lot of it.

I closed my eyes and thought for a moment.

Shortly after turning sixteen, I had decided to leave my small town along the Detroit River and run away from its ominous, puffing steel mills and lack of opportunities. I wanted college and a real career, and I saw no option or path beyond being a secretary and finding a husband—or two—if I didn't leave.

For three months, I plotted my escape with my best friend, Jenn. We would convince our parents to let us visit my mother in California. It didn't matter that I had rarely seen her during the previous ten years. I would visit, and once there, figure out how to stay.

To my and Jenn's surprise, our parents agreed to our scheme, and we flew to California with my youngest sister in tow. My mom planned a grand adventure for us: driving from Silicon Valley to Hollywood and Disneyland. As we cruised beneath towering redwoods and past the sparkling Pacific Ocean, I let California seduce me. There was no doubt in my mind I had found my place.

"I can't come home," I said through tears when I called Dad the next day. "Please let me stay in California." I hated nothing more than breaking my dad's heart, and in that moment, listening to his throat catch tore me to pieces.

Dad stayed silent, but his heavy breath rushed through the phone receiver. "Is this what you want?" he finally said. "Are you sure?"

The protective part of my mind screamed for me to go home and take the known path, but my heart longed for adventure and the unknown possibilities that came with it.

I had said the words. There was no going back.

"Yes," I said, sniffing.

"Then we'll send your things."

With his resigned blessing, my course shifted, and the inevitability of my previous life slipped away, leaving a world of possibility.

I had once been decisive and fiercely independent, but over the years, I had surrendered to existing only as part James and Bee, and as the boys' mother. Had I drifted so far from who I once was that she'd been lost forever? Was that girl still inside me?

I opened my laptop. Paris. I could go to Paris. I would be like Victoria and start my life over. I could do it, and James couldn't stop me.

Before he realized my plans, I transferred even more money out of our joint account into my personal one. Then, I bought the first available business class ticket to Paris, arranged for the boys to fly alone to my parents' home in Michigan, and began packing.

I was done trying to fix James. It was time to fix myself.

15

———

Music blasted up and down the crowded rue. Vendors sold light food in addition to wine and beer from street-side carts, and the mob around us moved in unison to the beat. Victoria grabbed my hand and pulled me through the throng of people.

"How do you like Fête?" she yelled over the enthusiastic shouts of the crowd. "You came at a great time!"

"It's amazing! Thanks for inviting me along!" Immediately after booking my flight, I had emailed Victoria with the happy news that I'd be in town for at least a month. I failed to explain why.

I had arrived in Paris earlier in the day. When I stepped off the plane, dozens of messages from James greeted me. He decided to fly with the boys to Michigan and had submitted their passport applications along with the notarized permission document I hastily secured before leaving. My hazy plan was to bring the boys to Paris if James and I were going to divorce. I didn't tell James this, though, and had insisted that it was so we could all be together in Paris as a family.

James had sent me detailed directions on how to find the

RER train at the airport because he had no faith that I could find it on my own. I suppose it was a nice gesture, but at the time it infuriated me, and I refused to answer his calls or messages.

So here I was, standing on a rue in Paris, looking up at Sacré-Cœur while a city-wide music festival raged around me. It felt like I was watching my life from above; that I was just a spectator of my misery.

"Where's your apartment?" Victoria's friend asked. I felt bad because I kept forgetting her name, but she had lovely, dark skin and big, brown eyes and was by far the prettiest woman I'd seen in ages.

"Le Marais. Rue Chapon."

The friend nodded. "Le Marais is nice. Touristy, but nice."

We bought wine from a flirting vendor and passed street performers dancing with glowing hula hoops. We danced and sang and danced some more, and for the first time in nearly two years, I didn't feel anxious or miserable.

I was free of James and his problems.

Victoria and I met a man who told us a terrible tale of love and loss, and for a minute I thought of everything I had lost with James, but then I remembered I was in Paris, and crying was illegal there.

At some point, we made our way to a nightclub. Victoria stood outside next to a motorcycle while her friend snapped pictures. She radiated happiness, and I decided that was the magic of Paris—if I tried hard enough, I could be happy again. But then I saw our group selfie, and despite my smile, my eyes were dull and vacant.

I was lying to myself. Again. Like I always did.

After midnight, Victoria and her friend walked me to the Métro and showed me how to read the map. Victoria put a Paris Métro app on my phone, and her friend told me to walk away from the water when I exited the station.

We double kissed good-bye, with plans to see each other soon, and I set off on my 1 a.m. adventure across town.

It was dangerous and exhilarating, and I knew I could do anything or be anyone, and I didn't have to define myself by James.

At the Hôtel de Ville stop, I climbed above ground and tried to figure out the direction of the Seine. I couldn't see it, so I started walking. My phone had died, and I couldn't remember where my apartment was.

Broken glass and empty plastic cups littered the street. I kicked at a wine bottle and watched it roll into the gutter. In the courtyard outside the Pompidou, I realized I had no idea how to get back to my apartment. I was lost in Paris, but I wasn't concerned.

Two police officers stood a little way off, chatting and watching the revelers. Bravely, I approached them and asked for help in slurred French. After conferring, they decided my street was farther down off Rue Saint-Martin. In a sleep-deprived, liquored-fueled haze, I followed twisting and turning rues. Finally, as purple light lanced the sky, I found my apartment.

It was only luck that let me remember the passcode to get through the enormous wooden door. I climbed five flights of stairs and forced my heavy, metal key into the exterior balcony door that separated the narrow walkway to my apartment from the stairwell. I skittered along the walkway, before stopping at my apartment door. The listing agent had told me to jiggle the doorknob while I turned the key, so I did, and it opened without a problem.

Exhausted, I collapsed on my bed and slept for three hours.

A deep obsession grabbed hold of me that day. When I woke, I immediately opened my laptop and began digging up everything I could about Khalie. To my horror, she had followed my author Facebook fan page and had even commented positively on a few of my posts. She also followed me on Twitter and on my blog.

I opened my notebook and made a timeline based off the limited knowledge I had squeezed from James before I left. He had sworn that the affair began in March and they had only slept together three times.

I didn't believe him.

I plunged into a rabbit hole and only left my apartment to eat a late lunch and get bottles of water. I stopped showering and sat in bed all day. Every phone call I received, I ignored, sending them to voicemail until it stopped taking messages. I searched and searched and searched, driven by a sense that there had to be some reason, something I did, that caused James to cheat.

I thought about myself before James's accident, immediately after, and during the last several months. I'd spun stories to make sense of our unraveling marriage, but what role had I played in his affair? And who was I really? A loving, devoted wife? A scared, clingy middle-aged woman? An overbearing control freak? Could I be all at once?

Did it matter? I racked my brain, searching for the reason this had happened, and arrived at one conclusion.

I wasn't enough. I lacked something that James, like my mother, could see.

On day three of my self-imposed isolation, I swallowed my pride and called James. I had questions and needed answers. My brain would not rest until I had some sort of closure.

"Bee?"

"Don't call me that." I was listening to Lady Antebellum's "As You Turn Away" on repeat and turned it up.

"Don't listen to that," James said. "It's not going to make you feel better."

"I'd feel better if you hadn't done this to me."

He didn't say anything.

"I hate you," I snapped. "I hate everything about you. You're a liar, and I will never trust you again."

James said nothing as I verbally beat him down. When I finished, tears streamed down my face, and I screamed, "Aren't you going to say anything?"

"I'm sorry. I love you, and I want to fix this." His voice hitched. "Please, Bee, let me try to fix this."

All my research told me that he needed to definitively end things with his mistress. "Have you talked to her?"

He hesitated. "She knows you're in Paris."

"You told her where I was?" I screamed. "You told her I ran away? She's going to think she won!"

"It's not like that." He blew into the phone. "I need to go to New York on Monday for work, but I'm flying with the boys to Michigan first." He paused. "I need to talk to your parents."

I broke into a cold sweat and zeroed in on the important information. "You're going to see her?"

"I'm going for work."

"She won," I whispered. "You're choosing her over me."

"Bee—"

"Fuck you." I slammed the black phone onto the receiver. I couldn't let him anywhere near Khalie ever again. I needed to stop whatever was about to happen.

In a fit of desperation, I pulled up James's company's website. Months earlier, I had met the head of HR, a woman named Sally who James worked closely with. My hand trembled as I pushed in the main office phone number. When the receptionist answered, I asked to speak with Sally in HR.

She picked up immediately. "Hello?"

"Hi, Sally, this is James Sutton's wife. I'm sorry to bother you, but I have a problem."

"Oh, hi! How are you?" She was a friendly woman with a big voice, and as we chitchatted, my plan coalesced.

"I'm sure you know James had an accident at the end of 2010?" I asked.

"Yes, I remember."

I chose my next words carefully. "Well, he never took any time off, and unfortunately, he's been struggling with PTSD and depression." I intentionally didn't mention the brain injury. "We're embroiled in a lawsuit, and he's struggling. I think he needs a break but is afraid to ask. What needs to happen to get him a leave of absence?"

Sally blew into the phone. "I had no idea he was struggling. I'm so sorry."

"He'll be fine." I didn't believe this, but what else was I going to say? "He just needs a break to regroup."

"We give a ninety-day medical leave. We'll need a note from his doctor to document it, but other than that, he just needs to contact me and let me know he wants to take it."

I frowned. I had hoped I could get the leave and then inform James. I didn't want a confrontation—I wanted it done. "He doesn't know I called," I confessed. "If he gets back to you today, would it go into effect immediately?"

"It would."

"He has a trip to New York on Monday." My voice shook thinking about how he was going to be with Khalie again. "I'm worried going will make him worse."

"I'll pull him off it. Everything will be okay."

"Great. I'll talk to him now."

After I hung up, I sat there for a moment, trying to gather my thoughts. I had to stop James from going to New York because I feared Khalie would convince him that my running away meant I didn't want our marriage anymore. Maybe there was truth in that, because my motivation for asking for the leave wasn't fueled by my love of James. I thought I despised him. My singular intent was to not let Khalie dictate the rules of my marriage anymore.

I gathered my courage and rang James. When he picked up, I said without greeting, "I called Sally in HR. You're going to get a note from your doctor detailing your injuries to give to her. That will get you a ninety-day leave of absence effective immediately." I paused. "You are not going to New York. That trip is off."

"You did what?" Anger permeated James's voice. "You told my company about the affair? Why the hell did you do that?"

I fought the hateful words building in me. "I did not tell them about the affair. I told Sally you have PTSD and depression, and that you need a break. You can either take it and try to fix things with me, or you can fly to New York and be with Khalie. Your choice, but don't say I didn't give you an option."

Without hesitation, he said, "I'll take care of it now."

After hanging up, I sank into my pillows. Khalie may have had the upper hand for months, but we were on equal footing now, and I had no intention of letting James be anywhere near her.

That night, I received the first email from Khalie. It was a collection of PDF files documenting handwritten notes between James and her. I pored over each one, studying the contents, looking for clues on why this happened, and adding my findings to a growing list in my notebook.

The thing that troubled me the most was a note dating from early December. In it, James described watching her sleep in the seat next to him as they flew to Asia. He told her that he had never felt anything so strong, so fast as his love for her.

Sitting in my tiny Paris apartment, I read the letter over and over again until I could recite every single word.

James had lied. I suspected, of course, but now I had concrete evidence. He did love her, and the affair had started in December. He had never mentioned taking Khalie on this trip, but he knew before he left that she would be there. He had basically run out of the house and thrown himself into her arms.

I read my detailed notes. The timeline didn't add up. James said the affair started in January and ended in March. So, was it a December through March thing? He told me the first time had happened after a team dinner when she came back to his hotel, and they had a drink in the lobby bar. He hadn't meant for it to happen. It just did.

I chewed on his story and the note from the plane. Did he fall in love with Khalie before he actually slept with her? What did that mean?

I rang James again.

"Did you use protection with Khalie?" I blurted

"What?"

"When you had sex with her in December, did you use protection?"

"Of course."

"I thought you didn't have sex until January." I paused.

He was hanging himself. "I don't remember."

I was tired of James's convenient memory loss. "Timing aside, you want me to believe a married woman carries condoms in her purse? Because if you bought them, then it was premeditated on your part."

"She . . . she had them. I swear."

"I doubt it."

James didn't say a word.

"That's what I thought." I clicked off.

December, I wrote in my notebook. It started in December, not January.

It was well past midnight in Paris, and warm, June-night air filled my room. There was no air conditioning in my apartment, and I kept the bedroom windows open, praying for a breeze. From the bed, I had a view of rooftops sloping at odd angles. Somewhere across the courtyard, people laughed and sang.

I reached behind me to the shelf over the bed and grabbed a bottle of water and my Klonopin. My doctor had given me a three-month supply when I told her my situation, and I had been taking them according to the directions. But that night, my mind wouldn't calm down, and I swallowed two pills at once.

I lay back in bed, cranked up the depressing music, and tried to eradicate the endless images of my husband in bed with Khalie.

I couldn't do it.

16

I knew James was coming. I had all but ordered him to, and yet, when he called from my building's front door, I burst into nervous tears. His arrival was an intrusion into the safe cocoon I had created, and as much as I didn't want to see him, something deep inside me wanted to see him more. I needed to look him in the eyes and demand answers to the questions Khalie's emails had raised.

As I waited for him to make the trek up five flights of stairs, I walked across the microscopic bedroom to the floor-to-ceiling window. Unlike every other day, the sun was hidden behind clouds, and a soft sprinkle fell from the sky. The hum of traffic mingled with the tinkling of piano keys from the music school a few doors down.

James had come. He had given his request for a leave of absence, didn't go on his trip to New York, and flew to be with me. Everything I had read on various affair recovery sites said marriages could be saved if the guilty party not only showed remorse but actively accepted blame. James had taken the first step toward fixing things, and I should have felt relieved. After all, it seemed as if I had won.

164

My sour stomach churned. Was I ready to see him? It had only been a week, and James had spent it with the boys at my parents' home in Michigan. He had confessed his crimes, and my dad, while furious, felt James wanted to save our family.

"What should I do?" I asked my dad. I no longer cried. I wanted facts, not emotions.

He paused for a moment. "That's up to you, but you need to really think about what you want for yourself and what you want for your family."

"I want to not be married to a cheating asshole."

"Hon, I think you should give James an opportunity to explain himself. Don't decide anything until after the two of you speak honestly."

With Dad's words swirling through my mind, I unlocked my apartment door and hurried back to the couch. I pulled a blanket over my knees even though it was a humid day, and I assumed a hardened mindset. I would not let James confuse me or make me feel pity for him. I needed to protect myself.

But when James appeared, framed by the screened-door window, my breath caught. He looked ragged, like he'd not slept in days. Our eyes locked.

I hated him. He needed to leave.

I loved him. I wanted him to hold me and fix things.

"Bee?" James said. "Unlock the door?"

I couldn't move.

"Sweetheart, let me in. Please." Sweetheart. He hadn't called me that in months.

I struggled to hold back tears. I didn't move. "How could you do this?"

He pressed his hand against the door frame. "Let me in so we can talk. People are going to wonder why I'm standing out here."

I kicked back the blanket, my cocoon of safeness, and stumbled across the tiny living room. I stopped short of the door. If I let James in, was I committing to trying to fix things? Did I even want to try to fix things? What the hell did I want?

"Bee? Are you going to open the door?"

I clicked the lock and ran back to the couch. When James stepped inside and dropped his bag on the floor, I felt his intrusion. He didn't belong here, and his shattered appearance annoyed me.

He gave me a hopeful smile, and I returned it with a blank stare. James sighed.

I'm not sure what he expected, but I'm positive it wasn't the complete indifference I exhibited. He glanced around my tiny apartment.

"It's cute." He hadn't left his spot near the door. "Do you like it?"

"Yes."

The apartment had a small bedroom at the rear, a mini bathroom with a washing machine, and a microscopic kitchen in addition to a living space. I had found a real estate agent the morning I discovered James's affair, and this apartment was the only Marais property available on a short notice. I had immediately sent the agent a month's rent.

James stepped tentatively toward the couch, toward my safe zone. "Can I sit down?"

I tucked my legs beneath me, making space for him at the far end, and wrapped the blanket tighter around myself. It was the only thing protecting me from him.

"Thank you for letting me come." James kept his head down. "I didn't think you would."

I wanted to scream, but my words came out flat. "You can sleep out here." I stood and dropped the blanket on the ground, exposing myself. I pointed at the apartment-sized L-shaped couch. "It's not uncomfortable."

James shifted forward, elbows on knees, and stared up at me without saying anything.

"What?" Every word, every gesture had an unbearable weight that crushed me and made me question my decision to let James come.

Before his accident, James and I had always been a team, and like any successful team, our strength came when we made decisions together. I had failed to understand that teams consist of individuals, and each one could change the outcome of the game. James stopped being a team player when he decided that he loved Khalie. He had made decisions on his own, with no regard to how they would impact me, our boys, or our marriage. I couldn't trust him.

"I'm sorry." Tears dampened James's cheeks. "Not only did I cheat on you, I emotionally abused you. I know that now."

I blinked at him. Other than the time James and I fought and I fell down the stairs, he had never laid a hand on me. "You abused me?"

James hung his head. "Bee, what I did was unforgivable, but I'm asking you to try. I want to fix this. I'll get therapy. I'll do whatever it takes."

I wanted to be firm and not let his emotions sway me in any direction. "You dangled me along for months while you fucked Khalie. You made me feel sorry for you." I narrowed my eyes. "I hate you."

A long sob rumbled out of him. He reached for me, and I stepped away, shaking my head.

"Can't I hold you?" he begged.

"No." I recoiled in repulsion. "You're disgusting. Do not touch me."

He wiped away his tears. "What can I do?"

I had no idea. Even though he had come, he hadn't really

chosen me. After all, until I got his leave of absence, he had intended to go to New York and to Khalie.

"I'm tired," I said. "I'm going to take a nap."

James studied me for a moment. "You don't look well."

Despite my hesitance about seeing him, I had showered, blown my hair out, and put on makeup. I wanted James to find me attractive, or at least as attractive as tall, dark, smiling Khalie. "I look fine."

He shook his head and stood. He took a step toward me, and I held my ground with my arms crossed against my torso. "Bee, you've lost weight. A lot."

I hadn't had much appetite, eating mostly dried apricots and almonds. Nothing else stayed down, not even salads. When I dressed that morning, my jeans had slipped off my hips, and I threw on a dress instead. Once it fit comfortably across my chest, but now the dress hung limply off my shoulders.

"No one loses that much weight in a week." I ran my hand over my boney hip.

"You have." James frowned. "We need to buy you some clothes that fit."

I studied him for a minute. "You want to go shopping?"

James nodded. "Just to get you a few things."

Going out was better than staying in my small apartment with someone I possibly, maybe hated. "Fine."

It was the first time James would try to make me feel better by filling up my life with things.

I stood in the dimly lit Levi's dressing room with a stack of discarded jeans on the floor. The sales associate kept bringing me more items. I started with a size 29 and was now waiting for her to see if she could find a 24. James wasn't wrong: I had lost an insane amount of weight in ten days.

When she returned, she studied my half-dressed body. "You are very tiny," she said in French. "We only have size twenty-five."

I shrugged. "Then I'll take those."

From outside the curtain, James asked, "Do they have your size?"

"No." I stooped over and pulled out two pairs of jeans before handing the pile to the associate. "I'm getting these." I held up the pairs I rescued. I jerked my head toward the waiting area. "He can pay."

"Your husband?" she asked in French. James couldn't understand us, and I liked that.

I held up my naked ring finger. As soon as I found out about the affair, I had taken off my ring. Like my marriage, it meant nothing.

I hesitated. "No. I am not married."

"He is your lover?" She smiled coyly.

"Hardly." I tugged my dress over my head. "But he'll pay."

After she left, I studied myself in the mirror. I had said I wasn't married, and it didn't feel strange. I could be not married to James, and it would be okay. Even more importantly, I would be okay. Hadn't I found an apartment and left for Paris in less than twelve hours, and learned to navigate the Métro and winding Parisian rues alone? I would survive without him.

I tore back the red curtain, exposing James, who typed furiously on his phone. My vision wavered. "Who are you texting?"

James jerked his head up and shoved the phone into his shorts' pocket. "No one."

The room spun. This is what he did with Khalie. He acted secretively and lied, and he was doing it again. "Is it Khalie?" I tried to stay calm, but panic welled inside me. "Is it?" I stormed toward him and grabbed at his pocket. "Show me your phone."

James grabbed my wrist. "Bee, it wasn't Khalie. I swear."

I broke free of his grasp. "Then who?"

His gaze flicked to the left. "A work colleague."

"Who?" There wasn't anyone else in the dressing area, and I raised my voice. "Who are you texting?"

James struggled to answer, and I shoved him before sprinting out of the store.

Before he could catch me, I melted into the crowd along Rue de Rivoli. It was the summer sale season in Paris, and the city brimmed with tourists speaking foreign languages and enjoying the now-gorgeous June day. I hurried in no specific direction, dodging shopping bags and sightseers.

An ever-increasing tempo banged on my heart. Eventually, I stopped walking and pressed my back against a cool, ancient stone building. No one paid me any attention as I muttered and wrapped my arms around myself.

I was safe. James couldn't find me. I was okay.

I walked past the Tuileries and found a small, shady park with benches encircling a fountain. There were only a few other people lounging and reading, and I took a seat. My phone vibrated urgently as text after text from James filled my phone screen. I deleted them without reading.

Images of James and Khalie laughing and having fun throughout Europe filled my mind. I struggled to think of something else, but nothing worked. My body shook with sobs.

How could James do this? How?

I pulled up my phone and typed in Khalie's name. She was everywhere—pictures, message boards, professional sites. In a fit of madness, I screen shot a picture of her smiling widely and saved it to my phone. I opened a site I had heard about on an infidelity message board, She's a Homewrecker.

My intent was to strike to kill.

Within minutes, I had typed up my sordid story and uploaded Khalie's picture. In that moment, I felt great satisfaction. I posted it and walked away from it, believing I'd never have to think about it again.

The hot, sticky day shifted into a slightly less sticky evening. I had to return to my apartment at some point. Avoiding James was impossible, but what then? How was I supposed to move forward?

As I shuffled home, through the thinning crowds, I planned a speech. I would tell James to leave. I would explain my plans to bring the boys over and start a new life without him. We were done, and I needed to show my boys that James's behavior wasn't acceptable. I had the strength to do it.

I climbed the five flights of marble stairs to my apartment. Across the courtyard, a dog barked and loud singing echoed off rooftops. How could anyone possibly be so happy that they would belt out French pop songs?

I stepped inside the dark apartment, crossed the small wooden floor, and dropped my bag on the bistro table. An eerie silence surrounded me. Exhausted, I entered the bedroom. James lay crosswise on the bed with his legs dangling off the side nearest me. He looked up from his phone.

"What are you doing?" I asked.

"Waiting for you."

My planned speech evaporated. "Why?"

He rolled over. "I was worried. You're not acting like yourself."

I had no roadmap on how to handle my husband's infidelity even though I'd spent hours, days really, studying various blogs. Without fail, the blogs gave tips on how to leave the marriage, but despite everything, forcing James out of my life felt wrong.

Staying with him didn't feel right either. I was stuck in a vast middle ground with no clear direction.

The sun had dipped over the rooftops, and yellow lights glowed through windows around the courtyard. It was well after ten, maybe almost eleven. I'd been up for nearly twenty hours.

"I need to change and go to sleep." I walked around the bed, toward the wardrobe. "You need to go to the living room."

James nodded and left. He didn't say good night when he closed the bedroom door, and I wondered what that meant. Would he sneak out in the middle of the night, leaving me before I had the chance to leave him? And if he did, would it make much difference? Yes, it would. He'd publicized his affair, so either I had to leave to save face, or he would leave and humiliate me more.

I fell into bed, counted out three Klonopin, and swallowed them with a gulp of water. As I listened to music through my headphones, my mind stilled, and I drifted to sleep.

I'm not sure how much later it was, but I startled awake from another nightmare. Out of habit, I reached for James, and in a half-asleep daze I rolled into his side, searching for him, but only found a cold, empty spot. It took me a moment to piece together where I was and why James wasn't in bed.

I got off the bed and found James, on his phone, in the living room. He looked up at me in surprise.

"What's wrong?" he asked.

"How could you do this?" I whispered. It was the only question that mattered. I stormed at him. "How?"

I lost control, my fists flying, and my words striking him over and over again. I called him filthy. I declared my hate for him. He ruined my life. I wanted a divorce.

Through it all, James stayed calm. When I exhausted myself, he picked me up and carried me back to the bedroom. He stretched out next to me, stroked my hair, and wiped my eyes. I didn't push him away.

I was simply too tired to fight anymore.

"I'm sorry, Bee. I know I can never make this up to you but let me try." He kissed my forehead, and I wailed. "Don't cry," he said. "Please don't cry."

It was well after two in the morning. Moonlight streamed through the open window, giving us both an unearthly glow. It had been ten days since I discovered the affair. Ten days. How could he expect me to not cry? For months, he had gashed at my heart. He had made me question my devotion. He had made me feel unstable and crazy.

"Don't ever say you love me again," I whispered. "You don't. You probably never did. Our marriage has been a lie."

Since childhood, I had searched for someone to love me; someone to take care of my emotions; someone to accept my proof of self-worth. I had saddled James with that tall order, which he had accepted and reveled in. I had trusted him completely to love me, and he hadn't. The pedestal I had erected for him was so high that I hadn't been able to entertain the idea of an affair—even when presented with concrete evidence. Now, his love was flawed, cracked, and possibly a mirage.

James held my face between his hands. He wiped my tears with his fingertips. "Please give me a chance. We can make this better."

All I had done for the past two years was try to fix our marriage. Did he not see that?

"What do you want?" I shrank away. "Do you want me to forgive you? Because I don't."

He flopped onto his back. "I want, no . . . I hope that you will try to fix this with me."

I sat up and hunched over on myself as I considered my

options. I could hurt alone, or I could hurt with James. There was no other way.

I don't know why, but I climbed across his lap, and when I had him straddled, I stared down at James and pinned his shoulders down—the hurt shoulders I had once protected. "I hate you. The thought of you touching me is revolting. You're filthy."

"I know." He placed his hands on my hips, and my breath caught.

I leaned over him, my lips hovering over his ear. I was driven by this deep urge to erase Khalie from his mind. I wanted to show him I could be everything she was and more. James and I had years of history between us, and that had to mean more than the months he spent with her.

Khalie may have been younger, taller, sexier, and more fun, but I knew James inside and out.

It was the first time we had hate sex. It was a pattern that would continue for months.

In the morning, James ventured to the grocery shop. He was appalled by my diet of almonds, water, and dried apricots, and was determined to make sure I started eating properly.

While he was gone, I showered. As the hot water washed over me, I let out a guttural cry because it was the twisted truth that as much as I hated James, my soul ached for him.

I had no idea who I was without him. For nearly eighteen months, I had put him absolutely first and expected everyone else to do the same. In my mind, the boys didn't need me as much as James. Plus, Molly was always there to step in and take care of all of us. But the truth was, I had ignored my children for months.

What kind of mother was I? I had abandoned them and run away. I slumped to the ground and consoled myself with the fact that they were somewhere with people who loved them as much as I did. My parents assured me they wanted James and me to use this alone time to figure things out before we said anything definitive to the boys. Plus, Molly had flown to Michigan to be with them, too. The boys were surrounded by love and away from the chaos. It was the best I could do in that moment.

I still didn't understand how James could do this. How did he look at us and not feel an immense sense of wrongness? How could he see the boys and not understand what he was doing to them?

I hated him.

I loved him.

I didn't know what I wanted.

I pressed my fingertips into my visible ribs. I hadn't disappeared yet, but the idea of not existing brought air into my lungs. I wanted to be done and float away and stop hurting.

Cold water pounded my chest, and I stood shivering with water rolling off me until James came home and found me. He grabbed a towel from the heated rack and wrapped me in it.

"It's going to be okay, Bee," he said. "It's going to be okay."

James hadn't wrapped my hair, and water dripped all over the couch when I sat down. "The couch is getting wet."

"It's okay."

Deep shame wedged itself in my heart. The night before had been a mistake, but that didn't stop me from throwing my arms around James and kissing him. When he pulled away, I gasped and sobbed. What was wrong with me? How could I long for James's affection and be repulsed by him at the same time?

"Are you okay?" James asked in confusion.

"Don't be nice to me," I ordered. "Don't be gentle. I can't do that."

"I don't want to hurt you."

I glared at him. "You already have."

I wrapped his fingers around my neck, and he blanched. "No."

"Hurt me. You like to hurt me."

"No."

"Then I'll hurt you." I slapped him across his face. When he didn't respond, I kissed him with more anger.

Somehow, we fell into bed again.

17

Over the course of the next few days, James filled his camera with photos of me: me in my tiny, pink running shorts posing along the Seine with the Eiffel Tower behind me; me in a cute dress in the Tuileries; me on the steps of Sacré-Cœur. Me. Me. Me. I had become the center of his world, and he was doing his best to prove it.

In the evenings, we would select the best photos and post them all over social media. I wanted Khalie to see that she hadn't destroyed me or my marriage. I wanted her to doubt everything James said and did, but I also needed those pictures to convince myself I was okay.

Most of what I remember during this time comes from those photos. When I stare at them, feelings bubble up, mostly confusion mixed with anger. I desperately wanted to control the situation, and at the same time, I wanted to run away. James kept insisting he loved me while I felt a strong break with any feelings of love I had ever felt for him.

My life had fractured into life before June 19th and life after June 19th, and nothing felt real. I couldn't make sense of how James betrayed me or how I naively believed his lies. Even more confusing was the way I clung to the very person who hurt me, and the more I screamed at James the worse I felt for not being able to control my emotions.

I wasn't the only one struggling. James later confessed he lived in a constant state of worry during that time because he had no idea what I would do. I'd always been steady and reliable, but my sudden decision to move to Paris threw him—just as I had hoped.

One afternoon, around the time of the Tuileries photo, I met up with Victoria for coffee. When I didn't arrive home on time, he called me over and over again, and I ignored him. Eventually, when I made my way home, I found James distressed.

"I thought something was wrong." He hugged me tightly. I refused to return his embrace and kept my arms firmly at my sides. It was a behavior that would continue for years. "You scared me." James's panic didn't stem from something actually happening to me, but rather him thinking I had run away, which was, in all fairness, a valid worry.

I shrugged away from him. My gaze landed on a beribboned, blue box on the small bistro table near the micro kitchen. "What's that?"

James grinned. "I got you something." He handed me the present. "I hope you like it."

It felt odd taking a gift from him, but I tugged the ribbon away and lifted the lid. Inside was a short, navy dress with a Peter Pan collar. The day before, I had spotted it in the window of a nearby shop, but I hadn't mentioned it to James.

"Do you like it? I saw it and thought of you." He stared at me expectantly. "Bee?"

I held the dress against me. James knew me so well. "It's a thirty-six," I said flatly. Despite our earlier shopping spree, I struggled to understand just how much weight I'd lost. "I hope it fits."

"You're tiny."

With his prompting, I tried on the dress, and it fit perfectly.

Heaviness settled over me. Nothing excited me—especially not gifts from James. "It's great." I pulled the dress off. "Thank you."

I wore it the next day when we visited the Louvre and the Tuileries. James and I found chairs in the shade near the round fountains and made up stories about the people around us. It distracted me from the disaster of my own life and helped us avoid talking about the state of our marriage. At one point, James had me stand so he could snap a series of pictures of me laughing and posing in front of the giant fountain. I dutifully posted them to Facebook with breezy captions, and the likes and loves rolled in.

I don't know how I did it.

I spent those days wandering around Paris in a daze. My brain couldn't separate the man who I loved from the man who betrayed me. I'd look at James and simultaneously be thankful he was with me while wishing he'd pack up and leave. If he had left, things would have been easier—there would have been no decisions for me to make about our future. I'd have the boys fly to Paris, and like Victoria, set up my new life. I'd move on in my own time, and eventually, the boys and I would be happy again.

After one particularly draining conversation about the affair, I called Dad again to ask what I should do.

"What do you want?" he asked in his comforting, flat Midwest accent.

"I don't know."

"Hon, if you have any hesitation about walking away, you owe it to the boys and yourself to see if you can make it work." He paused. "If you don't hesitate, you have your answer."

It wasn't that easy. By coming to me, James had shown his commitment to fixing our marriage. Still, I felt like a consolation prize. I had ripped him away from Khalie, and he defaulted to me out of fear of losing everything.

That night, as we walked home from having crêpes at Café des Arts, my messy brain clicked together another piece of the elaborate puzzle James had created.

"Have you spoken to Khalie?" I asked.

"Why would I do that?" He quickened his pace and dodged tourists.

I held his hand—something I started to do earlier that day—and pulled up short, yanking James to a stop. "Have you ended things with her?" I'd spent the past three weeks reading about affairs, and every expert agreed that affairs needed to be ended without question. There could be no open doors, no possibility of things rekindling. "Have you?"

James glanced away. "She knows I didn't go to New York."

Bile stung my throat. "You haven't told her it's over?" My voice pitched higher. "What the hell is wrong with you? Do you not want to be with me?"

"It's just . . . she's traveling. I thought I'd wait until she—"

"You're waiting because you don't know how things are going to go with me. That's why you've waited." I tore away from him. "You're unbelievable."

"Bee—"

I pivoted toward him. "You will call her when we get to the apartment or you will leave. Do you understand?"

"Yes."

We walked in silence the rest of the way to the apartment. Once inside, I pointed at the couch. "Call her."

James shook his head. "I need to make notes."

"You do not need to make notes. All you need to say is 'It's over. Do not contact me again.'" I sat down. "Call her now, with me sitting here, or you leave. It's simple."

He sat next to me and took his phone from his pocket. He studied it for what seemed like an eternity. "She's probably at the airport."

"I don't give a fuck."

James dialed her number as my heart pounded. When Khalie answered, her chirpy voice came loud and clear through the phone. "Where are you? Why haven't you called me? What's happening?"

James stared at the ground. "I'm . . . I'm in Paris."

"With her?" Khalie shrieked. "You're with her?"

I'd never heard Khalie's voice before, and I fixated on her low tenor. It was another thing that was different from me. Did James like her voice better than mine?

"I'm in Paris with my wife. What you and I had is over. Do not contact me again." James kept his eyes downcast.

"You can't do this! I love you!" Khalie cried. "We have plans."

Plans? How the hell did he make plans with a woman who is not his wife? Who makes plans with someone they've only slept with three times?

"It's over." James hung up and dropped the phone on the couch between us. "Are you happy?" he said softly. "Can I stay now?"

He hadn't ended things willingly. He hadn't wanted to. I had to force him. What did that mean?

I snatched his phone and ran to the bathroom, locking the door behind me. For the next hour, I sat on the ground and pored through emails, pictures, Facebook messages, and Instagram until I had dozens of new dates and plans. Plans like running the San Francisco Half Marathon and going to Napa

MIA HAYES

with Khalie over our anniversary. Plans like moving to New York and getting an apartment with Khalie, who apparently had already put a deposit down. Plans like divorcing me.

James had so many plans, and the only ones that involved me were divorce.

When I emerged from the bathroom, I was too exhausted to fight. I handed James back his phone and crawled under the bed's covers. James fussed over me, asking me what he could do.

I closed my eyes, defeated. There was no sane way out of this mess. Everyone would be better off without me. It was all there in the messages between James and Khalie. She painted a picture of me that was self-obsessed and a terrible wife and mother. James had agreed with her.

No wonder he wanted to leave me. I wasn't good enough. I had been too focused on my career, and not enough on James. I should have done more for him. I should have tried more.

I wasn't the one who ran James over, but how I dealt with the aftermath was one hundred percent my fault. I'd pushed James away by telling him over and over again he needed help. Khalie believed nothing was wrong with him. I was negative; she was positive. I was a short strawberry-blonde; she was a leggy brunette. I stayed home and raised kids; she traveled the world.

My thoughts tumbled over and over, forcing me to admit the obvious. I deserved everything that had happened.

I became quiet, unable to leave the churning mess of my brain. I sat and stared and slept most of the next day. I refused food and only sipped water when my throat hurt from dryness.

James lay next to me on the bed, rubbing my back and trying

to coax me from my mind. Before his accident, he'd doted on me and loved me. After his accident, I gave everything I had to fixing him. Now, I wasn't sure either of us had anything left.

Over the next few days, I stopped showering and didn't get out of bed. James brought me food that I left untouched. I didn't listen to music. I didn't talk. The movie of James and Khalie playing in my head was too powerful, and it was all I could think about.

———

One morning, James held out my phone. I had no idea what time or what day it was. "You should call the boys. They miss you."

"No." Talking to anyone seemed impossible. There was no way I could pretend that everything was okay—not even for my boys. Talking to them would only cause more damage.

"Bee, you need to." James held out the phone. "They need to know you're okay. They're scared."

I closed my eyes. "Because of what you did and how you behaved."

"No. They're scared because you've vanished." James shook the phone at me, and I took it. "Call them."

I turned on my phone, and it vibrated with incoming emails. I hit the mail icon and dozens of messages from Khalie flashed across the screen. My stomach dropped, and my gaze flicked to James.

"I have to use the bathroom." I clenched my phone and fled to the bathroom again. I locked the door and slumped to the ground.

James knocked on the door. "Bee? You okay?"

I didn't answer. Over the course of the week, Khalie had inundated my inbox with more letters and a link to a blog called *Our Journey into Love and Faith*. I skimmed the letters before opening the blog.

The picture James had painted of their relationship was vastly different than the one presented on the blog. Every day, James and Khalie posted a scripture and reflected on how it applied to their relationship. The James who wrote the blog was nothing like the man I knew. This version was religious and liked discussing what color and animal he felt like that day. I didn't know what to make of it.

There were also more details about the affair. It had started on his trip to Europe after he added her last minute to the production team, and the extra days he stayed in Rome had been spent with Khalie, vacationing. She came along on the Asia leg of the trip, and for her birthday, James put them up in the Hong Kong Mandarin Oriental complete with a couple's massage and walk along the beach.

He had used my book advance money to fund it.

I heaved into the toilet.

James rattled the doorknob. "Let me in."

I wiped my mouth with toilet paper. "You're a liar! It wasn't three times! It was a fucking relationship."

James rattled the doorknob. "Let me in."

I yanked the door open. "You promised you'd told me everything, but you're still lying." I hit his arm. "You. Are. A. Liar."

"I didn't want to hurt you." He caught my fists. "I thought it was better if you didn't know."

I ripped away from him and ran into the bedroom. I grabbed the Klonopin from the shelf near the bed. I had no plan, not in that moment; I only knew I couldn't take it anymore. I unscrewed the cap and dumped a bunch onto my hand.

"What are you doing?" James stood on the other side of the bed near the door.

"Like you care."

I popped the pills into my mouth and dry swallowed. Then I dumped more into my hand and took those, too.

This time, James lunged across the bed, but not before I swallowed the next batch of pills. "What are you doing?" Panic filled his voice. "Bee, stop!"

I didn't know what I was doing. I didn't want to die, but I wanted my brain to stop looping through images of Khalie and James together. I wanted my heart to stop hurting. I wanted to disappear. The pills could do that.

I lay down on the bed and pulled my pashmina over me. "I can't do this."

I remember James calling Victoria and asking what 9-1-1 was in France, and I remember telling him that I didn't need it. After that, I remember nothing.

I'm not sure why he never called emergency services, but when I woke it was mid-afternoon, and daylight poured in through the large window at the foot of the bed. James sat near my feet, staring at me.

"Hey." He touched my toes. "You scared me."

I turned my head. "You lied."

"It won't happen again."

"Do I know everything?" I cleared my dry throat.

"Yes." James nudged me. "Do you want to take a shower and go get some food? You've been asleep for almost a day."

I pulled my olive-green pashmina tighter around me. "I'm not hungry."

"Bee, you're wasting away. You need to eat."

I glanced at the bedside table. My pills were gone. "What did you do with my Klonopin?"

"I took them." He softened his face. "If you need one, I'll give it to you."

I had no fight left in me, and I knew I was spinning out of control. "I just want to stop hurting."

James pulled me into an embrace. "I know, babe. I'm going to help you."

My body sagged into his, but my arms hung limply at my sides. "Let me go. Please let me go. I can't do this."

James understood I didn't mean physically. I wanted him to abandon me. I wanted him to make my decision easier. Was his being here selfish or selfless? How was I supposed to know?

He pressed his lips against the top of my head. "I'm not going anywhere."

I mmediately after my pill-taking incident, James found a therapist for me. She was a lovely older woman with a crisp, British accent and beautiful office on the Champs-Élysées. Twice a week, James schlepped me to Vivian's. At first, she saw both of us, but by the third session, Vivian insisted on seeing me on my own.

Unlike most other people in my life, she had zero opinion on whether I should stay with James or not. The few family members and friends who had tried reaching out encouraged me to stay with him, and that added to my guilt because I still didn't know what I wanted. In Vivian's office, I was free to be messy and ugly, and there were no rules or expectations. I could solely focus on myself.

"I failed my husband, my children, and my marriage," I said one day as I sat across from Vivian. "I've never failed at anything before."

Vivian scribbled a few notes. "You feel responsible for James's actions?"

"No. I . . ." The hands of the clock Vivian kept next to her ticked loudly. "I'm a terrible mother."

"How so?"

My answer came fast. "I don't want to see my kids." The words caught me by surprise. "I love them, don't get me wrong, but I'm afraid of them seeing me like this."

"Because you feel out of control?"

"Yes, and I'm a bad mom. I should have protected them. Not sent them away."

Since arriving in Paris, I had isolated myself from nearly everyone—including my boys. I didn't call them, and I relied on James to tell me what was happening with them.

Vivian scribbled again. "Sending them to Michigan was a healthy decision. You had the foresight to know you couldn't care for them in your current state."

"Children need their mother."

"Leaving them with your parents was an act of love."

It didn't feel like it. It felt like I had abandoned them as their family imploded. Like me, they'd suffered through months of James's erratic, angry behavior, and they—like everyone else—knew he had had an affair, but I thought they didn't fully grasp what that meant.

I had failed them in so many ways and couldn't face them.

At my next session, I sat in Vivian's office clutching a soggy tissue. We'd been working through my insistence that James hadn't chosen me and instead defaulted because he didn't know what else to do. As I composed myself, Vivian placed her pen on her notepad. "You need to see your children at some point. You need to make a plan to reunite with them."

I pulled my dress lower over my thighs. James and I had spent the past few weeks shopping and replacing my entire wardrobe into something more Parisian. Gone were my impractical wedged shoes; in their place, I wore Repetto ballet flats. I had a collection of size 25 Levi's in my closet and more scarves than I knew what to do with.

But what I didn't have was a desire to see the boys.

"I don't think I can." I balled the tissue. "I know I should want to, but I'm afraid."

"Of what?"

I curled into myself. "I may scare them."

"How?"

I tightened my grip around my torso. "I feel out of control."

Vivian tilted her head. "We can talk about this next time, but for now, why don't you start with a phone call. They need to know you're okay."

"But I'm not," I whispered.

"It will take time and patience, but you will be." Vivian held the door open for me, and I stepped into the high-ceilinged hallway.

James waited for me in the lobby. He wrote Vivian a check for 110 euros and whisked me downstairs. We'd fallen into the routine of getting a snack and drinks after my therapy sessions. Sometimes I'd share my breakthroughs with him, and sometimes I didn't say a word. That day, I said nothing as I drank first one, then two, then three glasses of wine and ignored the cheese plate sitting before me.

"I talked to the boys while you were with Vivian. They went out on your dad's boat yesterday and had to be tugged into shore."

I absentmindedly swirled my glass of red wine.

"I guess the engine broke or something," James persisted. "They think it's hilarious. Your dad has the worst luck with boats."

I stared at the mid-summer throng of people pushing their way up and down the sweltering Champs-Élysées and fought the urge to melt into them and disappear. It would be easier than facing everything I had going on in my life.

"They miss you," James said. "You should call them."

"That's what Vivian said."

James reached across the table and placed his hand on my free one. I stopped swirling and didn't pull away. "You should listen to her." James stroked my hand. "She knows how to deal with these things."

The weight of not being able to mother the boys crushed me. History was repeating itself, and I felt unable to stop it. Maybe women in my family weren't meant to be good mothers? After all, until Molly came into my life, I hadn't had a true mother-figure. Like my boys, I had been abandoned by my own mother when she had run away.

I tensed my jaw. "They hate me."

James squeezed my hand. "They're worried, but I told them you are doing great. They're happy because we're together."

Everyone was happy that James and I were together. Everyone but me.

"So?" James took his phone from his shorts' pocket. "Do you want to call them?"

"You can." I rocked in my chair, trying to anchor myself and not run away.

A slight frown flitted across James's face. "They want to hear from you."

I stared at the restaurant exit. I could run away again, and this time, I wouldn't tell anyone where I had gone. "I can't call them yet," I said. "Maybe tonight."

James sighed. "Okay. Let's try tonight."

It would take me another week to make that call, and when I did, I felt nothing. They excitedly told me about their adventures riding quads, picking berries, and playing with BB guns, but I had nothing to add. I listened to their happiness and realized they didn't need me.

When I hung up, I knew I had damaged them, and nothing I did would ever make up for my abandonment.

During this time, I became obsessed with making James own his actions. I made him call our boys' principal, Mr. Hanley, and explain why the boys would not be returning to school in the fall (we still hadn't decided on living arrangements, but I knew I would not be returning to San Francisco). Mr. Hanley, who cared for the boys on the day of James's accident, was shocked but promised to support us in every way possible.

When I demanded James call Sally, the head of his company's HR department, and explain why he could no longer work with Khalie, he blanched. I persisted. There was no way I would let Khalie around him. She had to go. She was a contractor, not a permanent employee.

"She contacted your wife on numerous occasions?" Sally asked carefully over the speakerphone. "I would like you to send those messages to me."

"She's insane," I said shakily. "She's stalking me on social media—with your company's social media accounts—you have to do something."

James shook his head, telling me to stop talking. "I'll compile everything and send it this afternoon."

When we hung up, I felt victorious. Sally was going to get rid of Khalie. How could she not? After all, the evidence was damning. In email after email, Khalie stated how she had willingly entered into a relationship with James, and there were emails where she demanded James place her on better assignments or she'd reveal the affair to me.

In my eyes, Khalie had basically blackmailed my husband and tried to ruin my life. I wanted her punished.

The second week of July, James stocked the fridge with water and ice cream bars—the only thing I could eat other than almonds—and made me promise to eat while he was back in the States. He was flying to Michigan to see the boys before heading to San Francisco for the final mediation of our lawsuit. He'd be gone a week.

As soon as he left, I put on my shoes and walked to the neighborhood department store, BHV. I didn't know what I wanted to buy, maybe a strapless bra—mine was now too big—or a new handbag.

The store was crowded with sale-season shoppers. I had begun having what Vivian identified as panic attacks in confined places, and as I poked through the racks, a familiar tightening in my chest sent me searching for a quieter part of the store where I could regroup.

I ended up in the art section. In college, I had minored in art, and being among the paint, canvas, and brushes soothed my trembling body and racing mind. I studied the erasers and charcoal before picking up an X-Acto knife. The cool, metal handle hummed in my hand. I had no reason to buy the knife, but I carried it to the nearby cash wrap and handed over my euros.

Back in the apartment, I stared at the knife for a long while before touching it. I slid the plastic cap off the blade and pressed the metal into my left forearm. When the knife pricked me, I pressed harder, watching beads of blood follow in the wake. I pressed harder still, and a trickle of blood ran down my arm.

As blood splattered my dress, a sense of relief swelled over me. I could still feel physical pain, even if I felt nothing else.

Since arriving in Paris, no matter how awful I felt, I kept up my daily blog. At some point, our lawyer, Emily, instructed me to stop writing. She believed that James and my running around Paris didn't paint the image of a couple in distress. She also worried that I would disclose the affair, something she feared would derail my loss of consortium claim.

I ignored Emily and kept at it because I wanted to prove to Khalie I had the upper hand. Since talking to Sally, Khalie had sent me more emails, and on two occasions called me sobbing, begging me to send James back to her. Her behavior made me double down, and I wanted nothing more than to make her miserable, but to appease Emily, I promised to stop the shopping posts.

On July 13th, our final mediation started. It was well after six in the evening when I was conferenced in, and Emily very firmly told me that I was not to say anything. Apparently, my behavior was being called into question. I sat silently fuming while the mediator posed questions and worked out the sum of our payment from the driver's employer's insurance company. At some point, my being in Paris was brought up. As instructed, I said I was there on personal matters. The defendant's lawyer produced my blog posts, and Emily asked to speak to James and me privately.

"Our case is becoming weaker and weaker," she said. "If you disclose the affair, they will cite that as the reason your marriage has fallen apart. If you don't disclose it, they will argue that the two of you seem to be having fun all over Paris."

"What do you want to do?" James asked me.

"Don't disclose it," I answered. Even though James had posted his apology on Facebook, I couldn't handle having it as part of the public record.

"Are you sure?" Emily asked. "Your current behavior is not in keeping with the deposition you gave."

For sixteen months, the lawsuit had hung over us. This was supposed to be the payoff for all the tests and depositions, and my anger and pain had somehow messed it all up.

"Let's just tell them the truth," James said. "Emily can make a strong case that the affair is a result of the accident."

It was the first time either of us had made that connection, and something inside me clicked. James's affair began around the one-year anniversary of his accident. It started after he stopped taking his antidepressants because Khalie, who didn't know him before the accident, repeatedly told James there was nothing wrong with him and that I was projecting.

"Blaming your affair on the accident is a cop-out," I snapped, but he'd triggered a new line of thinking. If the affair were a result of his accident, then maybe I could have done more to prevent it. And if that were true, then maybe James's behavior wasn't so much his fault as it was mine for pushing him too hard.

Had Khalie been slightly right? Had I sent James into her arms?

In the end, Emily didn't disclose the affair, and the mediator negotiated a settlement for half of our original request. When James called me a little later, I was a hysterical mess.

"Your affair is not my fault," I sobbed. "I didn't do this."

"I know, Bee, I know." James tried soothing me through the phone, but his words meant nothing. The whole nightmare was of my own creation. If I had only taken James to work that rainy day, then none of it would have happened.

I hung up, found my X-Acto knife, and carved crimson lines into my right hip.

For a moment, I felt better.

19

Those early days in Paris weren't all miserable. Sometimes, James and I would walk miles and miles, talking and sorting through things. We'd stop and admire street art, pop into a museum, or just enjoy people watching while sitting at a café. My life was in emotional turmoil, but at least I had the steady rhythm of Paris to soothe me.

I snapped pictures of bridges and James snapped pictures of me posing by the shimmering Seine or with the Eiffel Tower in the background. I uploaded the pictures to my blog and Facebook page and created a narrative around our new life where everything was amazing. How could it not be? We were on an extended break in the most romantic city on earth.

As we walked back to my apartment after dinner one night, we heard the booming bass of a pop concert and decided to find the source of the music. It sounded like it was coming from Hôtel de Ville, the sixteenth-century town hall where free community events were often held. But as we followed the music, we wove through narrow, twisting streets, away from the Seine, and toward the 11th arrondissement.

Next to a small, gated park, a crowd gathered around a stage where a band banged out French pop music. Bottles of wine were passed around the crowd and poured into plastic cups, and cigarette smoke hung heavy in the air. The crowd was made up of all ages from toddlers to the elderly, and James and I squeezed into the middle of it.

James grabbed my hand and spun me around. "Want to dance?"

"Sure."

We swayed to the music, his arms wrapped around me, until the song changed.

James pointed at a small shop. "I'm going to get a bottle of wine."

I waited next to a bench and watched the crowd grow. The band wasn't bad, and I asked a guy next to me who they were. He explained that a local radio station was hosting the free event to help new artists gain exposure. I loved that about Paris. Everywhere we went, there was free music or art or simply culture.

When James returned carrying two plastic cups and an uncorked bottle of wine in a brown bag, I told him the name of the band. He handed me the cups and poured generously. Sultry, July heat swirled around us as we laughed, drank, and danced. At one point, I threw my arms around James's neck. He smiled at me as if to say, "See? It can be great again."

And I wanted to believe that. I wanted us to be okay.

Then the music ended and the stage lights dimmed, and James and I were just standing on a street with a bunch of other people. I stared at my beaming husband, the one who had willingly hurt me, and my chest tightened. The magic that had briefly whisked me past the pain had evaporated, leaving the bleakness of reality behind. I knew, in the dusky Paris twilight, that we couldn't keep pretending away our pain. We had to go through it.

As July dragged on, our drinking increased, and I took more and more pills to still my constantly racing mind.

James had returned the Klonopin to me before he had left for San Francisco and had picked up a new lorazepam prescription for me. It had been easy to get—I called my doctor, told her I was in Paris and the Klonopin made me feel sick, but I was still having anxiety attacks. What could she do? She sent a three-month order to the pharmacy, and James brought it to me.

Most nights, I'd drink a bottle of champagne on my own at dinner and come home, take one or two pills, and pass out for three or four hours. Nightmares haunted me, and I'd wake up crying and confused. I didn't realize it at the time, but I was repeating the self-numbing behavior I had detested in James.

On nights I couldn't sleep, I stalked Khalie, studying every picture I found of her. She was tall—maybe five foot ten—with wide-set brown eyes, dark hair, and a giant smile. Physically, we were opposites, and that convinced me James had grown tired of me. Maybe if Khalie had been more like me, I would have thought that he wanted another me—one that was more fun and didn't know the old him—and I would have understood. But he'd pitched me to the side and chose someone I could never be.

The last time Khalie called me, James was flying back to Paris on a red-eye. I recognized her number, but instead of ignoring it, I answered.

"This is your fault," she said, without a greeting. "You exploited his accident for your own benefit. You didn't want him, you wanted the pity."

I stared out my apartment window at the disjointed jumble of rooftops. Somewhere, a piano student tapped out a song, and laughter from the rue drifted up.

"Stop," I said sharply. But was she right? After all, how many times had I repeated his story to everyone around me?

"That's all you're going to say?"

"What do you want, Khalie? Just tell me what you want so you'll leave me alone."

She laughed. "He hates you. You know that, right? He wants to divorce you and move to New York." I didn't say anything, so she added, "You're pathetic."

"I'm pathetic?" I didn't want to egg her on, but my anger got the better of me. "How am I pathetic? I'm not the one begging a married man to come back to me."

Khalie made a strangled noise. "It's not like that. He loves me. You've read it yourself, so stop being delusional."

I hung up.

When Khalie had sent me letters where she and James discussed the children they would have together after the divorce, I wanted to vomit. But worse, Khalie repeatedly slammed my parenting, calling me lazy and heaping praise on James for being an involved dad.

James never corrected her, so was she right? Was I pathetic and a bad mom? After all, what kind of mother runs away and leaves her children?

When James arrived in Paris, he promised to get the therapy he had resisted in San Francisco, and after doing some research, he decided to find a therapist specializing in Eye Movement Desensitization and Reprocessing (EMDR) to treat his PTSD. The process involved him reliving the trauma of the accident in brief, guided spurts, and it wore him out. After a session, he would sleep for hours, but his nightmares lessened, and he no longer panicked at the sight of scooters zipping along Paris' streets. But, most importantly, his personality became more like his pre-accident self. He was gentle and calm again, and the franticness that had overwhelmed him faded.

As we walked aimlessly through the streets of Montmartre one day, James said, "I can still smell the burnt tires."

I stopped walking. "What?"

He kept his gaze straight ahead and led me through the throng of people choking the sidewalk. "The smell is wedged in my nose. I can't get rid of it."

It took me a minute to figure out what he meant. "The accident?"

James nodded. "I thought I was going to drown. The rain kept rushing at me, and I couldn't breathe."

Tourists swarmed around us, but that moment felt private. We walked up the hill, past trinket shops, and toward the white sanctuary of Sacré-Cœur where we sat on the steps, surrounded by people, and watched the street performers while roaming men sold beer from coolers. I didn't ask questions, out of fear of sending James spiraling backward.

After a while, James rested his head on my shoulder. "When everything stilled, I thought I had died, and I remember being mad that I wouldn't see you again."

"I thought you had died, too." I had never shared with James what I had been through that day, and my words were followed by tears. I couldn't tell him the thing that I knew to be most true: my selfishness put him on his scooter in that intersection, and I was the reason he'd been hit.

The more progress James made, the further I fell. It became harder and harder for me to distinguish between things that had actually happened and things I had only dreamed. I frequently woke up screaming that Khalie was outside my apartment trying to kill me, and I relied on James to soothe me.

When I shared with Vivian my fear that my brain had broken in an unrepairable way, she patiently explained that, like James, I had suffered traumas—first from his accident and the months of abuse followed by the discovery of his affair. I scoffed. I wasn't the one hit by the truck, so how could I possibly have PTSD?

"You need to be patient with yourself," Vivian said. "Healing from an affair is a long process, and with your shared history of PTSD, it may take five years or more."

"Five years?" I gaped at her. "I can't do this for five years."

"Trauma needs time to resolve," Vivian answered calmly in her British accent. "You both need time to heal."

I left her office angry. What happened to me wasn't as traumatic as what James had experienced. I was sad. Hurt. Maybe depressed. But I didn't have PTSD.

I wasn't that damaged.

Still, no matter how much I willed myself to feel better, I couldn't stop the pain and fell into a routine of berating myself and invalidating my feelings.

"We need to bring the boys over," James said one lazy afternoon. "They've been with your parents for six weeks, and they miss you."

I picked at my now cool shawarma. Noura had my favorite Lebanese food in Paris, and James and I often ate there after my therapy sessions, but as usual, I had very little appetite.

"I'm not ready."

"You're never going to be ready," James said with a sigh. "But you need to try."

I poured more champagne in my glass and sipped. "Do you think they should be exposed to this?" I set my glass down. "I don't want to damage them anymore."

"You can do it." James locked his eyes on mine. "You just need to try."

I wanted to tell him that he ran away when he was struggling, and that he'd left the boys and me behind for weeks, but instead I finished my drink in two gulps. "What do you think I've been doing?"

James looked away. "You . . . you need something other than yourself to focus on." He shook his head and back toward me. "Having the boys around will be good for you."

"And then what?" I pushed my barely touched food aside. "What if it's not okay?"

"We'll figure it out." James pressed his lips together like he wanted to say more but decided against it.

"Our kids are not an experiment. We can't just throw them into this situation and pray they're going to be okay." I paused and spat out my next words. "Besides, prayer only works for you and Khalie."

James blanched and held his tongue. We both knew things quickly escalated whenever I brought up Khalie.

"You're not going to say anything?" I badgered. "Nothing?"

He shook his head. "The boys need you, and they want to come."

"When?"

James gave a half-smile. "I think the second week in August is good. I can fly to Michigan to get them."

"You've already talked to my parents, haven't you?" My chest constricted, and I felt clammy. Plans had been made without my consent, and the boys were coming. "I'm a disaster." My voice wavered. "They can't see me like this."

"When you see them, you'll know what to do." James reached for my hand. His touch didn't repulse me anymore, but it still felt oddly intimate and violating. "You're a wonderful mother. You always have been."

I pulled away. "You're wrong. I'm too broken to be their mom."

"Bee, we need to put our family back together."

The high, coved ceiling held my attention as my head spun from the champagne. My marriage status was questionable and my mental health fragile. How was I going to handle three boys under the age of ten? How was I going to care for them when I could barely crawl out of bed most days? James was wrong. Vivian was wrong. I needed more time.

At least he wasn't forcing me back to San Francisco. I had already informed him that I would never go back after how he publicly humiliated me.

"I have no choice, then." It was a bad decision. I hadn't protected the boys from James in San Francisco, and now they were going to see me falling apart. They didn't deserve that.

James reached out again and squeezed my hand. "You can do this."

"I can't. I'm going to ruin them."

"Bee, they need you."

Strangely, the panic I had felt earlier had disappeared,

leaving behind a vacant flatness—like I had floated out of my body. I didn't want to be needed; I wanted to hide from everyone, but the decision had been made, and I had to prepare for it.

"Hey," James said. "We need to find a bigger apartment. The boys won't fit in your tiny one." As I tried to process what was happening, he added, "I called Ruth, and she's giving us a few showings tomorrow."

My shoulders sagged. Instead of being angry at James for putting a plan in motion without consulting me, relief flowed through me. I didn't have to do anything but go where he pointed me. "Okay."

"That's my Bee." He patted my hand. "You can do it."

After we paid the bill, we walked to the Métro, dodging tourists along the sweltering Champs-Élysées. James held my clammy hand like he was afraid to lose me. When we boarded the Métro, I focused on the black tunnel walls whooshing past and not the growing grayness devouring me. I had to try for the boys. I had to engage and seem like I was happy to see them despite my worries.

But what if I couldn't? What if I was right, and I damaged them? James didn't think it would happen, but I knew it could. After all, watching James slide into PTSD depression and living in the aftermath of his affair had broken me. Surely, I was stronger than three boys under the age of ten, so how would their not-fully-developed brains deal with everything?

Despite my apprehension, the next afternoon James and I toured two- and three-bedroom apartments in the Marais. I insisted on having a washing machine, and since we had no furniture, it had to come fully furnished. It also had to be a place where three young boys could play outside.

We found the perfect apartment on Rue du Trésor, a small, cobblestone street off the Rue Vieille du Temple. It was a car-free street that came to a dead-end just past our building. Cafés and shops lined the picturesque street, and I imagined the boys running around outside.

The apartment itself was on the fifth floor at the top of a grand, curving staircase that wound around a one-person elevator. Ten-foot, double wooden doors with a solid, old-fashioned lock guarded the entrance to the apartment, and inside, the foyer opened to a grand hallway with parquet floors. A micro kitchen sat to the right, and a salon with floor-to-ceiling windows was on the left. At the rear of the apartment, one bedroom overlooked a courtyard, and another larger room faced the street. Between them was a wet room and a bit down the hallway, a toilet.

It was bigger than our San Francisco apartment, and James tried to get a reaction from me, but I sat on the hard sofa and stared at the gaps between the floorboards. Ruth rattled off a few details before opening the windows to let the stuffy, overheated air out. Below us, Paris hummed with life, but in that room, I felt nothing but suffocation.

I needed out.

I wandered over to the window, pushed back the wispy curtains, and stared at the pedestrians and café patrons. We were on the fifth floor, which in France is the sixth floor. Even with the decorative railing, it would be easy to accidentally fall out the window.

"Bee?"

I turned slowly and raised my eyebrows as if nothing were wrong. "What?"

"You okay?" James walked over to me and placed his hand on my lower back.

I nodded. "This is a great apartment, Ruth. We'll take it."

"Perfect." She dug into her satchel. "I have the contract, and you can sign it now if you'd like."

I motioned to James. "He'll do it."

As far as I knew, Ruth had never mentioned the rental rate. But it didn't matter, I liked the apartment, so James would pay for it with the stack of cash I had in my wallet. I opened my bag and handed him the money.

"How much?" he asked Ruth.

"3,450 euros."

James counted out the money and gave it to her. Our lease was month-to-month since we didn't know how long we'd stay in Paris.

"You can bring your payment to our office on the fifteenth of each month," Ruth said, tucking the money into her bag. "Or you can wire it to us if that's easier."

"We'll bring it in," James said.

"Good." Ruth smiled. "You're going to have a three-day gap between leases. The owner of your current property has already rented it for the day you leave."

I hadn't realized this. "Oh. What should we do?"

"Perhaps a hotel?" Ruth offered.

James ran his hand over the stubble that now lined his jaw. "I'll figure it out."

Ruth gathered her things and guided us out of the apartment. "We can store your belongings for a few days if you'd like. That way you can travel a bit." She turned the large, metal key in the external lock. "Prague is lovely, or maybe London?"

There were too many moving pieces, and I couldn't sort out any of it. We had to move, get the boys, and find a place to stay for a few days. It was too much.

"We'll get back to you," James said as we walked down the flights of stairs.

After we said good-bye to Ruth, James and I strolled across the street to the café and ordered snacks and wine. Scorching mid-summer air enveloped me even though we had refuge under the shady awning. Beads of sweat slipped between my breasts and down my neck, dampening my dress. Paris had become uncomfortably hot.

"Where do you want to go?" James asked. He poured another glass of water from the carafe the waiter had left on our table. "Pick a place, and we'll go there."

"Why?" I stabbed a piece of hard cheese. "I like it here." The thought of leaving my safe Parisian cocoon terrified me. "I don't want to go to Prague."

"Ever?" James asked with disappointment.

I shrugged. "Not now. I want to stay here."

"Getting out of the city will be good for you." James's eyes pleaded with me. "Plus, it's too hot here."

I spun my phone around on the table while trying to think of somewhere James would never want to go. After a minute, I offered, "Nice?"

"The beach?" James didn't swim well. Growing up in San Francisco, where the wild Pacific pounded the coast and riptides frequently sucked people out to sea, he feared the water.

I fought back a smirk. "Yes. I want to go to the beach and drink champagne under an umbrella. Doesn't that sound fun?"

"Okay. I'll work on it tonight." He stared at his wine glass before looking at me. "I know you're stressed about the boys coming, but you can do it."

Red-hot pressure built in my ears. "I don't want to talk about it."

James sat silently while I poked at my food. His phone buzzed, and he picked it up before swiping and setting it down. It buzzed again, and he did the same thing.

I glared at him. "Who's texting you?"

"Work stuff." He picked up his phone and shoved it in his pocket, but not before it buzzed again.

My heart pounded. "Is it her?"

"No."

"Then who is it? You're on leave. They shouldn't be calling." Was it Khalie? Or some other woman? Did he have other women? He did. Of course he did. Cheaters always had other women, and James was a proven liar. I swallowed hard, forcing horrible words from spilling out into our conversation. "Why won't you tell me?"

"It's just work stuff." James didn't meet my eyes. "That's all."

I shook my head. "No. That's what you always say, and it's always a lie." I pushed back from the table and my foot caught on the leg, causing the bottle of open red wine to spill onto its side and over the white, paper placemats. Hysteria had overtaken me. "You lie about everything."

I grabbed my bag and ran down the cobblestone rue until I reached the corner. I turned left and ran some more, dodging mid-July tourists holding shopping bags and parents pushing strollers. I kept going until I reached the Seine. My yellow ballet flats pinched my heat-swollen feet, but I didn't stop. I walked and muttered to myself as other pedestrians gave me a wide berth.

I was going crazy. I knew I was going crazy. I didn't know how to make it stop.

As daylight slipped away, I made my way back to my apartment. Convinced James had left me, I crawled into bed and sobbed until I fell into a restless sleep.

Visions of James with Khalie crawled through my dreams. They were things I'd never seen but knew so well: James and Khalie holding hands in Rome; James and Khalie sharing drinks at a rooftop bar in London; James and Khalie having side-by-side massages in a firelit room in Hong Kong.

These memories didn't belong to me except in the PDF files Khalie had sent and in the emails I had read on James's phone. I never saw any of it, and yet they were vividly etched into my brain. In those early days, I returned to them time and again, looking for answers to my answerless questions.

When I woke, James was sitting next to me with his lips tightly together and worry filling his eyes. This new expression of concern had replaced his scowl.

"Did you take any pills?" he asked softly.

I shook my head.

He offered me a pill and a bottle of water. "You need to sleep. You'll be better when you've slept."

"I try, but I can't stop the dreams."

My dress bunched over my hips when I sat up to sip the water, and James gasped. His hand jutted toward me, and his fingertips hovered over my thigh. "What happened?"

Angry, red lines sliced my leg. I'd managed to hide them and had explained the one on my arm by saying I had cut myself on a sharp counter while out shopping. These precision cuts on my hip, however, I couldn't lie about.

When I didn't answer, James grabbed my hand. "Did you cut yourself? Did you do this?"

"It's not what you think," I whispered. "It helps me. I feel better when I do it, and you want me to feel better, don't you?"

He rubbed the back of his head. "You can't do this. It's not normal."

"Try to stop me." I had hidden the X-Acto knife under the couch cushion. He'd never find it.

James's breath caught, and tears welled in his eyes. "Oh, Bee. I don't know what to do. I don't know how to fix this."

He wrapped me in his arms, and his warm tears dampened my knotted hair. I stared blankly out the window, hardened to any soft emotion James expressed.

Five years didn't seem like enough time to fix the mess we were in.

Nice had moments of calm. During the day, we took chairs at the private beach and gorged on strawberries and cold glasses of Taittinger. Nighttime was different, though. The flashbacks came faster and lasted longer, leaving me an emotional mess and distrustful of James. I would lock myself in the bathroom and dig my knife into my flesh, eager for the release it gave me.

My life was chaotic. I took too many pills and mixed them with champagne. I railed and hit James. I insisted on having rough sex and hated myself for letting him touch me.

One morning, I collapsed at the foot of the bed, too weak to move, and curled into a ball. I hadn't eaten a proper meal in days, and my ribs were visible. The pictures James had uploaded to Facebook the night before received a mixture of jealousy over our trip and concern about my appearance. According to the scale in the hotel bathroom, I weighed forty-three and a half kilograms, or about ninety-six pounds. When James expressed concern, I shrugged. Disappearing didn't seem like an awful thing.

Many of my memories from that trip are tied to strong feelings of shame. Shame over James's affair; shame for not being able to control my emotions; shame for being a terrible mother.

But here's what I didn't understand at the time: once you give shame power over you, it will eat you alive.

It was devouring me.

20

We returned to Paris more battered than when we left. I barely spoke more than a few words at a time and struggled with my role in James's affair. Everything I had read online stated that an affair happens because of a breakdown in the marriage, but I believed I had given James everything I had. So, where had I gone wrong? Was it that I pushed too much? Had I made unreasonable demands of him? What exactly had I done to shove him into Khalie's arms?

The truth haunted me. If I had driven James to work that rainy November day, he wouldn't have been hit, and if he hadn't been hit, he wouldn't have had an affair. By putting my phone call with the editor above my husband's needs, I had sent us careening down this path. Me, not James.

His affair was, in fact, my fault.

Once back in Paris, James quickly set up our new house while I sat in the lounge and stared blankly. Raucous noise from the street below wafted up, and I closed my eyes, allowing it to wash over me. I was in Paris, and I was safe. Everything would be okay.

"It's hot in here," I said. "Can you help me open the back windows so we can get a cross breeze?"

As I undid the latch for one set of massive windows, James undid the other. When I turned toward him, I studied his face. It was leaner, more angular than it had been in the past five years of our marriage. He was almost too thin, and stubble lined his jaw. He stared back at me inquisitively.

I wanted to climb inside James's brain and open all the doors his accident had barricaded away. I wanted him to remember me and the boys and the happier moments of our life. I also wanted him to remember all the horrible things he'd said and done over the previous twenty months.

But I never wanted him to remember my role in his accident.

Even though I was against it, James insisted on taking me to Prague for our anniversary. It was a tourist-infested mess of orange-tiled buildings spilling down a hillside and puddling at the base. It was nothing like I had imagined from reading novels. It was more crowded and less refined.

I hated it the minute I spied it from the highway, and the trip, despite having a few happier moments, couldn't be over fast enough. James wanted to celebrate our sham of a marriage, and, too weary to protest, I let him drag me around the city with a private tour guide.

Fourteen years earlier, I'd spent the night before our wedding with my maid of honor, painting our nails and talking about my dreams for the future. With the nervous enthusiasm only a soon-to-be bride can have, I told her how I wanted five boys, my professional dreams for James, and how he and I would always be best friends. I believed we would celebrate every one of our anniversaries lavishly.

Prague was not the spectacular, romantic trip I had dreamed of. It was a kamikaze, make-our-marriage-survive Hail Mary. The life I had once dreamed of had come and gone, and I no longer had any idea of what I wanted my future to look like.

I had been type-A during my early marriage, and the uncertainty of having no plan terrified me. There was nothing or no one who could guide me through this heartbreak.

Stay or leave, leave or stay—did it make any difference? It wouldn't change what had happened. Our anniversary had become a painful reminder of the transitory nature of love.

21

We sat in the impossibly clean Prague airport waiting for our flight back to Paris while a piano player delicately plunked out tunes. Despite it being late afternoon, I had a flakey pastry balanced on my thigh and held a paper cup of steaming tea. Next to me, James jiggled his leg. He'd received an email from Sally the night before, and she wanted to talk.

"It'll be okay," I said. "I don't know why you're nervous. Sally loves you."

James clenched his jaw. "Sometimes that isn't enough."

His phone rang, and without making eye contact with me, he stood and answered as he walked toward the windows. Curious, I left our bags and went to him.

When he saw me, he shook his head and held his free hand up like a stop sign. I froze. Worry lines furrowed between his eyes.

What was happening?

James turned his back, his shoulders slumped, and he nodded his head a few times before walking back to our seats.

He took a pad of paper and pen from his bag and began scribbling.

I peered down at the paper. He'd written a series of dollar amounts and a date.

My heart pounded, and my legs grew weak.

James hung up. When his eyes met mine, he shook his head. "What?"

"Khalie is threatening a sexual coercion lawsuit. She's hired a lawyer." James's normally tan skin had taken a ghastly hue. "I think I should resign."

I gaped at him. "Resign? Why?"

He nodded. "If I don't, Khalie may file a lawsuit, and it could get really messy even though she was contractor and there's no rule against what we did."

"Why?"

James sighed. "You'll get dragged into it, and I don't think you can handle another lawsuit."

"So you need to resign?" My dry throat constricted. "For what? She's just a contractor who blackmailed you! It's in black-and-white. We sent her emails to them!"

Because James and Khalie had stupidly sent personal messages through their work email accounts, the company had access to everything that was said in addition to the private emails and PDFs James and I had supplied. Khalie had repeatedly requested a higher hourly fee, which James secured for her. In the few emails where James expressed wanting to end the relationship, she threatened to tell me everything before demanding James take her on trips like the one they had planned to take over our anniversary in Napa.

In my opinion, Khalie had preyed on my stupid, broken husband. Yes, he did what he did, but she created an environment that made ending things impossible.

"They can't do this!" I screamed, not caring that we were standing in the middle of a busy airport.

James grabbed my arm. "You need to calm down. Being emotional won't help the situation."

I yanked away from him. "I can be however I want."

He pressed his lips together. "No, you can't. That's how we ended up here. You kept writing about her on your blog, and she's pissed."

"So? She did it. She has to live with it."

James shook his head. "This is her way of getting back at you. The more you react, the more she'll attack."

I bristled. Khalie wasn't going to win. She had tried to ruin my marriage and family, but she wasn't going to ruin me financially. James and I needed to work together to beat her.

"Okay," I said, trying to calm the rage gnawing at me. "What do we do?"

James held up his phone. "I'm calling Emily. I need an employment lawyer."

Another lawyer and more money. Wonderful.

The lawyer James hired wanted all the documents we supplied his company. I stayed up all night, compiling everything, eager to prove our case. At some point in the night, James called Sally, and she asked to speak to me.

"Did you make a post on a site called She's a Homewrecker about Khalie?" Sally asked.

I had forgotten about that. "Yes."

"Khalie is requesting you remove it immediately."

I bit my lip. When I posted it, there was a lengthy disclaimer about not being able to edit or remove posts. "I can't. They don't allow you to take it down."

"You can't remove it?" Sally asked.

"No."

James stared at me quizzically.

"You do realize that your blog and that post are motivating Khalie's actions?" Sally said flatly. "You've tied our hands."

I couldn't control myself and shrieked into the phone. "This isn't my fault! Why are you blaming me?"

"Please give the phone to James."

"You need to fix this!" I screamed. "You have the emails! You saw what she said!"

"I'd like to talk to James now."

"Talk to me!" I yelled. "Since she hates me, talk to me!"

James tore the phone from my hand. I lunged at him. I wasn't done talking to Sally. She needed to hear my side of the story. I was convinced that if she did, she'd see why Khalie needed to go, not James.

With a firm push, James sent me falling onto the bed. He walked into the front room, and I scrambled after him. He didn't say much, just listened to Sally. When he was done, I pounced on him.

"What's happening? Why are they doing this?"

His eyes softened. "I know you're hurt, but you've got to calm down. You're not helping anything."

All the anger I had been trying to contain spilled out, and I pulled back my arm and punched James in the jaw. "You did this! Not me. Don't ever blame me."

He grabbed the side of his face and bent forward. He didn't yell out or cry. He just leaned forward and rubbed his jaw. When he peered up at me, he said, "You have a nasty right hook."

"You deserved it." I wanted to punch Khalie for causing our

current problems. Rationally, I knew James became responsible when he let her into his hotel room in London, but it was so much easier to blame Khalie—a woman I didn't know who seemed determined to ruin my life.

I glanced at James and felt no remorse over hitting him. He was the one who actively decided to hurt me and discard our marriage.

It occurred to me in that moment that the source of my pain was the person I was relying on to help me recover. Being with James was incredibly painful, and every day brought some new horror with it. First it was the uncovering of his never-ending lies. Then it was the full realization of what he and Khalie had done. Finally, now, it was the possibility that he had ruined us financially. And somehow, despite all these things, I believed I needed him to help heal my broken heart because I would have done it for him.

In the darkened room, James studied the separation letter closely. "I don't like it," he said without sharing the details. "My attorney won't either."

I rolled over in bed to face him. I had been trying to sleep, something I hadn't done in nearly forty-eight hours. "Why?"

"Don't worry about it." James typed rapidly on my laptop before shutting it. His hand gently massaged my shoulder, and he gave me a weak smile. "I've got everything under control."

I had no fight left in me. My head throbbed from crying, and I struggled with the fact that I couldn't leave James now—he had no income and no way to pay spousal support. If I left, I would have to support myself, and I had no viable skills or job prospects. I had, stupidly, allowed myself to become wholly dependent on James.

I was stuck.

In the morning, we received a lengthy response from James's lawyer. As predicted, he hated the offer and instructed James to not sign it. He would draft something new to send over.

"What's so bad about the offer?" I asked. "Is the amount too low?"

James shook his head.

"What is it then?"

"Let's get breakfast," he said gently. "We can talk there."

It concerned me that he wanted our conversation to happen in public. Did he think that would stop me from getting upset? Hadn't my past actions shown him that it wouldn't?

"Is it bad?" My stomach rolled. James had told me, before the offer came, that he would at least get his vacation and sick leave. Could they refuse that? Was that legal?

"Just get ready."

I threw on clothes and pulled my hair into a messy bun. James and I walked to the corner café and ordered a light breakfast even though I had no desire to eat. He didn't say a word until our food arrived.

His separation agreement was tied to me never discussing the affair with anyone other than my therapist, lawyer, and doctor. His company wanted to squash all mentions of it, and Khalie was demanding I remove my blog posts and the She's a Homewrecker post.

His attorney instructed James to refuse the offer since I was violative, and James and I were careening toward divorce.

"Do you want a divorce?" I whispered. James seemed hell-bent on making me happy, but was he still thinking of a divorce?

"No, but you may." He sipped his steaming espresso. "I have no idea what's going through your head."

I shoved my untouched *pain au chocolat* away. "You're saying you need to protect yourself from me?"

"I can't be responsible for your actions. They're erratic." James caught my eye. "You understand, don't you? You've threatened divorce numerous times, and we're not in a good place."

It was the frankest discussion we had had about the state of our marriage. He knew I was unhappy, and we both knew my emotions were unpredictable.

"What now?" I asked.

James sighed. "We're asking that they strike any mention of you from the agreement."

That sounded reasonable. "Will they?"

James shrugged. "We have to wait and see."

To no one's surprise, his company denied our request. However, they decided to make me a separate, independent offer. James's attorney couldn't represent me, so I had to find my own attorney.

My offer came with a substantial payout in exchange for my silence. My attorney felt signing was not in my best interest given that the company had expanded the scope of their request to include me never writing or discussing any affair or James's accident in any manner.

For three long days, James's attorney and mine went back and forth with the company's representation.

In the end, James and his company came to an agreement, but I refused my offer and walked away from the money even though it would have given me financial independence from James.

We had dwindling funds, no jobs, and no idea of where we'd end up or if we'd end up there together. I should have signed the agreement, but James's affair had stolen so much from me, and I refused to let it take my voice.

22

The first week in August, James flew back to San Francisco to retrieve the boys. Molly had flown to Michigan again to bring them home for a few days and to get them ready for Paris.

Before he left, James grocery shopped and stocked the fridge with ice cream bars, almonds, water, and fruit. He knew I'd eat little else while he was gone over the next three days, but he asked me to pick some things up for the boys and left me a detailed list on the counter, which I immediately forgot.

With James back in the States, I had no one to force me out of bed, so I lay there thinking about all the things I should have been doing but couldn't. I needed to write my book; I needed to get ready for the boys; I needed to leave the apartment.

Most of all, I needed to make a decision about James.

My fractured brain flipped endlessly through imagined memories of James with Khalie as I lay in bed. James loved her, and he didn't love me. He hadn't given her up on his own, and I had forced the decision on him. The more I sat in silence, the more convinced I became that James was only staying with me until it was safe for him to be with Khalie.

When he called to check on me, I either cut the calls short or didn't answer. I know I was unwell, and I didn't want him to hear the unsteadiness in my voice, because I didn't want him to have a reason to leave me.

Day blurred into night and back into morning. The boys were coming, and they would see me like this. They needed to believe they had one stable parent. I owed it to them to try.

Over the course of a day, I moved my things from the larger front bedroom to the back bedroom, leaving my clothes in the rickety built-in closet. I made the boys' bed with freshly washed sheets that I had air-dried over dining room chairs and scrubbed the bathroom. Nothing I did, though, erased the images of James and Khalie boiling in my mind.

As the crowd at the bistro down the street became late-night rowdy, I sat on the couch near the large, open windows and contemplated flinging myself onto the cobblestones below. If I died on that day, the boys wouldn't have to see it, and James could tell them it was an accident. Maybe they'd believe I fell out while trying to clean. If I sliced my wrists, he wouldn't be able to hide the truth from the boys.

I walked to an open window and laid my hand on the cool, wavy glass, which had warped over the decades. The windows didn't do much to keep the heat or sound out, but they were gorgeous, and like the herringbone floors and high, decorative ceilings, very Parisian. It was the type of apartment I'd envisioned living in when James had mentioned moving to Paris a few years earlier.

Down on the rue, people gathered for their evening post-dinner drinks. Cigarette smoke billowed from the patio in front of the bistro. *God, the French love to smoke and sing*, I thought as I watched friends air-kiss and laugh. No matter where I went in Paris, people embraced life, and I had hoped some of it would rub off on me.

With a sigh, I turned away from the window. These people hadn't had their lives upended. They hadn't experienced the deep, cutting pain that rippled through me nonstop.

James's ringtone broke me from my thoughts, and I reluctantly picked up.

"Hello?"

"Hey, Bee. We're at the airport in San Francisco. We'll see you in a few hours." James sounded upbeat. "Check your email."

He had sent a picture of the boys smiling and looking excited about their long flight. I flicked it closed. No matter how hard I tried, I couldn't muster even a glimmer of excitement.

When the boys were little, small enough to still need a stroller but too big for their baby carriers, I taught them to walk through our San Francisco neighborhood and cross the six lanes of Geary Boulevard traffic that separated our side of the Inner Richmond from where our church, the library, and all the good restaurants along Clement Street sat.

There was no stoplight or curb cut out at the corner of our street's busy intersection when we began the lessons. I would grasp Ryan and Leo's tiny hands and give them a quick squeeze, a hand hug, before stepping tentatively into the narrow space between the car parked closest to us and the curb. If a delivery truck had parked at the corner—or, even more commonly, double parked—I'd have zero visibility and would have to ease myself forward to assess while keeping the boys tucked behind me. If a car hit me, I prayed the boys would be spared.

Once all the SUVs, trucks, and sports cars had sped past us and the light a few blocks up changed to red, we had enough time to sprint to the median, if not make it completely across. It was dangerous, but my job as their mother was to teach them to navigate the world safely and, eventually, independently.

Before Tate was born, I met then-mayor Gavin Newsom at a party and shared my concern about our dangerous corner, and I suggested putting in a light and curb cut out. A few days later, work began, and within the month, the boys and I could safely cross the street without playing Frogger.

I think of all the hand hugs I gave the boys over those years as we crossed Geary. I'd squeeze and release, and they'd squeeze back harder. Even after the light had been installed, I held onto the boys, not because I was afraid to let them go—after all, preparing them to fly on their own was my job—but because I wanted them to know that no matter what, I'd always be there to keep them safe.

But now, I didn't miss my children, and I didn't want to see them.

Around three that afternoon, James and the boys banged on the apartment's door. I hesitated before forcing myself to stand and cross the salon to the foyer. I could do this. I could be Mom.

I wish I could say that when I saw them, all my fears evaporated, but instead of hugging them, I burst into tears. Here were three young boys happy to see their mother after eight weeks apart, and their hugs and kisses made me sob in fear.

I glanced up at James, desperate for him to rescue me, but he smiled, unaware of the turmoil swirling inside me. "I knew it would be okay," he said, mistaking my tears for joy. "The boys are here!"

I had crouched down to Leo and Tate's level, and the boys clung to me. I fought the urge to unwind from their arms and barricade myself in the bedroom, but they deserved better, and I had to try to give it to them.

"Leo," I said, breaking our embrace, "I got you something. Wait here." During one of my forced phone calls with the boys, my middle son, Leo, had asked if I could buy him "that fancy hat French people wear." Not wanting to let him down, I had dragged James to a tourist shop on the Left Bank and picked out a beret. It was red, Leo's favorite color.

The beret sat on my unmade bed. I picked it up, plastered on a smile, and returned to my family. When I held it out to Leo, his face lit up.

"I love it!" He immediately put it on. With his red striped shirt, he reminded me of *Where's Waldo*. "Do I look good?"

"You look French," James said with a laugh. He turned to me. "Did you get the groceries? We're starving."

"No."

James hid his frown quickly. "Okay. I guess we'll go out." He hefted a stuffed backpack over his shoulder. "Boys, let's get you situated, then we'll go eat."

While James and the boys decided on sleeping arrangements, I folded myself onto the couch and blinked back tears. I had hoped I'd be overwhelmed by feelings of love, but all I felt was worry and franticness.

"You ready?" James asked from the doorway. When I kept my hands over my face, he said, "Bee? You okay?"

I didn't want to let the boys down, so I exhaled and stood. "I'm fine."

"The boys are starving. We should go." James held my handbag. "Were you crying?"

I nodded as I slipped on my yellow ballet flats. "I'm just so happy to have them here."

James beamed. "See? I knew it would be okay."

The boys burst into the room. Ryan wore sunglasses, and Leo still had on the beret. Tate's faced needed a washing, but honestly, I didn't feel like doing it.

Ryan grabbed my hand. "Where are we going to eat?"

"Across the street if you guys like the menu." I followed my family into the foyer and out the door. Ryan had been a vege-tarian since the age of three, and I worried about how he'd fare in France. "There aren't a ton of vegetarian options, so you may be stuck with a cheese plate."

"That's okay." Ryan didn't let go of my hand until we reached the lobby. He ran ahead to shove the eight-foot-tall doors open.

"Do we live in a mansion?" Leo asked as we exited onto the cobblestone rue. "Our house is so big, and we have an elevator!"

James laughed. "No. We live in Paris now. It's going to be fun."

We stopped at the bistro across the street, and I explained the menu to the boys. James snapped a picture of the back of us, me holding Tate's hand while the other two boys—Leo in his red beret and Ryan with his arms crossed—stood next to me. It's a nice picture. We look like any other family, but every time I see it, I think, *I hated that day.*

Since we didn't have proper visas, we had to homeschool the boys. In San Francisco, I had homeschooled Ryan, and James had brought most of my teaching supplies and books back with him from home. I developed a curriculum, and James and I agreed to teach in the mornings and explore in the afternoons. I'd oversee reading, spelling, and French while James handled math and history.

In the mornings, before the boys and the rest of Paris woke, James and I would run along the Seine to the Tuileries and back to the apartment. I savored this time because I didn't have to be Mom or Bee. I just ran mindlessly, letting my breath match my pace. Sometimes, James would ask me to stop so he could take pictures of me along the river. As usual, he'd post these on Facebook, and I'd add them to my blog as more evidence that life was normal and his affair was nothing more than a nuisance.

Every day, however, I ignored and deleted messages from friends asking when I'd be home. I didn't return their concerned calls or respond to Facebook comments, not even the envious or complimentary ones. I wanted to run away from the life we had created in San Francisco and the overwhelming embarrassment I felt.

I even ignored Molly's calls. We hadn't spoken since the day before James's affair, and I equated my failing marriage to failing Molly. The day I discovered the affair, I had hidden in my flat, refusing to see her, until I left for the airport. As I had driven away, Molly had stood on the porch, watching me go.

Vivian worried I had cut myself off from my support network and relied too much on James to help me through my misery. While she was pleased that James was in therapy too, she frequently pushed me to examine the real reasons I stayed with him. I never had an answer other than I stayed because I didn't know what else to do.

Eventually, my appointments with Vivian dwindled from twice a week, to once a week, to once every other week. Therapy seemed pointless since James was treating me so much better. Plus, spending over two hundred dollars a week on therapy wasn't sustainable.

James structured our days so that he and the boys would set out on an adventure in the afternoons while I attempted to work on edits for my second book. My agent had given me a month extension to finish, but I couldn't concentrate long enough to get through a page. Instead, I'd waste my time staring at the walls or researching affair blogs, trying to puzzle together the moments of James's affair that felt fuzzy to me.

Even though I hadn't had any angry outburst since the boys arrived, I struggled with rage. I managed to play the role of mother until I developed a nasty, painful rash down the right side of my back. Not knowing what it was, James slathered me in Tiger Balm to help ease the pain, but it only made the rash blister and burn. Desperate for relief, I snapped a picture and sent it to my sister, an ER nurse.

"Shingles," she wrote back. "You've missed the window for treatment. Don't leave the house until the blisters heal."

"How did I get shingles?" I typed.

"Stress."

While I recovered, a crippling heatwave settled over Paris. The stone buildings and cobblestone streets radiated heat, and with very few buildings having air conditioning, the city sweltered.

Unaccustomed to hot temperatures, Tate began vomiting, and James and I frantically turned on the three small fans that had come with the apartment. We tried keeping the heavy curtains drawn in hope of blocking out the sun, but that didn't work, so we threw the windows open and prayed for a breeze that never came.

It was too hot to go out, so we downloaded a few movies to my laptop and gathered on our bed. Around noon, we were all drenched in sweat, and I thought Tate was running a temperature, so James ran to the nearby pharmacy to buy a thermometer.

When he returned, he smiled and handed me a bag. "McDonald's has air conditioning. Let's go there for lunch."

"Can we?" Ryan asked. "Please?"

I never let the boys eat fast food, but the heat was too much. "Sure." I unboxed the thermometer and ran it over Tate's head. A number in Celsius and a frowning face appeared.

James looked it up on his phone. "It's about 100.7, I think."

I frowned. I had been placing cool, wet towels on Tate's neck while James was gone. "Can you look up heat stroke?"

After determining that Tate was not dangerously warm, we headed to McDonald's. It was packed with others trying to escape the heat, and I headed to the basement with Tate where I found a small table we could gather around. Tate crawled onto my lap and rested his warm head.

"I don't feel good," he whimpered.

I rubbed his back. "I know, baby, but Daddy's getting you food and a drink, and I think that will help."

James, Ryan, and Leo returned carrying trays of food. "Mom!" Leo rushed toward me carrying a drink holder. "You order at a machine! Dad didn't have to speak!"

I laughed. "You could read the menu?"

"Pictures," James said with a grin. "It's my kind of menu."

"Dad thinks we ordered a chèvre sandwich," Ryan said. "It looks like a fried cheese wrap."

"Sounds just like what a vegetarian would want." I motioned to the three empty seats at our table. "Let's see what you have."

We sat there for hours, ordering more food and enjoying the air conditioning. We laughed and shared silly stories, and it almost felt like life before the accident.

When we arrived back at our apartment, I set the boys up in

the large, interior wet room with DVD players. The cold tile felt heavenly in the heat, and it was the coolest place in the apartment. James and I lay in bed while the boys watched movies and drank sodas. We told them they had their very own home movie theater, which they found funny.

"We live in a mansion, and we have a movie theater." Leo grinned. "I love Paris. It's so nice."

Since no one ate dinner before seven in France, we felt no need to move. I figured that when the boys became hungry, we'd venture across the street because cooking in the apartment would be unbearable.

A little after seven, I checked on the boys. Tate had fallen asleep, but Leo and Ryan wanted to know if they could go to the playground a few blocks over. It was still bright outside, but the heat wasn't as oppressive. Plus, other than our trip to McDonald's, they had been cooped up all day.

"Let me ask Dad." James and I often let the boys walk to the corner patisserie alone, and in San Francisco, they crossed six lanes of traffic to get to school. I didn't worry about them going out by themselves, and James also felt that it wasn't a big deal.

"The park closes at eight," I said. "When the park lady blows the whistle, come straight home." Neither boy had a watch or phone, but again, that didn't concern me. After all, I had had none of those things when I was their age, and there was a woman who closed the park promptly each night. The boys would know when to come home.

After Ryan and Leo ran off with promises to be careful, James and I climbed back into bed. Tate was asleep in the wet room on a pile of pillows, and it was the first time we'd had any real alone time since the boys had arrived. James leaned over and kissed my shoulder, and his hand danced over my stomach.

I turned my head and let his lips find mine. James's touch

didn't repulse me as much anymore, but I struggled against the invading images of him with Khalie. I sighed.

"What's wrong?" he asked.

"You. I can't get these images—"

Someone banged on the apartment door. James's brows drew together before he leaped from bed. I sat straight up but didn't follow because I wasn't wearing a bra and had on tight, tiny running shorts.

"Leo's hurt!" Ryan's voice echoed down the hallway. "I think he broke his arm!"

I charged toward the door. James had Ryan by the shoulders. "What happened? Where?"

Tears ran down Ryan's face, and his body shook. "Leo fell off the way-up-high thing. He's throwing up." He crumpled against James. "I'm sorry. It's my fault."

"Get my passport and wallet," James shouted as he shoved his feet into his shoes. "I'll meet you there." He and Ryan ran down the staircase.

I quickly dressed myself and woke Tate before collecting our passports and James's wallet from the dresser. I half-dragged, half-carried Tate as I ran to the playground. None of the boys had ever been hurt before, and I wasn't sure what to do. Did we take him on the Métro to the hospital? Did French hospitals have emergency rooms? What were we supposed to do?

An ambulance sat in the narrow street next to the playground, and a crowd surrounded Leo, who was lying on the ground.

James gestured wildly as he tried to communicate with the other parents and medics, but none of them knew English well. When he saw me, James ran toward me and grabbed my hand. "I can't do this." He pushed me toward the medics. "You need to go with Leo. I can't get in the back of an ambulance ever again."

"They're taking him in the ambulance? For a broken arm?"

My stomach dropped. Why wasn't Leo moving? Was he hurt more than Ryan had thought?

James tugged at his hair. "I don't know. I don't understand anything they're saying."

"Okay." I pushed through the crowd and knelt next to Leo. His arm stuck out at a strange angle, but he wasn't crying. "Hey, baby. I'm here. It's going to be okay."

"Are you the mother?" the medic asked me in French.

"Oui."

The medic asked me a few questions in French about Leo's health, and another woman described what happened. Leo had been at least twelve feet off the ground, hanging off parallel bars that sloped to the ground when he fell. He had stood, thrown up, and collapsed. He hadn't moved since.

I touched my son. "Baby, can you move?"

Tears formed in Leo's chocolate-brown eyes. "I can't move my thumb."

"Can you move your legs?"

He wiggled them, and I sighed in relief. As I explained to him what was going to happen, I realized I had lost James in the confusion. Ryan had Tate near the ambulance, but James had vanished. "Where's Dad?" I asked the boys as the medics loaded Leo into the ambulance. "I need to ride with Leo to the hospital."

Ryan had his arm draped protectively around Tate. "He went that way." Ryan pointed in the direction of our apartment. "Mom, I think he's scared. He started crying when he saw the ambulance."

James had to be having a flashback. That was the only explanation for his absence. I bit my lip. I couldn't leave Leo on his own, and I couldn't leave the other two boys by themselves while James melted down.

The medic told me to get in the ambulance so we could leave.

"Everything is going to be okay," I said calmly as I took the apartment key from my pocket and gave it and James's wallet to Ryan. "Go home and wait for Dad, okay? I'll call and tell him where Leo and I are."

"Okay." Ryan clenched Tate's little hand. He was only ten, and I had asked so much of him over the past year and a half.

"It's going to be okay, buddy," I said, trying to stay positive. "Dad will be back soon. If he's not at the apartment, sit in the hallway. It's cooler there."

As the medic shut the ambulance door, James rounded the corner. His hair stuck up at strange angles, and his pajama pants were twisted. He looked wild and frantic.

Please, I thought as we drove away. *Please be able to take care of our boys.*

Leo had to have immediate surgery to set his arm and required an overnight stay at Neckar-Enfants Malades Hospital. Like everywhere else in Paris, the hospital lacked air conditioning and the stay was absolutely miserable. James and the other two boys arrived via the Métro two hours later while Leo was in surgery. I didn't ask James about what he experienced, and he didn't mention it. We huddled with Ryan and Tate in a narrow waiting room under flickering fluorescent lights.

Finally, the surgeon emerged. She was young and had a pleasant smile. In French, she explained what they had to do and showed us the X-rays of Leo's arm. He'd broken it in two spots, but they were able to set everything without using screws. When he woke, they'd test to see if he had use of his thumb.

James paced around the room. "We shouldn't have let them go alone."

I had had the same thought. "He would have fallen even if we were there."

"Maybe not."

I frowned. "You said yourself that half the playground equipment wouldn't pass muster in the US."

"I could have caught him." James paused his pacing to stare down at me. "We're shit parents."

And that was it: we were. We'd left the boys for weeks in Michigan with my parents; we'd let two children under the age of eleven roam around Paris alone, and they didn't speak the language. James and I put ourselves and our decaying marriage first over and over again.

We were selfish, awful parents, and our boys were paying the price for our actions. Something needed to change.

23

James and I had never parented without Molly and Joe's support, and being alone with the boys in a foreign country terrified me, especially after Leo's accident. Instead of stepping up and trying to be the parent they needed, I called Molly. It was the first time we spoke since I fled San Francisco, but I missed her and her stable presence terribly.

"Come to Paris," I begged. "James and I will pay for it." Molly already had a passport because, a few years earlier, James and I had surprised her with a trip to Ireland for her sixtieth birthday. All she had to do was pack and show up at the airport.

"I can't."

"Why?" I didn't understand how she could abandon me. Molly had always been my rock, so how could she leave me when I needed her most?

"Honey, I love you, but now isn't a good time." She never said she didn't want to come; she only said she couldn't.

For days, I sulked and cried and whined to James. He called his parents multiple times and tried to convince Molly to change her mind, but she never did.

In a fit of misplaced anger, I decided I wasn't going to speak to her anymore since she clearly didn't care about me and had taken James's side.

What we didn't know was that Molly was hiding her descent into dementia from us. She believed I couldn't handle any more stress and put my mental health before her own need for support. She acted like a mother.

A sense of normalcy settled over us despite the unusual circumstances. We woke up, did schoolwork, ate lunch, explored the city, had dinner, went for a walk, and fell asleep. Over and over again. Since the boys had arrived, I occasionally believed things were going to be okay, but at other times, I feared the uncertainty of the future.

James continued to photograph everything, and I wrote cheery blog and Facebook posts to accompany them. I thought that if a photo could capture a split-second happy moment, then that happiness had to exist inside me. I just needed to dig harder.

To the outside world, James and I either looked like a miracle or insane. The comments were always positive and encouraging, and yet I felt like a weak failure. I couldn't properly parent, I couldn't make up my mind about James, and I couldn't control my emotions.

Still, the routine of our lives was good for me. I needed structure, and James made sure every minute of my day was spent doing *something*. He understood that leaving me alone with my thoughts would only send me spiraling, and every night, after the boys fell asleep, he'd plan the next day.

In mid-August, he decided we would rent a car and drive to Normandy as part of our World War II history classes. After surviving the crazy Parisian traffic, we whizzed past fields and out toward the coast. James had a list of sites he wanted to visit, and we stopped first at Le Mémorial de Caen. Here, we walked through exhibits documenting life in France, America, and Japan during the World Wars. The boys asked dozens of questions during the Holocaust portion, and we had to reassure Leo that he was safe now, in the present.

After the museum, we visited the German Cemetery at La Cambe and La Pointe du Hoc. Craters and pieces of concrete littered du Hoc. The boys ran over the bluffs, darting into the former German command center. Grass and flowers covered the craters and fields, and tourists posed for pictures next to machine gun stands.

To my surprise, the infamous beaches showed no sign of the battles. In fact, trucks drove over the sand and children flew kites in front of large, beachfront homes.

I realized that's how time is meant to work—either we forget or we adapt. I, however, was on a third path: erasing myself.

James and the boys were happy together, running along the beach while I walked lazily behind, not fully engaged, but present enough to pretend like I was enjoying the day. Grief had made me vulnerable; it had ripped my heart from the safe cage of my ribs and exposed my weakness. I had never emotionally progressed beyond a young woman desperately needing validation of my worth, and I had conflated worth with love from others. If James didn't love me—because how could he after what he had done—and the boys didn't need me, then I had no worth, or perhaps worse, purpose. I simply existed to occupy space.

After Normandy, we took a train to Amsterdam. My memories of that trip are nothing more than pictures. I know we went, but I don't remember much. The photos show a happy family riding bikes around the Vondelpark and posing in front of the Amsterdam sign. Our room at the Pulitzer Hotel overlooked the canal, and again, I know this from pictures on my hard drive.

When we returned to Paris, the summer heat slowly melted away. Ryan asked to have his birthday at Versailles, and James obliged. Ryan loved the palace, but he loved the Petit Trianon even more. We walked the gardens, took more pictures, and created images that captured a happy, loving family for social media. Meanwhile, I grew more distant and numb.

Our friends and family were impressed by how well we were doing. No one asked if I was okay or if I wanted to stay with James. And why would they? Our Facebook posts showed none of the distress I felt or the emptiness that surrounded me. I spoke to no one other than Vivian, who I paid, and James, who had hurt me.

Dark grayness consumed more and more pieces of my mind, and the only way I could fight it was through pills and drinking. I flitted through those hazy days, drinking heavily in front of the boys, but hiding my pill-popping. Every night at dinner, I'd drink and drink until my head swam, then I'd go home, take Klonopin, and pass out. James never objected, so I thought it was fine. Now, when I ask him why he didn't intervene, he says he thought I was getting better because I didn't cry or rage as much, and he honestly didn't know how many pills I was abusing.

One morning, as I struggled against my flat emotions, Leo asked if I needed my pills. When I asked him why, he answered, "Dad gives them to you when you are sad. I can get them."

I shook my head and buried myself under the sheet, unable

to look at my sweet boy. Someone saw how unstable I was. Unfortunately, it was my eight-year-old son.

Miraculously, I turned in my book edits at the end of August. My agent loved the dark direction I had taken with the main character and felt my writing was emotional. I wanted to scream that I poured my anger into that book. I blew up things because I couldn't do it in real life. My character snapped and bared her teeth, and she didn't put up with anything. Meanwhile, I was afraid of my shadow, possibly hated my husband, and worried about destroying my kids. I had written the woman I wished I could be.

Around this time, after years of ignoring my writing passion, James badgered me to read my first book, and I refused. During his affair, he accused me of loving writing more than him—something Khalie had said in her emails—and I was hesitant to share my work with him. I had written a heartfelt dedication to him in my first book, something he didn't know, and in light of my naivety over his affair, it rang hollow.

He was persistent, and I gave in. When he finished, James plowed through the second book and asked if I'd written anything else. I reluctantly gave him a manuscript I had been secretly working on before his affair upended my life. It was a contemporary young adult novel about a privileged boy finding his way in life. Parental infidelity played a central role, and in hindsight, I wonder if I had somehow known about James's affair before I admitted it to myself.

James devoured that book, often staying up late reading.

MIA HAYES

When he finished one evening, he looked at me and said, "You really wrote this? It's amazing."

I nodded. "Kathleen doesn't think there's a market for it."

"It needs to be published," James said. "The world needs Fletch."

"Tell that to Kathleen and the Powers That Be."

I rolled over and, despite the sweltering heat spilling in through the open window, pulled the sheet tightly around me. James only gushed about my books because he had to.

Time ran away from us until I officially overstayed the limit for US visitors in France. I could no longer leave the country without fear of not being able to get back in, so James and I began to discuss what we wanted to do next.

I wanted to stay in Paris and thought we should apply for a long-term visa, but James didn't have a job and my writing income couldn't support our family. James suggested he find a job in London, but I didn't want to go to London. I only wanted to be in Paris.

He kept throwing ideas at me: New York, Los Angeles, somewhere else in Europe. I'd meet all his suggestions with silence.

"Bee, you've got to help me figure out where we're going," James said one night after the boys had gone to sleep. He'd been on the iPad for hours, trying to find anything that appealed to me.

I didn't want our friends and family to know our life in Paris had been a façade, and the thought of facing the schoolyard moms terrified me. "I'm not going back to San Francisco. It's too embarrassing."

James sat at the end of the bed next to my legs. "I understand, but we've got to go somewhere."

I pointed at my laptop sitting on the dresser. "Give me my computer."

James handed it to me, and I googled "Best Places to Live in the US." Several top ten lists popped up, and I selected one about halfway down the page. "What about Provo, Utah?"

"Utah?" James furrowed his brow. "Isn't there anywhere else?"

I liked the sound of Utah. They probably had lower infidelity numbers and would be more family focused. "What's wrong with Utah? It's supposed to be gorgeous."

"Where would I work?"

I shrugged. James's job tied him to major cities, but he didn't have a career anymore. He could reinvent himself if necessary.

"Where else?"

I hesitated. Before the boys were born, James and I had discussed moving to Northern Virginia and working in DC. He aspired to work in politics, and I wanted to work for the Department of State. "Leesburg in Northern Virginia is on the list. It could be nice."

I waited for him to say something about our past dreams, but there was no recognition. "What does it say?"

I read the entry for Leesburg, which had taken the number three spot. When I finished, James nodded his head. "It sounds great. Let's go look at it."

"How?"

James took my laptop. "Let me work on it."

He spent the next few hours tapping and typing while I tried to ignore him. Every so often, he'd ask me a question, but he didn't share what he was doing until he was finished.

"We're going to have a four-day layover in DC," James said.

"I've reached out to a real estate agent who's going to show us a few properties."

"To rent or buy?"

"Rent. I don't want to buy just in case we hate it."

That made sense. "What's next?"

"Can you narrow it down to a few neighborhoods that interest you?" He watched me carefully, almost like he was asking too much of me. "The agent will show us around on Friday and Saturday."

A lumped formed in my throat. "Next week?"

James touched my hand. "This week. We're leaving in two days."

"But our lease—" Panic nibbled at me. I needed more time to wrap my brain around all the new developments.

"I already emailed Ruth. They'll prorate us for the month."

"You bought tickets?" I whispered.

He nodded. "We have to go back to San Francisco for at least a few weeks. It will be okay."

"For who? You? The boys?" I slapped his hand away. "Am I supposed to just show up at school and pretend my life is amazing, and I spontaneously moved to Paris for the hell of it?"

"You don't have to see anyone if you don't want to." James stood and stripped off his T-shirt, revealing his overly thin frame. "If you want to hide out in the house, that's fine."

"We're leaving?" I asked flatly. Even though I wanted to be upset, I couldn't find the emotion.

"Yes. On Wednesday."

As our departure date crept closer and James made more plans, I panicked. My anxiety attacks came harder and faster, and I spent the early mornings, before the rest of Paris was awake, running along the Seine, taking pictures to calm myself. I knew that I hadn't had enough time to work through my emotions, and I was being shoved down a path that I wasn't sure about.

"You're one of the strongest women I know," Jeff, the only one of our friends I would speak to, said over the phone. He was James's best friend from college and a pastor. I had called him tearily a few times during James's affair, but not since. On this day, I had called him out of desperation. I no longer saw Vivian and needed guidance. "Pulling through this will require a tremendous amount of grace and strength," Jeff said. "But I know you, and I know you can do it."

Jeff wasn't alone in his beliefs. James, the boys, and my parents told me over and over again how strong I was and how much grace I was showing, but to me, it felt like no one cared about how much I hurt as long as I stayed with James.

On our last day in Paris, I went out for an early morning run. I found a secluded place on a set of stairs leading down to the Seine and contemplated not going back to the apartment. I didn't want to be married anymore. I could leave James and be okay. I had some money left from the amount he gave me from the lawsuit and could go someplace where no one knew me. I could move on and maybe, one day, be whole again.

But who was I if I wasn't James's wife and the boys' mom? I hadn't had a real job in thirteen years. My life was my family. That's all I was good at . . . except I wasn't anymore. I wasn't good at anything.

As gentle waves lapped at the stairs, I fought the two voices in my mind: Go and Stay. Go wanted me to file for divorce and give James full custody of the boys as soon as we landed on US soil. Stay told me that I could get through this if I just tried harder.

With the weight of my thoughts pressing on me, I made it back to our apartment. James and the boys were up, eating breakfast, and I paused in the doorway. A strange sense of calm filled me. I felt nothing. No attachment, no love, no hate. Just nothing.

While James and the boys finished packing our things, I sat on my bed and studied the medallion on the ceiling. I closed my eyes and allowed the feeling of the apartment to fill me, committing the warm air and the sound of laughter from the street to memory.

Since we had ten large suitcases, James arranged for a van to take us to the airport. I didn't cry like I thought I would as Paris slipped away. Instead, I welcomed the numbness that now consumed me.

Feeling nothing was better than hurting.

24

W e arrived at Dulles airport, collected our rental car —a giant Suburban that would have looked out of place in Paris and San Francisco—and drove toward DC. I stared out the window, watching the Northern Virginia scenery pass by. The leaves had started to turn, and while it was pretty, I hated seasons and missed the towering ancient buildings of Paris.

Strike One.

James maneuvered the behemoth rental car into the hotel parking lot, and I sat in the car as he unloaded everything onto two trolleys with help from Ryan and Leo. Tate dozed in the back seat, and I didn't want to wake him.

"I'll stay with Tate," I said. "Just leave me a key."

James frowned. "Wait here. I'll be back as soon as I drop this off at our room." He had selected the Embassy Suites in Tysons Corner, and Leo excitedly told me about the buffet breakfast James had promised him in the morning. I pretended to care, but really, I didn't. I just wanted to curl up in a dark room and disappear.

After a while, James returned to carry Tate inside. "You'll like the room," he said. "There's a private sleeping area for us."

"Great."

"Bee, just try. Please."

I clenched my jaw. "What do you think I'm doing? Every day I stay with you is a day I tried."

I understood James didn't cling to the old version of me because he didn't remember it. I think that made things easier for him—he only needed to fall in love with the mess of a woman currently before him. I, however, had to let go of three different versions of my husband: Pre- and Post-Accident James along with Affair James. I had to let go of the beautiful life and dreams I had meticulously crafted and of the pain that accompanied the planned version of my life vanishing. I had to trust the latest iteration of James was permanent. But I couldn't, not when I didn't understand how he could change overnight from wanting to leave me to never leaving my side.

James cared for me out of guilt. That was clear.

I followed him inside to the elevator. Tate slept soundly on his shoulder. When we arrived at the room, Leo and Ryan had neatly set up their space. James placed Tate on the couch and draped the blanket from the closet over him. He pressed his finger against his lips, telling the older boys to be quiet as they sat on the floor and played cars. It was the middle of the night in Paris, and they had to be exhausted, but they weren't whiny.

"Why don't you grab dinner downstairs," James said. "I'll stay with Tate."

"I'll stay with Tate," I snapped as I sat next to him. "I'm not hungry."

Now immune to my outbursts, the boys kept playing.

James tried taking Tate from me.

"What are you doing?" I tightened my grip on Tate. "He's tired."

"He needs to eat." James lifted Tate from my arms. "We'll eat as a family."

I sulked in the stiff upholstered chair near the desk. "I'm not hungry."

James ignored me. "Boys, get your shoes on. We're going to dinner."

They immediately jumped up and did as they were told. James slipped on Tate's Velcro tennis shoes. "Let's go."

I didn't move.

"Bee. Stop. You're being ridiculous."

He was right. I was being ridiculous, but I couldn't stop, and tears formed in my eyes. "I can't. I don't want to leave the room."

James sat Tate down and knelt next to my chair. His warm hand touched mine. "You can do this. It's just dinner."

"And tomorrow," I sniffed. "How am I supposed to do tomorrow?" Before we left Paris, James had reached out to every person he knew in Northern Virginia and managed to arrange two job interviews for himself. The boys and I would be alone in DC for the day. I hadn't been alone with them in months, and the thought of entertaining them in a strange city filled me with fear.

"You'll do fine tomorrow."

"I have to feed them and play with them and show them around." The boys were listening, but I didn't stop. "I can't do it!"

Ryan wrapped his arms around me. "We'll be good, Mom. I'll help you."

"I will too, Mom." Leo stood near the door, his right arm still encased in a cast.

I swallowed hard. "I can do this?"

Ryan squeezed harder. "Yes."

It didn't occur to me how odd it was that I was relying on my eight- and eleven-year-old sons to pull me through the day. I'd hit a new low.

———

While James interviewed, the boys and I explored the Smithsonian museums. A few years earlier, James and I had brought Leo to DC as a First Communion gift. We had arrived the night Osama bin Laden had been killed, and all our tours had been canceled. This time, DC hummed with activity, and I kept thinking, *I may be able to do this. I could live here.*

With an energy I hadn't felt in months, I guided the boys around the city, riding Metro and trying different food trucks. As we walked past the White House and along the Mall, every nerve in my body buzzed. It wasn't Paris, but DC had an invigorating energy.

A little after five, James called to say his interviews were over and he was waiting at a restaurant for us. When we approached the table, James beamed.

"What?" I asked in a chipper voice.

"I got an offer."

I raised my eyebrow. "Already?"

"We're working out the salary, but it's a solid offer." He darted his gaze away.

"What?" I asked.

"It's going to be a pay cut, no matter what. No one wants to pay my old salary."

A twinge of anger hit me. That bitch Khalie had taken my marriage and financial security from me. "How big of a cut?"

"A lot."

The buzzy feeling evaporated. I didn't speak as I pushed food around my plate. I should have felt relieved that James had a job prospect, and we'd have an income again. Instead, I was furious. James's actions had led us to this place. We would have been happy and secure in San Francisco if he had just kept his pants zipped, but now we were contemplating moving across the country for a job that would pay substantially less.

I was angry, but I didn't see any other option.

The houses in Virginia were gigantic: four- and five-thousand square feet with five bedrooms and multiple bathrooms. I wandered through each rental, nodding and pointing out things to James while pretending to not be in awe of all the space.

Leo was again convinced we were rich since the homes were five times the size of our San Francisco house. He'd walk slowly through each one, making comments, before running off to find the bedroom he wanted to be his.

We had focused our search on two Northern Virginia exurbs: Leesburg and Ashburn. I wanted something completely different from the life we had had, and both seemed to offer that. No one would know our story, and we could start over. We may not be happy, but we could be an enviable family again.

What I failed to see was that we were fumbling forward despite James seemingly having a plan. Neither of us knew who we were as individuals or as a couple, and our literal running away wasn't going to help fix either of those issues.

After seeing three homes which didn't grab me, the agent took us to a picturesque neighborhood that nestled the banks of the Potomac River. We drove into the development as the middle school let out, and James excitedly pointed at kids walking home and carrying musical instruments. Hazy, yellow-orange light cast a warm glow over the neighborhood. Stately homes towered over perfectly manicured and wide streets, and it felt as if we'd stepped into a magazine.

"The boys would be able to walk to school if we lived here," James said.

"They could." We stopped to let a group of kids cross the street. To my surprise, the students were racially diverse—something I didn't think I'd see outside of San Francisco or off the coasts.

We pulled into the driveway of the rental, and our agent hurried to open the front door. As we entered, sunlight spilled through the back windows. I stopped at the stairs and sat down.

"I like it," I said. "How much?"

The agent stared at me. "Don't you want to look around?"

I glanced at James, who kept his eyes trained on me. The boys had run up the stairs already. "I guess," I said. "But this is the best house we've seen."

James offered me his hand. "Let's check out the rest of the house before we make a decision."

"I want this house." It was odd, the connection I had to that space. Maybe it was because I didn't want to move back to San Francisco, but I had to have that house. I wanted to plop my kids down in the middle of what seemed like nowhere and hide. I wanted to disappear and drag my family with me.

James rubbed the back of my hand with his thumb. "Are you sure?"

"Yes."

He turned to the agent. "How much?"

"Thirty-two hundred a month. You'll have to fill out an application, and I'll need to verify three months of your income." The agent rattled off some numbers, and I tuned out. James hadn't accepted the job yet, and his new salary most likely wasn't enough to qualify us for the house.

"Okay," James said as if the number didn't scare him. "Do they consider savings, too?"

I turned and climbed the stairs before hearing the agent's reply. James was going to let me down again. We'd go back to San Francisco, and I'd be the laughing stock of the schoolyard. I'd have to face my shame and guilt. I couldn't do that.

Moving to Virginia was the only thing that made sense. It had to happen.

James came up behind me in the master bedroom. "Hey, you okay?"

I turned around. "We won't be approved for this house."

"I'll take care of it," James said. "If you want this house, I'll get it for you."

"I doubt it."

"Bee—"

"Don't 'Bee' me," I growled. "You're a fucking disappointment." I stormed off to find the boys.

When the agent saw me, he smiled. "So?"

I gestured over my shoulder at James. "He'll handle it."

The agent gave James a stack of papers, and he filled them out. He explained he didn't have three months of income because he'd been on sabbatical, but he'd show our bank account information. The agent said we'd also need to supply an offer letter from James's new employer.

James and his new boss, an old friend, worked out a deal where James was given an offer letter based on salary and bonuses. His new income was one-third of his former one, and I knew, at some point, our savings would run out, but I pushed it from my mind.

On the flight back to San Francisco, I bounced between excitement over our new adventure and horror of having to be in the city again. To calm myself, I drank several glasses of wine, took lorazepam, and excitedly told James all the things I wanted to buy for the new house. I made lists of furniture we'd need to fill up the space and sketched out ideas for decorating.

It was the first spark of passion I had shown for anything in months, and James latched on to it. He squeezed my hand. "We'll start over, okay?"

I nodded. "Okay."

THE AFTERMATH

25

When we arrived in San Francisco, I refused to see Molly and Joe because in my mind, when Molly hadn't come to Paris, she had chosen James's side. I felt unloved and unwanted, and I locked myself in our flat and counted the days until I could flee to Northern Virginia.

James shifted into do-it mode. He found movers and handled getting the boys school and health records while I lay in bed all day. I barely ate, and I cried constantly. San Francisco was my home, and now I couldn't show my face. I was no longer a PTO parent who chaired numerous committees; I was no longer plugged into my community; I was no longer able to give my friends marriage advice.

I was a disgrace, and being back in the city forced me to confront my embarrassment and James's betrayal.

While I hid, James planned a cross-country driving trip for us. Leo would stay behind with Molly and Joe to celebrate his ninth birthday early with his friends. The rest of us, along with our two cats, would pile into our minivan and drive the southern cross-country route. Leo would fly out ten days later.

The morning we left, I sat silently in the car while James,

Ryan, and Tate said good-bye to Molly and Joe. Tate clung to his grandparents, and Ryan bounced with excitement. Joe kept a stiff upper lip, but Molly cried as she hugged the boys. I knew I was breaking Molly's heart, but it didn't stop me from ripping my children from the only life they'd ever known.

When Molly came to the car to say good-bye to me, I gave a curt nod of my head and only said, "Thank you" when she said she loved me.

We headed south, toward Arizona, stopping at the Grand Canyon. We'd taken the boys a few years earlier in May and had found ourselves in a snowstorm. This time, the weather was gorgeous, and we posed for pictures along the canyon's rim. I staged each picture of James and me to look as happy as possible because I had a suspicion Khalie was stalking me online. James and I laughed and kissed and pretended the affair was behind us as Ryan took pictures.

While we drove, James and I had endless hours to talk, but to me, it felt like we weren't saying things that needed to be said. Instead, we discussed our new house, James's job, my trying to write again, and how the boys would do going to public schools for the first time. We talked but didn't say much.

After Arizona, we crossed into New Mexico and the Texas panhandle. Somewhere in Oklahoma, between all the empty conversations, I decided to start an anonymous blog, one that was just for me. In the days immediately after discovering James's affair, I had devoured hundreds of affair blogs, looking for answers on why this had happened to me and how I could fix it. Most of the blogs discussed how to *leave* a cheating spouse, but what I really needed was a blog about how to *stay with* a cheating spouse, and I was sure other betrayed spouses did, too.

Since I no longer had Vivian, I needed to talk about what I was going through, and journaling in a letter format felt right. Each night, after I updated my official blog with happy photos, I would type a post to James, telling him how I felt that day. My thoughts swung from wildly optimistic and excited about our new adventure to depressed and angry. I didn't tell James about my new blog, because I wasn't ready for him to see my innermost thoughts, but I signed every letter, *Always Yours, Bee*.

I think I meant it. I wanted to love James again, and I believed the love I could no longer find was buried deep inside me, waiting for me to make sense of everything—my feeling about James, my feelings about mothering, and most of all, my feelings toward myself.

I typed on my phone as we drove through pastures and big cities. Even though I couldn't share my blog with James, I shared it with the world. I used popular affair hashtags and commented on other blogs, and by the time we reached Chattanooga, I had a solid following.

Somewhere along the way, we learned of a hurricane bearing down on the East Coast and rerouted our journey. Originally, we were going to drive through Georgia and the Carolinas, but instead we turned north through Tennessee. When we arrived in Northern Virginia two days early, the remnants of the hurricane pummeled the area. Unable to move into our new house, we stayed in a nearby hotel and sneaked our cats inside.

As the wind and rain lashed the hotel windows, I couldn't help but feel it was appropriate that we arrived in the middle of a storm.

There was no power. The storm had knocked it out, and turning it on in our new house was a low priority for the electric company, who had to reinstate existing customers first. I didn't want to stay any longer at the hotel, so James and I drove to

Walmart and bought blankets, pillows, and blow-up mattresses. The hurricane delayed the delivery of our belongings by a week, so all we had was what was in our suitcases.

We spent a week "camping" in our new house. The boys huddled together on a mattress in Tate's room to stay warm while James and I slept in the gigantic master bedroom that was larger than our entire San Francisco flat. We ate every meal out, and it felt like a vacation.

Leo's flight to DC was delayed for hours and rerouted from Dulles to Reagan Airport at the last minute due to the hurricane. We arrived forty-five minutes late, and the airport staff had to search to find him. I panicked, thinking we'd lost our not-yet-nine-year-old son, but Leo was found and we were, once again, a complete family.

The next day, on Halloween, James and I enrolled Tate in kindergarten and Leo in fourth grade at the neighborhood elementary school. Due to his late birthday, the school wanted to place Leo in third grade, but we had his glowing report cards and excellent test scores and insisted on fourth grade.

"He'll be the youngest in the class," the secretary told us.

"So was I," James said. "I've done just fine."

Getting Ryan enrolled was more difficult. Because I had homeschooled him in fifth grade and he had a September birthday, the school balked at placing him in sixth grade. Again, we insisted, and the school agreed.

The boys started school on November 1st, Leo's birthday. He came home excited because the entire fourth grade was going to Jamestown the next day on luxury bus coaches, and could he please go? James and I eyed each other. Our parochial school in San Francisco didn't have the type of facilities our new public school district did, and field trips in San Francisco had mostly been walks to The Academy of Sciences. Jamestown sounded elaborate.

What kind of free-education Nirvana had we landed in?

The next morning, James woke at four thirty to drop Leo off at school. When James returned, he gushed about the teachers and parents. "You're going to fit in, no problem."

James started his new job the following Monday, leaving me completely alone for the first time in months. I spent the day wandering around our empty house, talking to the cats, and trying to write.

My brain wouldn't rest. Every time I tried to focus on my manuscript, images of Khalie and James tormented me. I convinced myself that James wasn't really at work; he was with Khalie, plotting to take my boys and leave me. I called James sobbing and demanded to know where he was. Nothing he said could calm me.

After my fourth hysterical call, I hung up and found my X-Acto knife. I dragged the point across my forearm until blood trickled out. It didn't hurt enough, so I pressed deeper, creating a pattern of hatch marks across my arm. Blood ran down my arm and splattered the front of my dress, and I sank to the ground.

What am I doing? Why can't I control myself?

I stayed on the bathroom floor until the boys rang the doorbell. I pulled my sleeves down, hurried to the door, and greeted them with the biggest, fakest smile I could muster. As they excitedly told me about their days, numbness settled over me again. I hovered over my body, watching and knowing what to say, but unable to do it.

Leo stopped talking at some point and hugged me. "Maybe

you need to rest," he said, leading me to the couch just like James did. "I'll make Tate and me a snack. You just rest."

I curled into a ball on the couch while my middle son banged around in the kitchen, making snacks. No matter how much I internally yelled at myself to go help them and engage, I couldn't move.

By December, I deeply regretted moving my family to Northern Virginia.

The boys were flourishing; they had tons of friends and loved the freedom that came with living in a quiet suburb, but I had never felt so alone. After his first week, James transitioned to working from home. He said it was due to the hellish commute from our house to Chevy Chase, Maryland, but the real reason was his fear of leaving me alone. Plus, I had no car and no way to get around. Unlike in the city, I couldn't walk to stores or really do anything. So, I sat in the house all day long, waiting for the kids to get home. I couldn't even watch television, because I couldn't focus or follow story lines. I simply sat on the couch with my cats and stared out the window.

With James home, my day had structure again. He'd get the boys off to school before prodding me from bed. We'd either go for a walk or workout in our new home gym for an hour. Then I'd shower and try writing while James got to work in our shared office. We had gone on a furniture-buying spree to fill up most of the vast house, and our office was my favorite room. We each had a desk, but I preferred working on the loveseat. James had decorated the walls with my book covers and made sure I had enough room to create elaborate plot boards.

Despite all this, I rarely wrote. Kathleen had passed on my teen boy book and wanted me to write the final book in my trilogy. I had no interest in finishing that trilogy. It was too painful. When I started Book One, I wrote it with the love I had felt for James; Book Two was written during his affair and was filled with anger; I had no idea what Book Three should be—after all, how do you reconcile two characters who have caused each other so much pain?

Two weeks before Christmas, Kathleen called in the late morning with the news that Audible had picked up the rights to my first two books. I hung up, my faith in my writing restored, and wrote a chapter of Book Three. It was a small thing, but it felt like a victory to me.

James and the boys took me out to dinner to celebrate. As we ate, my email dinged. Kathleen had told me to expect the term sheet later in the day, so I eagerly opened the message from her. I scanned the email, froze, and read it again in disbelief.

"What is it?" James asked.

A lump wedged itself in my throat, and I set my phone down. "She doesn't want to represent me anymore. She thinks I'll never finish another book because my life is too chaotic."

"What?" He grabbed the phone from me. "Are you sure?" As I watched him read the lengthy email, anger rolled over his face. "She sold your rights this morning and dumped you? What the hell?"

I couldn't stop shaking. "I have to leave. I can't stay here."

James nodded and handed me the car keys. "We'll finish up and meet you at the car."

I locked myself in the car and sat silently. Not only could I not keep my husband happy or care for my kids, but I was also a professional failure.

I had nothing.

I needed an agent if only to give me the illusion of being able to work. I hadn't written much in over a year, but it had always been waiting for me, and I didn't understand why Kathleen couldn't wait for me to get through my issues. It cost her nothing to keep me on her list. Eventually, I latched onto the idea that Kathleen realized something about me I failed to see: I was a fraud.

The next day, at James's insistence, I queried a few agents. I found one quickly, but it did nothing for my confidence. Like James, Kathleen believed I wasn't good enough, and like James, she had abandoned me. It was just a matter of time before the new agent did, too.

2 6

———

At the end of January, James's uncle died, and we flew back to San Francisco for a week. Even though I still felt embarrassed, being in the city made me realize how big of a mistake we had made by moving.

The hum of the city surrounded me, and I didn't feel alone for the first time in months as I sat in my favorite coffee shop writing my daily post for *Always Yours, Bee*. As people came in and out, some of the tension of the past two years eased. Being alone in the bustling city was different from the stillness of the suburbs, and I craved the energy of people rushing around and cars whizzing past and deals being made.

I missed San Francisco, and I missed my old life.

My daily blogging had led me to realize that it hadn't been my devotion to James that had nearly killed me, it had been guilt and shame. Those two powerful forces had driven me from my home in San Francisco, isolated me from concerned friends and family, and whispered in my ear that I deserved everything that was happening. I had believed the voices, and even though I knew they were wrong, I couldn't fully rid myself of them.

But in that moment, the desire for my old life led me to

texting my friend Ann to see if she could grab lunch. We quickly made plans and met at Delfina. Over pizza, I explained to her how lonely and bored I was in Virginia, and I detailed all the ways the people there were different, and in my mind, less cultured than us.

"You could come home," she said, cutting her thin crust pizza into neat pieces. "We all miss you."

My phone dinged with a text. Thinking it was James, I looked at my phone. It was a neighborhood woman I had met the week before at Leo's lacrosse tryouts. She was inviting me to a party at her home.

"What is it?" Ann asked.

I showed her the text. "I think it's a mistake."

"Why would she not want to invite you? You're fun, and you have so much to offer."

"It's just weird. None of our other neighbors have come over to meet us. Isn't dropping off banana bread an established rule of suburbia?"

Ann finished chewing. "You should go. It'll make you feel less lonely for at least one night."

When I texted James to ask his opinion, he was thrilled that I had made an effort to talk to someone.

See, he responded. *You just need to put yourself out there.*

A few days later, my reentry into suburban life was brutal. I cried every day and begged James to please let us move back to San Francisco. He refused, saying that the boys loved Virginia, and our opportunities were better. I screamed over and over again that it wasn't better for me. That I was drowning. That I needed out. But James insisted I keep trying and used the party invitation as a sign that things were improving for me socially.

The day of the party, I agonized over my outfit. People in Virginia dressed differently than they did in San Francisco and Paris, and I wanted to fit in. I picked out a cute, navy dress with a small bird pattern, navy tights, and ballet flats. I twisted my hair up and put on dangly earrings. I looked polished, but still casual. More importantly, I looked like someone who I thought people would want to be friends with.

James gave my hand a squeeze before we entered the party. I had only met the hostess briefly, and James didn't know anyone. The party was going strong, and there were at least a hundred people filling the first floor. I guided James through groups of strangers to find the hostess in the kitchen. After welcoming us, she handed us off to another couple who promptly walked away.

As the night went on, I drank heavily and made small talk with the women.

"Paris," everyone exclaimed when I said where we had just come from. "How exciting!"

"I loved it there," I responded over and over again. "The food, the culture, the city life. I'd move back in an instant."

Whoever I was speaking to at that moment would eventually spot a friend across the room and wander away, leaving me standing by myself, waiting for someone new to talk to.

I smiled and laughed when necessary, but I felt like I didn't fit in. In San Francisco, women and men mingled at parties. Here, the women hung out together in the kitchen while the men gathered in the family room around the TV. I found it odd.

As I watched the women take numerous group photos, part of me longed to be included, but I couldn't make myself engage.

"Let's have lunch this week," voices around me said.

"Oh, what about a girl's night?" other voices answered.

I wasn't included in these conversations and stared forlornly as the women left me out of their coffee dates and plans for the next weekend.

When James and I left, I was emotionally drained and borderline miserable. James, however, felt I did great and praised my efforts. He cited my laughing and smiling as signs that I had enjoyed myself. When I explained how I felt left out, James waved my concerns away with a dismissive, "It takes time, Bee."

He didn't understand that I didn't have time. My loneliness was driving me into a downward spiral.

In mid-February, a flyer came home asking for volunteers at the elementary school's annual Carnival. James encouraged me to sign up for something as a way to meet more people and maybe see a few of the women from the party again. To him it made sense. After all, in San Francisco I was the fundraising chair and entrenched in the PTO, and in his mind, my only job, other than caring for the boys, was to make friends.

I logged on to Sign-Up Genius and committed to decorating, bringing a cake, and manning the popcorn station for an hour. I was determined to try even if it meant suffering through another social event.

I reported to the school promptly and was handed a spool of crepe paper streamers. "Go find Nicole," the volunteer told me. "She'll tell you what to do."

I spent the next three hours hanging streamers and no one other than Nicole, who was very sweet, spoke to me. When James picked me up, I broke into tears. "This is the least friendly group of women I've ever met. No one spoke to me. No one gave me a Welcome Buddy. They basically ignored me."

"Bee," James said, shaking his head, "you need to try approaching them."

"It's a clique!" I yelled. "And I'm not wanted."

Still, I baked my cake the next day, dressed in a cute outfit, and went to the Carnival. Nausea rolled through me when I stepped into the school. The boys happily ran off with their new friends while James and I stood awkwardly in the crowded hallway, waiting for someone to talk to us. Eventually, I had to report to the popcorn booth, and James wished me good luck. At least I'd have a partner and someone new to meet.

But when I checked in, the woman who was supposed to help me told me she was leaving because her friend needed help in the Cake Walk room. Defeated, I forced a smile as I filled bags of popcorn and handed them to excited children. I made small talk with the few dads that came through, but at the end of my shift I told James we had to leave.

"I hate this," I whined. "It's awful."

"The kids are having fun. Let's stay a little while longer," James said, and how could I argue. I couldn't ruin the boys' fun just because I couldn't make friends.

I needed to put my family first and stop being selfish, so I pressed my back against the cinderblock wall and watched the small, chattering groups of women around me. I remember thinking, *Is anyone here the slightest bit friendly?*

For Valentine's Day, James surprised me with a new SUV. "Here," he said, handing me the keys. "Now you won't be stuck in the house."

It did feel freeing to be able to drive where I wanted without having to arrange it with James first. I could go anywhere and not tell him. It felt dangerous.

On my birthday two weeks later, he gave me a ring I had admired at the David Yurman store. I no longer had wedding rings, and James wanted me to have something since I refused to consider replacing my bands. While I loved the ring, the thought of accepting it upset me.

James was trying so hard to win back my trust, but I wasn't ready to give it to him. By accepting the ring, I was encouraging James and giving him hope that our marriage could be repaired —something that felt more and more unlikely with each passing day even though I pretended to be optimistic.

James took pictures of me wearing the ring and posted them on Facebook. The comments and likes poured in, and once again, James and I were praised for our commitment to our marriage.

When I ask him now, James tells me that he truly believed I was getting better because I didn't yell as much. He worried about my crying, but felt it was normal given what we'd been through. I think it was easier for us both to ignore how deep into depression I had sunk.

At the end of March, Molly, Joe, and James's Aunt Jill came to visit. I couldn't get out of bed to greet them, and when I eventually did a day later, I sat quietly and didn't engage in the conversation.

Jill had brought a camera with her, and James thought it

would be a great idea for us to take family pictures with the cherry blossoms. I reluctantly showered and put on my favorite dress before helping the boys pick out outfits.

Jill took dozens of pictures of us laughing and playing in the fallen blossoms. When she showed them to us, all I could think was, *How do I look so happy?*

After pictures, Jill, Molly, and I sat around the picnic table on our deck. It was a lovely, warm spring day. After a few minutes of small talk, I turned to Molly and blurted, "I want a divorce. I can't do this."

She and Jill glanced at each other in shock. "Are you sure?" Molly asked. "You seem to be doing well."

I sat there for a moment. Did we really seem okay to others? And if we did, then maybe we really were? Maybe I had unrealistic expectations on how fast my healing should take? Maybe my recovery didn't matter as much as James's?

Without saying anything else, I excused myself and went upstairs to my room. I typed up an *Always Yours, Bee* post detailing how hopeless my life had become and how I couldn't keep pretending. I hurt. Deeply. And I needed out.

In a daze, I dug into the back of James's bathroom drawer and found my knife. I stripped off my dress so that I didn't ruin it and put on a T-shirt and yoga pants. Then, I dug the knife into my forearm harder than I had ever done before.

The emotional pain didn't stop.

I cut again, harder and deeper. This time, blood spurted from my arm, flowing quickly down my wrist and dripping off my fingertips. I stared at the blood and sat on the ground, letting it puddle on the floor.

I grew light-headed and needed to stop the bleeding. The Band-Aid box was empty so I tried wrapping gauze around the cuts, but the blood soaked through it in seconds.

After contemplating my options, I decided to get James. I

pulled myself up and lost my balance, smacking my head on the counter. When I regained my stance, I walked calmly to the stairs. About halfway down, I spied James in the kitchen with Joe.

"I need help," I said with no emotion. I held up my arm. "I think I hurt myself."

Rivulets of blood ran down my arm.

Someone gasped, and James rushed toward me. "What did you do?"

I blinked. Wasn't it obvious? "I cut my arm."

"You did this on purpose?" James's voice was calm, but his eyes showed fear. "You hurt yourself on purpose?"

I nodded. "I told you, it makes me feel better."

Molly rushed to James's side. Her face was ashen. "Oh, sweetheart." She glanced behind her. "Get her upstairs, James. We'll take care of the boys."

James picked me up and carried me to our bedroom, where he lay me down on the bed. "Why did you do this? We had such a good day."

I closed my eyes and tried to disappear. "I can't do this. I need the pain to stop."

James kissed my forehead and went into the bathroom, returning with a damp cloth. He wiped down my arm and changed the bandage. At some point, Molly came into the room and sat on the edge of the bed.

"How are you?" she asked softly.

I gritted my teeth. "Okay."

"Honey, you don't have to pretend. It's okay to not be okay."

I rolled over and turned my back to her. She pressed her hand against my back, and I stiffened. I couldn't stand her kindness. I didn't deserve it after taking her grandkids from her.

Molly walked across our massive bedroom to where James stood. "She needs therapy. Immediately. This is not normal."

They left a few days later. I spent the time hiding in my room, too embarrassed to come out even for meals. I was damaged, and now our family knew the extent of my instability.

I rejected the idea of therapy and insisted my problem was our marriage. I cried over and over again that I needed a divorce and to move out of Virginia. I needed to be in a city where I could be surrounded by people and energy while still being alone.

Determined to take control of the situation, I read up on Virginia divorce laws and discovered James and I could separate without living in different homes. With that in mind, I moved all of James's clothes to our basement guest room while he was at a client meeting, and I made an appointment with a divorce lawyer.

When James came home, I told him I wanted a separation, and he was no longer welcome in my part of the house.

He stared at me in disbelief. "You don't know what you want," he cried. "Bee, please. This is insane."

I shook my head. "Being here, with you, is killing me. You either give me a divorce and let me go, or I'll kill myself. There's no other way out of this for me."

James pleaded with me to change my mind, but in the end, he accepted the situation because I agreed to marriage counseling—if only to get him to leave me alone.

The marriage counselor James found was an older man with a strange beard and graying hair. His office was cluttered with a mishmash of styles. I didn't like him.

He made us do a questionnaire before arriving and submit it

to him. As we sat on the couch, shoved into opposite corners and not touching, the therapist assessed our situation and asked several questions. At one point, I burst out laughing, and the therapist pursed his lips.

"What do you find amusing?" he reprimanded. "Your marriage is in crisis. I hardly think that's anything to laugh about."

Chastised, I refused to answer any more questions. At the end of the hour, the therapist shook his head. "I can't help you. I don't say that often, but there is nothing I can do for you because you"—he pointed at me—"aren't willing to take this seriously."

"Should I curl into a ball and sob at your feet?" I asked. "Would that make me fixable?"

The therapist didn't reply.

I raised my eyebrow, and a small glimmer of satisfaction rolled through me. "We're hopeless then?"

He shook his head in exasperation. "I didn't say that, but I can't help you."

I smirked at James. "See? We can't be fixed."

James didn't say anything as we walked to the car, but once inside he let loose. "I'm going to find a different therapist. We are not beyond hope."

I rested against the door, as far as I could get from him, and said softly, "Just let me go."

James shook his head. "I'm not giving up on us or you."

27

J ames found another therapist, a woman named Katie, who I liked—mostly because she called James out on his controlling behavior on our first visit. She also gave me a referral to a psychiatrist in her practice because she felt I might benefit from taking an antidepressant in addition to my anxiety medicine.

Dr. Sims saw me the next day. She had a calm, caring demeanor and reminded me of Vivian. On my first visit, she did the standard intake questionnaire, pausing a few times as James and I described my thoughts and behaviors over the past two years.

"Before the accident, you never had periods of depression?" she asked.

"No," I answered.

"She did everything," James answered. I had asked James to come with me because I was nervous to go on my own. "She never slept and was always busy."

"How much sleep did you normally get?" Dr. Sims asked.

"Ummm . . . four or five hours?"

"And you functioned?" she asked

"Without a problem."

After asking about my history with drugs and alcohol, which I conveniently altered so I didn't sound like a pill-popping alcoholic, Dr. Sims directed her next questions to James, and I tuned out. At the end of her inquiry, Dr. Sims set her pen down on her notepad. She folded her hands and said softly, "Has anyone ever discussed bipolar depression with you?"

I blinked. "What?"

"It's not unheard of for a traumatic event to trigger bipolar II disorder. I want you to schedule an appointment to see Dr. Lisa, a psychiatrist here who has extensive experience with this condition. You need a deeper exam, but my first concern is to make sure you are stable." Dr. Sims studied me carefully. "Do you feel like you may hurt yourself?"

"I . . . I don't know." I stared at my hands. Since the wrist-cutting incident, I had struggled with intrusive suicidal thoughts and nightmares. I fluctuated between hating James and wanting nothing more than to keep him close, and I often fantasized about escaping my seemingly inescapable marriage. "I feel okay right now, but I can't control my thoughts."

Dr. Sims wrote several prescriptions. "I want you to start with these, and I want to see you back next week, okay?"

I nodded. Bipolar disorder? How was that possible? I was depressed, I knew that, but was I really mentally ill? "Am I going to be okay?"

"If you have bipolar disorder, it's manageable," Dr. Sims said. "We're going to get you leveled off first so you can start to get better."

I stood in the lobby and fought back tears while James scheduled my next appointment. James's accident, brain injury, and affair had broken me and made me crazy. I always thought I was a strong, resilient woman, able to handle anything thrown at me, and being told I wasn't, even though I knew it was the truth, terrified me.

My life became nonstop therapy appointments punctuated by thrice-daily medicine breaks. James dutifully doled out Lamictal, Abilify, Benztropine, and anti-anxiety pills and watched me swallow each one. Every time, he'd stare at me expectantly as if I should suddenly feel better. But I never did. In fact, I slipped into a deep, medicated fog that left me unable to function. When I brought this up to James and my therapists, I was told I needed to give the medicine time to work and my complaints were common during the first few weeks of medicating. It would get better, I was assured.

I stopped getting out of bed altogether, and the only times I interacted with the boys was when they'd visit me in my bedroom. They'd approach softly, waiting for my consent, and sit on the side of my bed. They'd tell me about their days and how much they loved me, and I would promise that I'd try harder the next day when the medicine started to work.

The truth was, I still felt nothing. Not for James or the boys or myself. A dull, gray fog hung over me, sucking out every emotion I had: anger, love, sadness, excitement. I truly felt nothing other than terror over feeling nothing.

Most nights, James would sit with me after the boys had gone to bed and show me old pictures on his phone. He'd ask me about them, and I'd tell him what I remembered, but it wasn't old photos I wanted to discuss. I wanted to understand why he lacked so many memories of his affair if it happened after his accident. I understood not remembering the things the truck had knocked out of his mind, but how could he not remember details of the affair when he had been so in love with Khalie? Why was I burdened with every single scorching detail that I had gleaned from their emails and blogs but he wasn't?

Even though I insisted we were separated, James often slept on the couch in my room because he feared what I would do to myself in the middle of the night. It was a valid concern, and I didn't fight him.

Our conversations during this time usually involved James explaining how my leaving was his wake-up call that he needed help. He claimed he had tried to end things with Khalie, but the fear of her exposing the affair to me kept him with her.

During one of our talks, he also revealed that he'd begun seeing a new therapist, who, like his Paris therapist, specialized in EMDR therapy.

"I almost feel like my old self," he said.

"Really?" I lay on my bed with the sheets tucked around me like a barrier.

James nodded. "I still have memory issues, but I'm not having flashbacks, and my emotions are under control."

His patience convinced me he was getting better and gave me some hope about my own therapy. I shared more with my psychiatric team and set small goals for myself, like scheduling my own appointments. Once I mastered that, I began setting timers for my medicine and took a more active role in my recovery. The constant desire to disappear was still present but became easier to ignore.

At some point, the haze surrounding me lifted slightly. With my therapist's advice and James's encouragement, I decided to try yoga, but taking the steps to find a studio overwhelmed me, so I let James find one and sign me up for a class. The first day I went to the studio, I placed myself in the back, near the door, so I could run out if necessary. I had never taken a yoga class and didn't know what to expect from the 'mixed levels' class James had chosen.

The teacher, a lithe young woman with hair flowing down her back, greeted the packed room with a smile. She guided us through a gentle series of stretches, and I felt a little smug. Yoga was easy.

Then she put on music and told the class to stand at the top of our mats. The tempo picked up. I had no idea what was happening. I folded, lifted, did some weird push-up thing, and tried to remember the all-important breath the teacher kept talking about. Sweat poured down my face, and my arms trembled.

I wasn't thinking. For the first time in months, my brain turned off and I simply moved. I breathed. My thoughts were still.

When the active portion of class ended, the teacher asked us to lie flat on our backs with our arms by our sides and legs slightly apart. We were to close our eyes and purge all thoughts from our minds.

I fell asleep, only to wake when the teacher gently touched my shoulder.

"You found peace," she said with a smile.

Yoga became my obsession, and I attended at least one, sometimes two, sessions a day. James bought me an unlimited monthly pass, and I eagerly folded and bent and stretched until I could exist without attacking myself.

———

One day, instead of going to yoga class, I went to see a divorce attorney. Even though I was unsure of how I felt about my marriage, I wanted to know my options and had saved the $250 consultation fee over the previous few weeks.

Rebecca's office was in her home not far from mine, and she ushered me into the cozy space. As I explained my situation and concerns, she took notes and nodded.

"How long have you been a resident of Virginia?" she asked.

I shrugged. "How do I establish residency?"

"Do you have a driver's license?" She frowned when I produced my California license. "You need to have six months of residency in the state of Virginia to file for divorce."

Since I didn't have a Virginia driver's license or any bills in my name, I had nothing to show that I'd been living in the state since the end of October. "Can I file for a legal separation?"

Rebecca shook her head. "We don't have legal separations in Virginia."

Getting a divorce was more difficult than I thought. Was this a sign I shouldn't be there? "Is there anything I can do?"

"Start locking down your finances," Rebecca said. "Document everything. Keep him in the basement."

"What about the boys?" This was the real reason for my appointment. I needed to know what my rights would be concerning my children.

"Do you want sole custody or joint?"

"I have bipolar disorder and no consistent job." I hated naming my weaknesses out loud. "Will anyone give me sole custody?"

Rebecca tilted her head. "It does make things more complicated. Have you ever been hospitalized?"

"No."

"Good." She made another note. "Are you taking medication?"

"Yes." I sank lower in the leather chair. The boys were the one thing in my life that I didn't want to lose even though I struggled to parent them. "I won't get custody, will I?"

"Not sole custody." Rebecca softened her face. "Joint custody isn't out of the question, but it will be tough."

I left the meeting defeated. If I walked away from my marriage, I could possibly lose my boys. Was leaving James worth it?

When I arrived home, James and Tate sat at the table, working on homework. "Hey," James said. "How was yoga?"

I wasn't my normal sweaty, post-yoga mess, and James noticed. "You okay?"

"Yes." I burned in anger. I was trapped in a marriage to a man who did nothing but try to redeem himself, and I hated it. I hated his sincere apologies and concern, and I hated the way he always spoke to me like I was one step away from breaking.

I had to face reality. I was a thirty-seven-year-old with three little boys and a mental illness. I couldn't support myself or them. James claimed he loved me. And he stayed with me, put up with my breakdowns, and made sure I took my medicine.

Rebecca made my decision clear: I needed to stay with James even if I didn't love him.

In April, Victoria told me about a masquerade ball being held at Versailles at the end of June. She was buying tickets, and she'd get me one if I wanted to come. Without asking James, I committed.

That night, after the boys were in bed, I told him about my plans to go back to Paris. Instead of telling me it wasn't wise, he nodded. "I think that will be good for you."

"I want to go for a month."

James didn't blink. "Okay."

I contacted Ruth about my Parisian apartment, and she blocked out June 13th–July 13th for me. I spent the next two months planning my trip and 18th-century costume. I would attend Le Bal followed by Fête de la Musique.

James arranged a business trip to London and would take the Eurostar over for the last two weeks of my trip. I wasn't happy about him intruding on my alone time, but I also didn't fight him. Our separation was truly only sexual since we spent all our time together, and that confused me more.

I didn't want to destroy my marriage. I wanted to blow myself up. There were so many pieces of myself I hated: the selfish bit that hadn't driven James to work that rainy November day, the neglectful bit that was a bad mother, and the overbearing bit that shoved my husband into another woman's arms. Mostly though, I hated the weak parts, the ones that made getting out of bed or connecting with my boys impossible.

The desire to hurt myself emotionally and physically drove me to share my *Always Yours, Bee* blog with James. I didn't ask him to rescue me, and I certainly didn't want to be saved by him, but I needed him to know that he was, in my mind, the reason I was self-destructing.

I believed if he realized I'd be better off without him, he'd ask for a divorce and maybe allow me parenting rights.

I sent him the link as I sat on the office loveseat and waited impatiently for him to open his email. When he did, he glanced at me, and I left the room.

I lay on the sofa and waited for some sort of confrontation.

The boys were at school, and I felt no urgency to face James and what was sure to come.

An hour later, James came to find me. His eyes were red, but soft, and he shook his head with a sigh. "I know you're hurting, but I didn't understand how much."

I twisted my mouth into a smile-grimace and tried to still my banging pulse. "Are you mad?"

"No, Bee, I'm not mad. I'm heartbroken, but not angry at you."

"Do you want me to stop posting?"

James sat at the end of the sofa. "Does it help you?"

"Yes."

He kneaded my foot. We didn't say anything else about the blog, but the next morning I woke up to a lengthy email from James. He wrote about his desire to ease my pain and protect me. He asked me to try trusting him again and begged me to let him help me. He promised he had changed and would continue with therapy and working on himself. Could I please give him a chance?

His earnest proclamations of love rang hollow, and the thought of trusting him scared me. Yet, from that day on, every time I wrote a blog post, James responded in the comments with his own thoughts. We wrote back and forth, with random people weighing in, trying to say what the other person couldn't hear, and for a brief time, it worked.

28

I spun before the mirror, admiring the cream-and-rose print ballgown I wore. The owner of the theatrical costume shop, Gregory, had cinched me tightly into the back-laced corset, and I stood rod straight. I had driven forty minutes to Alexandria to visit this store, and Gregory and I had spent a fun hour trying on different gowns.

"What do you think?" Gregory asked. "Gorgeous, right?" He was a robust man in his mid-thirties with a handlebar mustache, and he completed his steampunk ensemble with a monocle. "I sewed this beauty myself."

I ran my hand over the full skirt. Beneath it, I had on a petticoat and panniers to make my slender hips look wider. "I love it. Do you have a wig?"

Gregory clapped his hands in excitement. "Girl, you know I do!" He looked me over and nodded his approval. "You are going to be the Belle of Versailles!"

I left in two weeks for Paris and had just finally gotten around to finding my costume. Victoria had offered to pick out something for me, but I wanted to choose my own gown.

I studied the voluminous dress. "I'm going to have to pack my extra-large suitcase just for this."

"Oh, yes, honey. This girl needs her own transportation." Gregory slipped into the backroom and emerged with a black binder. "Let's find you the perfect hairstyle."

We flipped through the laminated pages, and Gregory pointed out period-appropriate hairstyles. Eventually, we decided on a towering Marie Antionette-style wig. "It will be heavy," Gregory said. "And you'll need to stuff it with newspaper, so it doesn't cave in."

"Okay."

"It should get here by Thursday." Gregory held out his hand for my credit card.

"That's fine." I handed it to him. "I don't leave for two more weeks."

"In that case, why don't you pick it all up at once? Three days before you leave? That way I don't have to charge you for all those extra days."

"Okay."

Gregory waved his hands. "Oh! I forgot. I must get a picture before you leave!"

I posed with my hand on my hip while he snapped a few pictures with his phone. When he was done he unlaced me, and I changed back into my jeans and blouse.

"So, June 15th?" I asked.

"Perfect!" Gregory air-kissed me, and I left.

On the long drive home, I blasted music and sung along, trying to steel myself against my return to boring sameness of the DC exurbs. Just before the county line, my phone rang, and I answered over the car's Bluetooth.

"Hello?"

"Honey! It's Allison! How are you?" Allison's warm, bubbly voice made me smile. After hiding from most of my San Francisco friends for over a year, I found myself wanting to reconnect with them. Allison was the best person for the job; she was always happy, and I had recently confided in her about my troubles with James.

"I'm good! What's going on?" I navigated through the toll area and merged onto the next freeway.

Allison launched into a convoluted story about a cat, Botox, and a taco bar before saying, "I'm coming to DC! Do you want to meet up?"

"Of course!" Seeing someone other than my cats and family was just what I needed. "When will you be here?"

"Tomorrow night," she answered. "I don't get in until after dinner. Maybe we can have a drink at the hotel bar?"

I was desperate to talk to an adult that wasn't James. "Sounds great!"

"Awesome! I'll text you the info."

I hung up and gunned the engine. Not only was I going to escape suburban hell but I was also going to see Allison. Things were looking up.

———

Not all of us fall apart in the same way. Maybe you implode —but more likely pieces of you fall away, chip by chip, until you have nothing left to give yourself. That's when you're the most dangerous, because you don't notice what's happened. Losing yourself feels normal. For me, I expended considerable energy searching for reasons—why James was hit, why he cheated, why I wasn't enough. I desperately wanted to fix whatever was wrong with me, even as the search to find the elusive 'it' destroyed me.

It was in this state of mind—this feeling of less than—that I walked into a hotel bar the next night. Allison wasn't there yet, and my gaze landed on the only person sitting at the high table running widthwise across the room: a handsome man with dark facial scruff and closely cropped hair. Our eyes locked, and my breath caught.

He flashed a devious smile, and when I smiled back, he stood and walked to me.

"Hey," he said in a deep baritone before leaning over and wrapping me in his solid arms. He felt like a favorite, old coat that I had misplaced, and I returned his embrace.

When I pulled away, I stared up at him in confusion. "Hi."

"Hi."

I spied Allison standing in the lobby, and she waved.

"I'll be right back."

My high heel sandals click-clacked across the polished floor. "Hey," I said to Allison. "I don't know who he is. Weird, right?"

"Not weird. You look so cute I'd hug you, too." She winked.

I spun in a circle, showing off my fitted sheath dress and size 2 body. "I do look pretty cute."

"Indeed." Allison made an exaggerated yawn. "I'm tired. Can we catch up at dinner tomorrow?"

I shook my head at her, disappointed that my big night out was a bust. "But—"

"Tomorrow." Her oversized handbag had slipped off her shoulder, and she adjusted it. "I'll text you in the morning." She lifted her chin toward the man. "Go have fun."

When I was nineteen, Allison gifted me expensive lingerie as a birthday present. "This is just for you," she had said as I unwrapped the present. "It's to make you feel good and not for any man." Over the years, she had gifted me many things and always made a point of telling me that it was for my well-being —things like spa days and new lipsticks.

With this in mind, it didn't strike me as odd that Allison would leave me alone with a man at a bar, especially since I had shared that James and I had separated. Allison hadn't been shocked and instead asked what had taken me so long. She had been the only person who mentioned leaving James before I found out about his affair. As she had put it, my happiness didn't need to be tied up with crazy.

After she disappeared down the hallway, I considered my options, staring first at the elevator exit then at the bar. I could go home, but I didn't want to waste my night out.

The man smiled and beckoned me over. "I'm not going anywhere if you want to hang out."

"Sure." It seemed a shame to get dressed up to just turn around and go home. I climbed on the tall stool, my feet swinging above the footrest. "What are you drinking?" It seemed like the best way to start a conversation.

"Whiskey." He rattled the square ice cube. "What would you like?"

I tried to think of something sophisticated, but only came up with a vodka cranberry. "Are you waiting for someone?"

"Just you." He kept his gaze fixed on me, and a thrill raced through my body.

Allison was definitely behind this. "Do you know Allison?"

His deep-set hazel eyes showed his confusion. "Who?"

"Never mind." Despite his reaction, I was positive Allison had set me up somehow, but I didn't press him, because there was something intriguing about his personality that made me want to keep talking to him.

He caught me staring and grinned, showing off his wide smile and perfectly aligned teeth. "I'd ask if you come here often, but that's a cliché."

"And we're at a hotel bar." My voice was an octave higher than normal. Flirting with this guy was easy and felt good—like flexing a muscle I'd forgotten I had. "Why don't you tell me your name?"

He raised his eyebrows. "It's Rob. What's your real name?"

What a strange question. "Mia."

Rob rattled his whiskey glass. "Let's enjoy our drinks and talk. Maybe you won't hate me." His mischievous eyes teased me. "Or maybe you will."

Rob wore his hair closely shorn. It wasn't quite a buzz cut, but it looked like something a former military man would wear. His clothes—dark jeans and a light-blue button-down shirt with the sleeves rolled up—were immaculate, and his squared nails were neither too short nor too long. A massive watch encircled his wrist.

Aside from the smooth groove on his finger where his wedding band had once sat, he looked perfect.

As he spoke, he leaned closer to me, not too much, but enough to make the space between us more intimate. I often read articles on body language and how to create connections with people, and curious about whether Rob was flirting with me, I rested my hand on the high-top. When he touched it, I didn't pull back, and excitement rushed through me.

Rob kept his deep voice playful but controlled. His accent was tinted with a hint of Midwest flatness, but it also sounded as if he could hail from anywhere, USA. He wouldn't answer my question about his hometown and instead told me to guess.

"Omaha?" I asked.

Rob shook his head. "Try again."

"Ohio." His slight accent reminded me of my family in Southern Michigan, but it wasn't as pronounced.

Rob sipped his drink and kept his eyes locked on me. "Why Ohio?"

Ah. So, I was right. "You sound familiar."

"To what?" He peered deeper and deeper inside me like he could see something long forgotten.

"My family in Michigan." I blinked, breaking the thrall he had over me.

"But you're from San Francisco?" Rob hailed the bartender for two more drinks.

"I was before I moved to Paris." He asked me a few questions about life in Paris, and I gave practiced answers. Everything in Paris had been wonderful. I had moved there to focus on writing. We lived in Le Marais, in a beautiful apartment, and I missed it terribly.

"Do you travel?" I picked up the cocktail the bartender had placed before me. It was my third of the night, and my brain felt a little fuzzy.

"I've lived all over. In some places you'd like to visit and in some that will never be on anyone's vacation list."

"Like where?"

He hesitated before answering. "Bulgaria. Iraq. Norway."

"That's a random group." His clothes told me he was a businessman of some sort. "What do you do?"

"Government stuff." His answer was vague, but I had learned that most people in Northern Virginia were vague about their government jobs, and I didn't press for more details.

As the night grew later, we discussed a variety of topics, but neither of us mentioned spouses even though we both had indentations around our ring fingers. It didn't seem relevant.

Rob was controlled, measured, and deliberate—everything James wasn't—and it drew me to him. Over time, I learned Rob rarely made mistakes, and when he did, he quickly covered them.

We talked until it was nearly nine. Rob's deep voice calmed me, and I felt like my old self—engaged, interesting, and fun.

When we both needed to leave, Rob flagged the bartender for the bill. I opened my wallet, exposing my passport.

"Do you always carry that?" Rob pointed at the dark-blue book.

"I like being able to leave when I want." The passport was an illusion. I was stuck in Virginia and could only leave when James let me.

Rob narrowed his hazel eyes and laid a pile of cash on the table. "I'll get this."

As we walked to the parking garage elevator, he laced his fingers through mine, and my heart fluttered.

When the doors slid shut, I leaned against the side wall to steady myself against the rush of excitement and one drink too many. Rob pushed the button and turned toward me. When our eyes met, I nodded, and he leaned into me, kissing me deeply. My head swam. His lips were foreign, but like James, he had beard scruff. It felt familiar, and I liked that.

When the doors opened, I stepped away from Rob.

"My car's this way." I turned left, and he followed me. I paused next to the car door. "Call me?" I asked. I didn't know what was happening, but it felt completely sane.

Rob placed his hands on each side of me, pinning me. His massive frame dwarfed mine, but I wasn't afraid, and this time when we kissed, there was more urgency, more desire.

Rob smiled down at me. "Give me your number. I'll text you."

He didn't text me. Instead, he pulled up behind me at a stop-light in my neighborhood and followed me home.

"Do you know what I thought when I saw you in front of me?" Rob asked when he rolled down his window.

I darted through raindrops and leaned in. "Kismet?"

"Serendipity," he answered. "Get in the car."

My wet clothes stuck to me, and my hair clung to my face.

In hindsight, I question my judgment and inability to see the red flags. Why was he at the hotel bar? How did he come to be behind me at the stoplight if he hadn't followed me? Why did he insist on paying cash?

However, in that moment, my thoughts focused on one thing: a handsome, intriguing man was interested in me.

I climbed in. Rob tore off down the street.

When Allison inquired about Rob the next day, I feigned modesty, and she didn't pry for details. Later, when I asked Rob why he was at the hotel bar, he said some divine force had planted him on that bar stool, but he never really answered my question.

I overlooked the consistent oddities of Rob's story because it felt good to be dating someone . . . or were Rob and I dating? Could you date if you weren't divorced? Did a separation count as being single? I struggled with the hazy parameters of my marital status. In California, there were legal separations with documents; in Virginia, there were no such things. You simply agreed upon a separation date and could divorce one year after that.

Over the next two weeks, I squeezed in as much time with Rob as I could: going for runs along the Potomac, having dinners with too much wine, and enjoying feeling desirable again. Rob had a way of making me forget all the chaos in my life, and I lapped up his attention.

The night before I left for Paris, Rob and I drank too much wine, and I confessed I was going to miss him.

"It's going to be hard to be away from you, too." He motioned me around the table and pulled me onto his lap. Rob was six feet three inches of solid muscle, and his size made me feel safe.

Despite this, my anxiety reared its ugly head. Would Rob forget me and move on if I wasn't around for a month? Why did I have to meet him right before my trip?

The next evening, James drove me to the airport and helped me check my bags. At security, he squeezed my hand and pecked my forehead. "Have fun, Bee. I'll see you next week."

I hesitated. I didn't want to go anywhere with James. I didn't want the confusion and wished there were some way for Rob to meet me in Paris instead.

"We'll have fun." I slung my computer bag over my shoulder.

James nodded. "I have a bunch of surprises planned."

Why was he trying? What was the point? "I can't wait."

I disappeared through security. James had upgraded me to business class. I took a Xanax, stretched out, and slept the entire flight.

The next day was a blur. I somehow made it to my apartment and met Ruth. She helped me carry my oversized luggage upstairs. After she left, I hung up my clothes and arranged my toiletries. I called the boys to let them know I arrived safely and that I missed them. Then I headed to Monoprix to buy a few groceries.

At six, I hopped in a taxi with my giant suitcase and headed across town to Victoria's. She lived near Sacré-Cœur, and the ride took nearly forty-five minutes. She and her still-stunning friend greeted me. We spent the next several hours getting ready for Le Bal, and I snapped a few pictures of me in full makeup and sent them to Rob.

"Hot!" he wrote back, and I squealed in delight.

Victoria asked what was funny, and I gushed about Rob. After asking me about James and our marriage, she nodded her approval. "Rob sounds like he's what you need right now."

"He is," I answered.

After squeezing into our dresses, the three of us piled into a taxi for the ride to Versailles. We hobbled over the cobblestones to the famous golden gates and posed with other partygoers as tourists took pictures of us. At dusk, we made our way into the gardens where the fountains danced to music and fireworks exploded overhead. At eleven, costumed attendants ushered us down a wide staircase to L'Orangerie.

Inside, a naughty, topless mermaid read dirty fairytales in French, and white tigers prowled inside cages. Music thumped around us as performers splashed and danced in bathtubs on a central stage. A huge bonfire roared in the courtyard, and couples sneaked off into the bushes for some nighttime activity.

We danced and drank until five in the morning when we were moved to the amphitheater for breakfast. Exhausted, Victoria, her friend, and I made our way through the gardens to exit. The train didn't run that early, and there were no taxis, so we waited while Victoria called around to find a ride. When a taxi arrived, we crammed ourselves and our giant dresses inside.

I fell asleep, and Victoria woke me up when we arrived at her house. "I've paid for this part of the ride. He'll take you home."

I nodded and forced my eyes open as the taxi sped along empty Saturday morning Parisian streets. At my building, I paid and hefted myself out of the taxi. After climbing the five flights of stairs in my dress, I collapsed on my bed and slept.

James and I passed our weeks in Paris eating, drinking, and shopping. We did friend things, not couple things. I didn't worry about the boys because they were enjoying their time at my dad's, and unlike the year before, I missed them and called frequently. The only guilt I felt was over wishing Rob were with me instead of James.

James and I traveled to Nice again, and this time I didn't scream or rage. Instead, I sent Rob dozens of pictures and felt slightly guilty about ignoring James. When Rob asked for a bikini shot, I slipped into the bathroom, stripped down to my lacy panties, and snapped a picture. His quick reply made my heart race.

James waited on the balcony where he unsuccessfully tried to seduce me. James who had hurt me. James who had felt I wasn't enough. James who I had caught in lie after lie. James who had lost his job and took another that paid a quarter of his old one.

Compared to Rob, James didn't seem like much of a catch. That's what I told myself.

29

The day we returned to DC, I immediately made an excuse to run an errand and met Rob near the river. We danced around each other, unsure, until he grabbed me firmly and kissed me against a tree. In that moment, I knew I needed to come clean with James. He deserved to know we had no future, but it was a messy separation, wasn't it? James kept trying to fix things, and I encouraged him by letting him travel with me.

For two years, I had tried to smash the pieces of James and myself back into a familiar, recognizable shape. I had pounded and forced, but that old shape stubbornly would not appear. What I really needed was not to hold on to what I felt I had lost, but rather accept that the shape of my world, and me in it, had changed.

The moment Rob kissed me, I knew I desperately needed Rob to want me, and I could no longer be with James.

The next night, Rob and I went to dinner.

"Malbec?" He tapped the wine list.

"I prefer Médoc." I winked.

"You're expensive," Rob said with a laugh.

"And you"—I reached across the table and touched his hand —"like expensive things."

Rob flashed his brilliant smile. "And pretty things."

"Are you calling me pretty?" I let the words dance playfully from my lips.

His grin grew. "Maybe."

With Rob, I didn't feel broken. Instead, I was a normal, non-mentally ill person who had suffered a traumatic event, and I absolutely did not feel depressed or like I had bipolar disorder. I was just me, and unlike James, Rob liked this version of me.

For some reason, Rob followed me home after dinner and waited for me to park. I got out of my car and leaned through his window. He reached over and kissed me good-bye before taking off. When I turned toward the house, James stood on the porch, his arms hanging helplessly by his side.

"Who was that?" he sputtered.

I wasn't ready to talk to James about Rob, so I pushed past him into the house.

"Bee," James said, catching my arm. "Who the hell was that?"

I shrugged. "Rob."

James's face fell. "How long?"

"We met before I left for Paris." I kicked off my shoes and headed to the kitchen where I poured a glass of ice-cold water and guzzled it.

James slumped against the counter. "Were you talking to him while we were in Paris?"

I nodded.

Hurt flooded his eyes. "Bee, I thought . . ."

"You thought wrong," I snapped. "I told you I wanted a divorce. I settled for a separation."

"You're cheating on me." James's defeated voice infuriated me.

"Cheating on you? No." I glared at him. "There is no us right now. I can do whatever I want, as can you."

James shook his head. "We can't work on things if there's someone else."

"Maybe I'm done trying." I set the cup of water down. The house was quiet. "Where are the boys?"

"Asleep."

I jerked my head toward the sofa, and when we were both sitting, I said, "You put us here. You."

"We can make this better."

Why was he making this difficult? "Cats have nine lives, not marriages."

"Bee—"

I held up my hand. "I don't care. You broke us. You chose to sleep with Khalie. Not once or three times like you originally said, but over and over again." James tried to interrupt, but I cut him off. "You told her you were going to leave the boys and me and move to New York for her. You used my money to fuel your fun around Asia."

I paused and glanced at the stairs, aware that any slight elevation of my voice would bring the boys out of their rooms. "You do not get to tell me what I can do any more."

"It's been a year," James said. "I've done—"

Rage overwhelmed me. "A year? You expect me to be over this in a year? Are you serious?"

"Bee, I'm sorry." I yanked my hand away when he touched me, and James frowned. "If we have any chance of getting through this, bringing someone else into the mess isn't the way to do it."

"I've spent nearly two years running around behind you trying to fix this mess while you were screwing Khalie and lying about therapy." I stood. "Two years of heartbreak and feeling like I had failed you."

James sighed. "So, this is payback?"

"It's not payback. It's me feeling happy for the first time in two years."

"I can make you happy." James stood. "I love you, and if you let me in, I can make you happy again."

James's frequent declarations of love enraged me, and that night was no different. I struggled to reconcile his past actions with his claim that he had never stopped loving me. He had explained numerous times that he hadn't loved himself and that's why he had the affair. In his mind, it had nothing to do with me or what I had or hadn't done.

That's what upset me the most: I had nothing to do with his affair, and no control over it. I had always believed I controlled my circumstances, and my will to succeed was enough to make things happen.

I had no say in James's affair. The husband I had believed to be unwaveringly faithful had shown me how quickly things changed, and this is what distressed me as it made me feel completely helpless in our relationship.

"You don't love me. You just don't want to fail." I walked toward the stairs. "I'm going to bed. It's your turn to get the boys to school tomorrow. I'll see you in the afternoon."

As I climbed the steps, I wanted to apologize to James. He was trying. He no longer yelled and was completely engaged with the boys. He made sure that I had everything I needed and refused to give up on our marriage. Was I wrong to not return his devotion? Was it wrong to feel happier when I was with Rob?

I stopped on the landing and turned around to apologize, but James was gone.

Rob and I spent the rest of the summer texting and having dinners in between our respective kid duties. James mostly moped around, which drove me crazy. I tried my best not to flaunt my growing relationship with Rob, but James always knew when we'd been out because I only had one friend and she was a daytime friend—someone I had lunch with but not much more.

In September, Rob told me he had to go away for a week for some training, and he wouldn't be able to contact me while he was gone. It would be the longest we had been apart since I went to Paris.

"I don't know how I'm going to do it." He lifted my hair off my neck and kissed the top of my head. I was kneeling, tying his shoe as he sat on the edge of my bedroom sofa. He had insisted on taking a shower and smelled like my soap, and I had a tooth-brush for him, which made it feel like we had moved onto a more significant type of relationship. "I hate not seeing you every day." He pulled me up and kissed me softly. "I won't be able to call or text."

I sighed. James was in Atlanta for work, and the boys were asleep. Rob came over and sneaked into the house shortly after I told him they were in bed. It wasn't the first time he'd been over —always when James was gone and after the boys were asleep. I wasn't ready to explain Rob to them. They were confused enough by James sleeping in the basement.

Rob had two children near my boys' ages, and we often compared parenting stories and challenges. He was extremely proud of his kids even though he said their fighting drove him crazy. I adored how involved Rob was with them, being a spelling study buddy and driving them to sports practices. He reminded me of pre-accident James, and in a twisted way, I found that attractive.

Rob towered over me when he stood. "God, I'm going to miss you."

I flashed a flirty smile and threw my arms around his neck. "I'll miss you, too."

We walked out through the garage door, and as Rob drove away, my brain told me something was off, but my heart spoke louder. I pushed the niggling thoughts away.

Later that night, well after midnight, he texted, "I want all of you. Every single piece, and that scares me."

I set my phone down and buried my face in a pillow. Tears scorched my cheeks. Rob wanted all of me, but he didn't know about my mental illness or really anything about me beyond the fun person I was when I was with him.

He wanted a fantasy I knew I couldn't deliver.

When James returned from Atlanta, he was an anxious mess. I hadn't returned his calls while he was gone, and he demanded to know if I spent my free time with Rob.

"I hate him." James tossed his laundry into the machine. "I'm serious, Bee. If this continues, you can't live here."

This was a new development. James had already cut me off from all our joint money by moving his paychecks into an account I couldn't access. He said it was because he worried about me over-shopping and spending obscene amounts of money, but in our fifteen years of marriage, I had never over-shopped. It was purely a way to control me. I had no money of my own since I hadn't published in over a year, and I had no books in the pipeline. I was 100 percent dependent on James financially.

"You know I can't leave," I said.

"Then you need to stop seeing him."

I had never done ultimatums well. "Fine. You're going to have to pay for my apartment. I'll contact my lawyer and have her draw up an agreement."

James blanched. "Bee, you don't have to do that. You—"

I had called his bluff and was inwardly pleased. "You don't want me here, so I'll go," I said. "But the boys come with me."

James bristled. "No."

Since Rob had come into my life, I was less depressed and more engaged with the boys. We played games after homework and went for hikes and bike rides. Leo and Tate helped me make dinners, and I drove carpools for Ryan and his lacrosse friends. The four of us had hit a rhythm, and I was once again the mom I knew I could be.

"I'm not going anywhere without the boys." I crossed my arms, determined to fight for my kids. "If you don't like it, you can continue to stay in the basement, and I'll stay upstairs in my room."

James's shoulders sagged. "Fine, but I don't want *him* coming here anymore. Go to his place."

In the four plus months we'd been seeing each other, Rob always came to my house, and until this moment, it hadn't struck me as odd. His soon-to-be ex-wife and he had a strange agreement about dating, and he was worried that if she found out about us, she'd be able to claim a larger portion of his pension and income. He had once asked if I thought James had me followed, and I laughed it off.

Was he afraid of his wife following him?

"Whatever." I used a phrase James found irritating.

James frowned and disappeared into the basement without a fight, and I smirked. He controlled me financially, but I controlled everything else.

Shortly after Rob returned from his work trip, my only friend in Virginia invited me out for an afternoon of shopping, and I eagerly accepted. I craved friendship and still struggled to meet people. The moms at school all had their cliques, and my neighbors were a bit insular. James was the only adult other than Rob that I socialized with regularly, and our relationship wasn't healthy.

Mary and I dug through the racks at Nordstrom, holding out clothes for the other to approve or not. When I gathered an armful of cute things, we headed to the dressing rooms. We laughed and commented on how different our styles were—she was more conservative in a posh Tory Burch way, and I liked dresses and tights. Eventually, we selected our items and paid.

As we walked out of Nordstrom, Mary said, "I got invited to a leisurewear party Thursday. Want to come? It's a bunch of fun girls."

"Sure." I was excited that Mary liked me enough to invite me to a nighttime event.

She pulled up her phone and opened the Facebook invite. With a flick of her finger, she scrolled through the list of women, asking if I knew any of them.

I kept shaking my head no until a face flashed across the screen. My heart dropped. A pretty, blonde woman faced the camera . . . and Rob was kissing her cheek.

"Who's that?" I tried to keep my face steady. It had to be Rob's wife. There was no other explanation, but why would she have this picture if they were divorcing? And why would she be invited to a party in my neighborhood?

"Oh, that's Katrina Diaz. Do you know her?" Mary glanced at me. "Are you okay?"

"I . . . I know him." I touched the screen. "Is that Rob?"

Mary drew her brows together. "You know Rob?"

I nodded. "But his last name isn't Diaz, it's Granati." There had to be a rational explanation as to why Katrina had a picture of her and Rob as her profile. "They're getting divorced, right?"

Mary slowly shook her head. "I was at a party with them last weekend. They are certainly not getting divorced."

"Are you sure?"

"Absolutely."

My legs trembled, and my throat constricted. Rob had lied. He had lied about going through a divorce, and he had lied about his last name. "Can we go?"

Mary studied me. "I don't know what's going on, but if it involves Rob, you should stop immediately."

Air didn't want to fill my lungs, and I felt faint. "Oh. I met him once." My voice shook. "I swore he said he was getting divorced."

"If he did," Mary said, "he lied to you."

The boys were still at school and James was at work when I returned home. I sent Rob a vague text asking him to call me. Then I called and left a message, keeping my voice upbeat and pleasant. I didn't expect to hear from him until after four thirty since he couldn't have his personal cell phone while at work.

The boys came home, and I made snacks and helped with homework, but the entire time I kept my eye on the clock, waiting for Rob to get off work. When my phone rang, I lunged for it, excused myself to the office, and shut the door.

"Hey," Rob said in his smooth baritone. "What's going on?"

Nausea consumed me, and beads of cold sweat formed along my hairline. "Is your last name Diaz?"

Silence.

"Rob?"

"Yeah. Ummm . . . can you meet me tonight?" He sounded flustered, and Rob was never, ever flustered.

"What time?" I forced back the lump in my throat.

"Six?"

James would be home by then. "Where?"

Rob gave me the name of a restaurant not too far from my neighborhood, but far enough away that I suspected he was trying not to be seen.

My heart thundered against my ribs as I moved through the rest of my afternoon routine in a daze. There had to be a reason Katrina used a profile picture of both of them. Was she keeping up appearances? Was she in denial? It's something I would have done with James to convince the world we were fine.

The more I reflected, the more convinced I became that Rob was not getting divorced. He was elusive and never spoke much about his life and, instead, always dodged my questions by asking about my life. He told me what I wanted to hear, and I never questioned his vagueness.

Like James, Rob was a liar, but damn if I didn't want him to have a rational explanation.

Rob had already selected a bottle of wine before I arrived at the restaurant and had polished off at least one glass. He stood and flashed his oh-so-charming smile at me. "We have a lot to talk about." He pulled out my chair. "I hope you'll hear me out."

On the drive over, I had sworn I'd tell him off. After all, I had been in his wife's position. I had been betrayed, and I absolutely could not play a role in hurting another woman. I couldn't.

But then Rob touched my hand, and tears formed in my eyes. "You're not getting divorced."

"Not yet."

"Not ever." Anger dripped from my words. "You're just running around behind your wife's back while she stays home and raises your kids and takes care of your life." The rage I felt over James's betrayal spilled out onto Rob.

Rob glanced away before focusing his laser gaze on me. "We're not a couple. We're roommates. That's it."

Roommates. James had written that about me to Khalie. It had been a lie about us, and I was sure Rob was lying now. "You live in my neighborhood, don't you?"

He clenched his jaw. "Yes."

"Where?"

He said his street name. I didn't recognize it, but we lived in a large development.

I struggled with my next words. "I can't see you anymore. I can't be part of whatever you're doing."

Rob swigged calmly from his wine glass. "You mean everything to me. We can make this work."

"I'm not helping you cheat on your wife!" But the truth was, I wanted him to say he was leaving her for me. I wanted him to choose me. James hadn't; he had only defaulted to me. But Rob could choose. He could decide that I was worth a chance.

I sat there, listening to Rob's endless explanations, and my resolve melted away. I justified what had happened. Clearly, Katrina and Rob had issues or he wouldn't be with me. Maybe she was a wonderful mother but a terrible wife like he claimed? Maybe they had run their course after nearly twenty years together?

Did it matter?

It absolutely should not have mattered. I should have stood and walked out. But I didn't. We finished our meal, and I let Rob escort me to my car. When he kissed me, I knew that walking away from him was something I wasn't ready to do, and I hated myself for it.

few days later, James didn't come home. He had promised to take the boys to dinner, and it was nearly eight. He wasn't answering his phone, and worry grew in my mind, but I gave the boys baths and tucked them into bed with the explanation that James had to unexpectedly work late. He'd make it up to them tomorrow.

After I turned off Ryan's light, I stumbled down the long hallway to my room. My brain was a frantic mess. James always answered his phone. Always. I tried texting and calling again. I waited a few minutes, changed into my nightgown, and washed my face. My phone sat next to the sink just in case James called.

At ten, despite it being late, I texted the only friend he had in Virginia, a neighbor a few doors down. He didn't respond either.

Rob called and texted me good night, but I ignored him.

By midnight, I was a complete wreck, pacing the house and crying. I searched the internet for any information about accidents that had occurred on James's way home but found nothing.

James was never late. He may have been upset with me, but he wouldn't disappoint the boys. Where was he?

Every moment of the day of his accident flashed through my mind until I was a hysterical mess. The hurt and rage that permeated most of my interactions with James slid away, exposing my fear of losing James again. Even though I wanted Rob to choose me, I couldn't truly picture my life without James. Before the accident, he had been my everything, and after, I was committed to fixing him out of love. And didn't he show me day after day that he loved me? Didn't he try when I made trying nearly impossible?

I acted angry and mean because I was afraid James would toss me aside again. Even worse, I so desperately wanted someone to love me that I stayed with Rob despite knowing he was committing adultery.

As I waited in the family room with my phone glued to my hand, I cried and promised myself that if James came home in one piece, I'd work on fixing things. I'd leave Rob and focus on my family.

At five in the morning, my phone rang. An unfamiliar but local number flashed across the screen.

"Hello?" I croaked. My parched throat hurt from crying.

"Hi. Is this James's wife?" a woman asked. She didn't sound concerned or business-like. In fact, she sounded a little drunk.

I drew my brows together. "Yes. Do you know where he is?"

She snorted. "Passed out on my couch. What's your address? I need him out of here before my husband gets home."

Heat rushed up my neck, and my ears rang. The fear I had sat with all night evaporated. "He's been with you all night?"

"Only after we left the bar. Now what's your address? I have a cab waiting."

I rattled it off and hung up. For nine hours, I had worked myself into a state of panic while James was out drinking and doing God knows what with some random woman who apparently had a husband.

Was this what we had become?

James could say whatever he wanted, but at least Rob and I were respectful, and I didn't intentionally neglect the boys. Plus, I had climbed beyond my depression and was fully engaged as a mother again.

James was being reckless.

Forty-five minutes later, he stumbled through the front door. His clothes were askew and he reeked of alcohol. When he spied me on the sofa he gave a half-wave. "I didn't know I'd get a welcoming committee."

"Not cool." I kept my voice low even though I wanted to scream. The boys didn't need to see this mess.

James knew nothing about childhood divorce trauma, and I believed he couldn't understand the immense pain and guilt children of divorce feel. He acted as if our increasing arguments didn't impact the boys and were contained solely within the boundaries of our relationship. He didn't understand that our actions had spilled onto the boys and were harming them.

James could hurt me, but I wouldn't let him hurt the boys again.

"I'm sorry." He collapsed onto the club chair next to the sofa. "I started drinking, and I don't even know how I ended up at the woman's house."

I clenched my jaw. "Do you even know her name? Or does that matter when you're banging someone else's wife?"

"I don't know. Does it make a difference when you know the wife's name?"

"This isn't about me." I kept calm, but how did James know that? "You're disgusting."

James rested his head against the back of the chair and stared at the ceiling. "Can you just stop? I fucked up. I know it."

I waited for him to tell me I was a monster too, but he said nothing. After the emotional night I had, I was too wrung out to fight and sank down on the chair across from him. "Did you forget about the boys?"

"What?" James rubbed his bloodshot eyes.

"You promised them dinner." I studied his confused expression. "You seriously don't remember?"

"Oh, God." His deep-brown eyes, the ones I once believed would never hurt me, filled with horror. "What did you tell them?"

"That you had to work late."

James leaned forward and rested his elbows on his knees. "I think I need rehab. I've been drinking too much, and I don't think I can stop. I feel like I'm slipping into my old patterns."

He was right. We both had drinking issues, but his had spun out of control since finding out about Rob. He had happy hours every weeknight and guzzled whiskey while sitting on the deck on the weekends. Occasionally, he'd have a flash of anger, but he generally kept his emotions in check. I never brought it up because I drank heavily too, and as long as we could parent, I didn't think it mattered.

Was James saying he could no longer parent?

"Rehab?" I asked. "Are you sure?"

He nodded and removed his phone from his pocket. "I want to find a place today."

"For how long?"

James shrugged. "For as long as I need."

"I'm not going to rehab," I said, worried that he would want me to go, too.

"No one is asking you to."

I sighed in relief. I wasn't as bad as James, and he knew it. "I'm going to bed to get a little sleep before I have to get the boys ready for school." I pointed at James. "Go downstairs. I don't want them to see you like this."

James wobbled and clenched his phone. "I'll stay out of sight."

———

James found a rehab facility about an hour from our house. We told the boys he had a work trip, and we didn't know how long he'd be gone. After Ryan left for school, I drove James to the facility. We didn't speak the entire way there, and I didn't escort him in, just dropped him off at the door.

James hadn't left me any money, and I couldn't access his bank accounts. The boys and I would be fine with food for a week or two, but if James had to stay longer, the pennies in my account weren't going to do much. If I found his checkbook I could have forged a check to myself, but I wasn't sure where he hid it.

I walked through rooms, making a list of things I needed to do: find money, call his boss, figure out what bills needed to be paid, and most importantly, take care of the boys and shield them from the latest parental fuck-up.

How had we come to this? James and I were once a solid team. Now we were a wreck. I didn't trust him, and he had allowed his anger about Rob to spiral into a drinking problem. We were trapped in a pattern of hurting each other and ourselves.

As the days passed, the boys and I settled into a routine, and while I was concerned about James, I was also majorly pissed. Over and over again, he had begged me to give him a chance and forget about Rob, but he'd run off with a random woman the first chance he had.

I shouldn't have been mad. We were separated. But I was furious and deeply hurt. It took James going missing for me to realize how much he still meant to me, only to have him ruin it by being a drunk who slept with another man's wife.

I wasn't any better. What I was doing with Rob was wrong, and I was terrified to let go of him. Unlike James, Rob was steady and reliable—even if he was committing adultery. When I was with him, every worry I had vanished, and I believed Rob was the reason I had climbed out of my depression.

Yet, I ignored Rob's calls, texts, and emails. I focused on the boys and spent the long nights crying over everything I had lost since James's accident. For the first time since I ran away to Paris, I had to sit alone and reflect on what I wanted, and I had to acknowledge my actions were wrong. I craved the safety, security, and love Rob offered, and rejected the broken version of myself James saw. As much as I adored Rob, his moral compass —and mine—was no better than James's. He had offered me a reprieve from my life, and I had eagerly and stupidly gobbled it up.

When the rehab center called and asked me to come in, I hesitated. James's caseworker felt it necessary to include me in his recovery plan, and I disagreed. She patiently explained why my help was necessary, appealing to my desire to protect the boys, and I agreed to come in later that afternoon when my neighbor could babysit.

At the center, I was led to a small, poorly furnished conference room. The counselor was a woman slightly older than me and wore a frumpy blazer over a T-shirt. She didn't bother to introduce herself before shoving a brochure across the table toward me. "James is sick, and he needs support. You need to be that support."

I blinked. "Did he tell you we are separated?"

"He said it was complicated." She tapped the table with her fingertip. "He won't be successful in his recovery without a support network, and from what I can tell, you're all he has." She paused. "You do live together?"

"Yes."

"Then he needs you to be on board with his program."

"What does that mean?" I didn't want the responsibility of fixing James again. I had tried in the past, and it hadn't worked. James needed to fix himself.

The caseworker pulled out another glossy brochure. "First, we need to address your codependent relationship."

I had never heard that term before. "Excuse me?"

"You and James are stuck in a cycle of trying to fix each other, and you need to end it."

"Isn't that what marriage is? Lifting up the other person when they need it?" How could trying to fix your broken spouse be wrong?

The caseworker shook her head. "No. A marriage is two independent people who agree to work together."

I screwed up my face. "Well, that sounds very business trans-actiony."

"You need to take this seriously." She was annoyed. "James won't get better unless you both address your codependency issues."

It was true that James had assumed my previous role as care-taker, and it seemed to give him a distraction from our compli-cated lives. In fact, the sicker I became, the more attentive he was.

"How will that help his recovery?"

"It will be difficult, but you need to end the cycle you're in. You will both need to do the hard work individually."

It was ridiculous. She was not my therapist, and she most

likely had no idea of what James had put me through. I shoved my rolling chair away from the table. "I think we're done here. James did this to himself. He can fix it himself. I'm done trying."

The counselor studied me with a resigned look. "Take the brochures. Read about it. If not for James, for your children. It's not healthy for them to live like this."

How dare she bring my kids into it. I knew they saw and heard too much. I knew I was a terrible mother. I didn't need some woman I had never met to explain that to me.

I tossed the brochures into my bag and stormed out of the room.

James was his own person, and he needed to take responsibility for his drinking. The accident wasn't his fault, but his affair and alcoholism were. He had taken responsibility for Khalie, and I knew he was working hard to convince me he was no longer the mean, angry man he had been, but in my opinion, alcoholism was an excuse for his shitty behavior. He had cited it as a reason he cheated, and I was not going to accept any responsibility for his inability to control himself.

I invited Rob over that night after the boys were asleep. It had been two weeks since we'd seen each other, and I found myself craving his attention. I had naively believed that with time apart I'd get over him, but when he called to ask if I was okay, I caved.

As we settled onto my bedroom sofa with a bottle of wine and fresh-baked cookies, Rob spied the brochures I had left on the side table. He fanned them out before studying them. "What's this?"

I sighed. "James's rehab center thinks we're codependent, and I need to be more supportive." I had taken two Xanax before Rob arrived, and my brain was fuzzy. The wine added to my giddy feeling.

"What the fuck does that mean?" Rob asked.

I shrugged. "I really don't care."

"Neither do I." He threw the brochures across the room and held out his arms. I crawled onto his lap and rested my head against his shoulder. "I missed you," he said. "When you stopped answering my messages, I hated not knowing if I'd ever see you again."

In my mind, I had broken up with Rob a thousand times. I had told him off and pushed him away, but in reality, I had done none of those things. I continued to make every wrong decision when it came to him.

At one point, after we had finished a bottle of red wine, he looked at me and asked, "What are we doing?"

It was such a loaded question. "I don't know."

His hazel eyes locked on me. "You're my girlfriend."

"You can't have a girlfriend when you have a wife. You can only have a mistress." The words slid off my tongue. Mistress. I had degraded myself to a woman who willingly sleeps with someone else's husband. After everything I had been through, I was an active participant in hurting another woman.

"You're my girlfriend because I'm leaving her. I have to. I realized it while you were MIA." Rob stroked my cheek. "I want to be with you."

It was exactly what I had been waiting for . . . and it felt wrong. I didn't want to be the reason two families fell apart.

Rob frowned at my silence. "Think about it. I'm going to move out this week, and I want you to be with me."

"I can't leave my boys."

Rob's hand drifted across my back. "When James gets out of rehab you'll have more ammunition."

"We're codependent, remember? I need to aid in his recovery." I didn't understand how those two ideas went together, and I laughed.

"Mia . . ." Rob rested his palm against my cheek. "Trust me. It's okay if what you want in life has changed from what you wanted at twenty." He kissed me softly. "It's okay to let go of something that's not working."

My heart clenched. Rob was choosing me and asking me to choose him. All I had to do was agree, and yet, I couldn't commit. "You're going to tell Katrina about us?"

"It's time."

After Rob left to go home to his family, I stood in front of my bathroom mirror and studied the stranger staring back. She had the same strawberry-blonde hair and large hazel eyes as me, but I didn't know her. This woman knowingly hurt another woman and her children the way James and Khalie had hurt my family. This woman put her own selfish desires before the morally correct thing to do.

What was wrong with me? Why was I justifying my actions?

I leaned in closer to the mirror as if my reflection had the answers, but all I saw was a monster.

By morning, guilt had seeped into every crevice of my mind. In a daze, I managed to make lunches, pack backpacks, and hand out good-bye kisses to the boys.

The house was silent when I sat down with my laptop. Over the course of an hour, I composed a dozen different versions of a "Dear John" letter, and each one was more pathetic than the previous. In frustration, I decided to go for a run.

About a mile in, I knew what I needed to say. I stopped, opened my email, and composed a letter while standing on the sidewalk.

Dear Rob,

Go be a good dad. Laugh with your kids, tuck them into bed, love them unconditionally, break up fights, tickle them. Give them the gift of time.

Love your wife. She's held your family together and deserves your respect. Hold her tightly and tell her how much you appreciate her. Maybe the sex isn't what you wish, but there's companionship and a deep understanding that comes from knowing someone completely. There's that warm sense of just knowing this person has your back no matter what, and that you'd be worse off without them in your life.

I will miss you, and I'm crying while I type this, but I know it's the right thing to do.

You will always have a special place in my heart.

xoxo,

Mia

I hit send before I could change my mind and found I didn't regret it one bit.

31

The day James returned from rehab, I scrubbed the house from top to bottom, baked his favorite thumbprint cookies, and ran through different scenarios of how things would play out. Would James act differently? Would I? How prepared were we to "do the hard work" as his caseworker said?

I was relieved that I hadn't heard from Rob since sending the letter two days earlier. Our clean break would make my plan of committing to James and my family easier.

A little after two thirty, James slinked into the house and dropped his suitcase next to the stairs. My nerves prevented me from getting up from my spot on the sofa.

"Hey." He kept his head down. "How are you?"

I didn't know what to say or if it was even okay to have a frank talk yet. "Fine."

James sat in the chair diagonal from mine. "The boys at school?"

"Yes."

My phone buzzed, and I half-heartedly looked at the screen. Rob's name appeared, and I tensed.

"Who is it?" James asked.

I shrugged. "Unknown number." I flipped the phone face-down. How did Rob know the exact moment to call?

"Jesus Christ. I've been home ten minutes, and he's already blowing up your phone?" James didn't raise his voice, in fact, he seemed more hurt than angry.

"I told him we couldn't see each other anymore. We haven't spoken since."

James tilted his head. "Then why is he calling you?"

"I don't know."

"Bee, I had a lot of time to think in rehab. I didn't end things with Khalie well, I understand that now, but you have to believe me that I love you. There's no one but you for me." His voice hitched, and I fought back tears. For over a year, I had insisted James defaulted to me because I forced his hand. "Please let me back in," James said. "I know you don't trust me, but can you try taking down some of the wall between us?"

I digested his words and tried to separate the man before me from the one who had hurt me. "How can I trust you won't do it again?"

"Because I love you."

"You claimed to have loved me before."

James knelt beside me and took my hand. "I hated myself. I hurt myself emotionally and physically because I didn't know how to deal with my feelings. Unfortunately, that spilled over to hurting you and the boys."

"I can't love you." Tears filled my eyes. "I can't do it again."

"Can't love me or don't want to love me?" James stroked the back of my hand, and it sent a crack rumbling through me.

"I'm scared." It was the first time I admitted to myself that I was terrified of James breaking my heart again. "I loved you so much. Maybe more than I should."

"I love you. You and the boys are my world." He touched my

phone. "We can start fixing this if you'd stop seeing Rob." When I didn't respond, James sighed. "I'm going to put my stuff away. I'll be back in a minute."

After he walked downstairs, I sat quietly and ignored my buzzing phone. I couldn't call Rob back if I were serious about ending things. I had told him to focus on his family and how he'd be worse off without Katrina in his life, but had I really written that for myself? James and I had been through so much, but at the end of the day, he understood me better than anyone. Didn't that count for something?

While James unpacked in the guest room, Tate and Leo burst through the front door, full of loud boy-laughs and giggles. Our home was open concept, and I could see them from my spot at the back of the house. They flung their shoes and coats every which way and tumbled into the family room.

Tate launched himself at me and wrapped his arms around my neck. "Momma!"

"Hey, baby! Do you want a snack?" I didn't mention James being home. I had decided to let him surprise the boys.

Leo sat down at the breakfast table. "Popcorn?"

"Pomegranate!" Tate named his favorite food.

I threw a bag of popcorn in the microwave and prepped the pomegranate for Tate to tear apart. We had a system where I would slice it open and submerge the chunks in water. Tate would break open the pods under the water. This way, red juice didn't spray everywhere.

Leo turned on the TV and took the popcorn from me while Tate set to work on his fruit. I kept glancing at the basement stairs, waiting for James to emerge, but he didn't. Eventually, I told the boys I'd be right back and headed to the basement.

James lay face down on the bed. A repulsive smell I hadn't noticed earlier radiated off him.

"Why do you smell weird?" I asked.

He rolled over, revealing his red, swollen eyes. "Detox medicine."

"What's wrong?" I sat on the edge of the bed near his knees.

"I'm committed to trying. Are you?"

For months, I had railed and cried and hurt myself, unable to express what exactly was causing me pain when James had consistently put me and my wants first. He had tried; I hadn't.

"Bee, we can do this. I love you, and I think you still love me somewhere deep inside there. You have to let yourself feel something."

Normally, this would have sent me into a rage, but James was right. I numbed myself; I drank too much; I took too many pills; I had stayed in a relationship with a married man. I self-harmed in so many different ways, I had lost count.

Why?

Because I was too scared to let anyone close to me. In Rob, I sought a protector and savior, but neither of us had been completely honest with the other, and we didn't know the messy sides of each other.

My phone buzzed again. I knew it was Rob without looking. James did, too. "I thought you broke things off?" he asked. "Did he not get the memo?"

"Come say 'hi' to the boys." I ignored my phone. "They don't know you're here."

I stood so James could swing his legs off the bed. When he pulled himself fully upright, he seemed so small and lost. I held my arms out, and he folded his trembling body into them.

"I messed this up. I did this. I'm so sorry, Bee. I'm so sorry."

His sobs chipped away at my closed-off heart. I wasn't going to make excuses for James's behavior, but the man I had married and was married to until his accident would never have done any of this. That had to be worth something.

"Don't give up on us because of a bad eighteen months, Bee.

Please." James wiped his face. "We can work on this."

He was repeating something I had said before I knew about his affair when I believed we were only dealing with a brain injury and PTSD. I had been so desperate to fix whatever was going wrong with us that I had forgotten to care for myself. It had left me a broken mess.

Yet, despite all the hurt James had caused, I wanted to try. I had told myself over and over again that I didn't love James, but the truth was I didn't want to love him. That was an entirely different beast.

My phone rang again, and this time I looked. It was Rob. My face gave it away, and James frowned, but he didn't comment. Instead, he took my hand and led me upstairs to our waiting boys. To our family. The one we needed to fix.

That night, James offered to run to the grocery store to buy bread for lunches. It was a quick trip, but after he'd been gone for an hour, I wondered if he had actually gone to the store. I tried calling him, but it went to voicemail.

Ten minutes later, calls and texts from Rob flooded my phone. I stared at his messages. James had gone to confront him at home. His wife had heard, and Rob wanted to know what the hell was going on?

When James returned home, he nodded at me. "He'll leave you alone now."

"What did you do?" Panic trilled across my nerves. "He said you told his wife."

"No. I rang the doorbell, and he answered in his pajamas. We stood on the porch, and I told him to stay away from you, and that he should focus on his own wife."

I gaped at James. "How did you know where he lived?"

"Google."

"You shouldn't have done that, James. You just hurt his wife." I was shaking, but not from anger. I didn't want to hurt Katrina, and I also didn't want Rob to get in trouble. "You overstepped." I headed toward the stairs so I could respond to Rob from the privacy of my own room. "I'm going to bed."

"Can we talk?" James seemed confused as to why I wasn't doing backflips over him blowing up someone else's life.

I shook my head.

"Bee, do not call him." James took my phone from my hand. "We need to talk about us and our future." His eyes pleaded with me. "Things are done with him. You said so yourself."

"What do you want?" I asked. "I ended things, and you threw kerosene on it. What else is there to discuss?"

James held out his hand. "Just talk to me for a little bit."

I allowed him to guide me to the sofa, and we spent hours discussing mine and Rob's relationship, James's affair, and what role my mental illness had played in my lousy decision making. I wanted to own my bad behavior, but James insisted I wasn't okay. He made excuses for me, and I accepted them. "How many pills do you take a day, Bee? How much do you drink?" He grabbed my arm and flipped it over, exposing angry, red marks. "You're still cutting yourself."

I yanked my arm away and tugged my sleeve down. I hadn't cut my arm in a week, but my hip had more recent slices. Rob had asked about the cuts a few times, and I had made up some bullshit answer that he had never questioned. In fact, if Rob had suspected anything was wrong with me, he never asked even though the number of pills I took in front of him should have been a sign. As I sat there, I realized I knew nothing about Rob, and he didn't know me. I had spent a considerable amount of time with him, but he was a stranger, and our relationship was built on lies and omissions.

At one point, I couldn't take James's breakdown of our problems and locked myself in the bathroom. I wanted another lorazepam, but James had hidden them again while I had been busy with the boys. I stormed out of the bathroom. "Where are my pills?"

"You don't need them."

I flew at him, fists balled. "You don't get to decide that." I pummeled his chest. "Just because you went to rehab doesn't mean you are an expert on pills."

He captured my hands. "Do you think Dr. Sims will keep writing you prescriptions if she knew you abused your pills and mixed them with alcohol all the time?"

"I need them," I cried. "They calm me down."

James folded me into his arms. "You are supposed to take one a day, and that's all I'm going to give you. You can hate me if you want, but I'm terrified you're going to overdose."

A dam broke inside me, and I sobbed. "I hate waking up. Every single day, I want to disappear."

"I know, baby, and we're going to work on that. The boys and I need you to get better."

I curled into his side, comforted by his presence. James saw my self-destruction and loved me enough to help me face the hard truth. I had a problem, but I didn't want help. I wasn't ready to expose my flaws openly yet.

"I don't want to be needed by anyone. I want to be alone," I whispered.

James wrapped me in his arms until I fell asleep. It was the first time in months that we had been that close while sleeping, and it didn't feel wrong at all.

A few days later, as I walked across the Panera parking lot, a large, black SUV followed me. It trailed me in my car until I stopped at a light. When it pulled up next to me, I immediately recognized the driver: Katrina. She motioned for me to roll down my window.

"I know who you are," she screamed. "You're a mother! How could you do this?"

I wanted to tell her I was sorry, but the words were lodged in my throat. When the light turned green, I rolled up the window and hurried home. To my relief, she didn't follow me, but seeing Katrina's raw emotions rattled me and brought back my own feelings about James's affair. I had sworn to never sink to this level, but I had, and I had hurt a woman who didn't deserve it.

James was working from home, and he heard me when I burst through the door, hysterical. Thankfully, the boys were still at school.

"What's wrong?" He pressed me against his chest.

"Katrina knows who I am. She screamed at me." My tears were stupid because I deserved so much more than being yelled at.

James released me and disappeared into the office. When he reappeared, he had a large folder overflowing with paper.

"What are you doing?" I asked.

"I'll be back." He grabbed his keys.

"Where are you going?" I yanked on his arm.

"Don't worry about it," he said. "Do not go anywhere, and do not contact Rob."

I had made a mess. I had hurt Katrina and maybe even her kids. What was wrong with me?

An hour later, I needed to meet Tate at school for a bike safety event and left the house, even though James had said not to. As I watched Tate pedal around cones, James called. "Are you home?"

"No."

"Go home now. Leo and Ryan are there alone, and Rob is on his way over."

"What?"

"Just get home now," James said.

I ran toward Tate, grabbed his little bike, and tucked it under my arm. "Daddy needs us home."

I had no idea what was happening or why Rob would come to my house, and James wouldn't pick up his phone. When I pulled into my garage, my nerves were raw from anxiety.

I paced my front room, staring out the window and unable to concentrate on anything. An hour later, James returned, but Rob hadn't shown.

"What the hell?" I said quietly so the boys won't hear. "What did you do?"

"I talked to Katrina. She was under the impression you seduced her husband and we had an open marriage."

"What?" I exclaimed. "Why would she think that?"

"You tell me."

Rob had lied about us. Of course he did. He lied about everything.

"Bee, she won't come after you again. I gave her a file of the emails and texts he's sent you. I found multiple online dating sites he was on and shared those, too."

"What?"

"He was on Ashley Madison and Match.com."

"What?" My vision blurred. "What is happening?"

"Let's just say, Katrina knows what a dick he is now."

I stood perfectly still, shocked that Rob had been actively

trolling for women. I wasn't sure why I was surprised. He was cheating on his wife with me, but I thought . . . why in the world did I think we met by chance? Why was he in a hotel bar anyway? Why had that never occurred to me? I needed to talk to Allison.

"He was on a dating site?"

"Lots of them." James jerked his head to the right. "You're probably not his only girlfriend."

It was a blow, but I didn't think James meant it that way. I think he was trying to make me feel less guilty, but it had the exact opposite effect. "How was I so stupid?"

I knew. Rob had offered me a sense of security, something I lost when James was hit. Rob felt steady and interested—except he wasn't ever any of those things.

Why hadn't I seen this before?

That night, I called Allison and asked if she had met Rob before I had. The story in my mind—that he just happened to be at the bar—had never made sense, but I wanted to believe it.

Allison hemmed and hawed before answering, "I set up a dating profile for you."

"You what?"

She giggled. "I knew you wouldn't, so I took initiative. I picked a cute picture of you, and I emailed with him at least a dozen times to make sure he wasn't a psychopath."

"Allison . . ." I broke into the sordid story of what was happening.

"Oh, honey. He was supposed to be a gift. Something to get you back into the dating world." She paused. "You never told me it was serious."

"Maybe it wasn't, after all."

3 2

I refused to leave my house, and on the one occasion I did leave the house with James, we saw Katrina at the store. She was everywhere.

Guilt devoured me, and James's patience wore thin. "You don't blame him enough." He never said Rob's name. "Why do you feel solely responsible?"

How could I explain it to someone who had never been on the receiving end of betrayal? I had lowered myself to base standards. I became exactly the person I hated. I was no better than Khalie.

At one of my biweekly therapy appointments, Dr. Sims said, "You need to move. Go somewhere more vibrant. Go back to city life." She folded her hands on her lap. "You need to get out of your neighborhood and away from Rob and Katrina."

When I shared this with James, he balked. "We are not uprooting the boys again."

"I can't stay here," I cried. "Please. Let's go back to San Francisco."

James shook his head. "We're not going anywhere. The boys love it here."

My shoulders heaved. "So, the only way for me to get out is to die."

He recoiled. "Don't say that."

I think this is the first time he realized how destroyed I was by the situation. He had been able to cut Khalie off and never see her again. He had been able to move on without the constant reminder of his bad decisions. But me? I was stuck in a place where I risked seeing Rob or Katrina over and over again.

To help me feel better, James surprised me with a membership to our neighborhood country club. "Maybe you'll meet some friends." He sounded hopeful, like being social would cure everything that ailed me. "It could be really good for you. We can take up golf or tennis."

The last thing I wanted was to socialize. I wanted to lie in bed all day and hide, but I let James sign us up for a gingerbread house-making event the following week.

The day of the event, I showered and brushed my hair for the first time in days. James helped me dress because even that was too difficult for me. He made sure the boys were dressed appropriately. Then we climbed into our car and made the five-minute drive to the club.

I knew no one, but we'd been assigned a table with the pieces of a gingerbread house stacked neatly on top, so I felt okay. I could hide at my table and focus on the boys. I had also taken two hidden Klonopin before leaving the house, and the effect had kicked in.

"Do you want a drink?" James asked. "They have mimosas." He didn't know I had medicated already.

"Okay." I kept my head down, my long hair falling in my face. I knew I looked depressed, and I didn't want to be that woman. I wanted to be the woman I once was, chatting with people and being social. But I wasn't her anymore. She had disappeared and the worst thing had happened: I had abandoned myself. I was no longer the confident, outgoing woman who loved being involved socially. Instead, I was a timid, nervous, worried woman who constantly second-guessed herself. I longed for the old me.

When James walked away, I glanced toward the entrance and froze. Rob stood there with his wife and children, smiling. Katrina hugged a few people, and the kids took off. When he noticed me, Rob's smile faltered before stretching wide again. He turned his back.

My hands trembled, and my knees buckled. I caught myself against the table.

"Are you okay, Mom?" Ryan asked. "Should I get Dad?"

I shook my head. "I'll be right back."

I exited the far end of the room, away from Rob and his family, to the verandah and leaned against the railing. I wasn't wearing a coat and bitter December air pricked my skin, but there was no way I could go back inside. I couldn't look at Katrina. I couldn't see her and watch her pretend that what Rob and I did hadn't gutted her or made her question every-thing about her marriage. I couldn't watch her put on a brave face.

I couldn't face the pain I had caused.

I slunk to the ground and stretched my legs out straight in front of me. I considered writing Katrina an apology letter and promised myself that I'd lie to her. I would say that what Rob and I had was nothing and that he never told me he loved me and we never made future plans. I'd tell her all the lies I wish Khalie had told me.

I tipped over onto my side and hugged my knees into my chest. The cold cement floor stung my cheek and bare arms. Snow floated softly from the sky and melted when it touched me.

I don't know how long I was there before James found me.

He scooped me up and lifted me off the floor. "Bee, you can't let him win. You need to be strong."

James was under the impression that Rob held me in his thrall, but he couldn't have been more wrong. I saw Rob and his lies clearly. It was Katrina that gutted me.

I rubbed my face against James's chest. "I want to go home."

"You need to try."

"This is unfair. You never had to do this. You never had to see Khalie's husband."

James clasped me to him and rubbed my back. "I know, but you have to make this work."

I shook my head. "Take me home."

"The boys are almost done with the house, and we have lunch reservations. They're starving."

I had no energy to argue and let James guide me back inside to our table. I reached down and grabbed my purse and took out a bottle of Klonopin I had hidden in there. James had given them back to me the day before, after I had sworn I'd only take one at night. I shook a pill into my hand and washed it down with the mimosa James had gotten me. He raised his eyebrows but didn't stop me.

Somehow, in a drugged haze, I made it through the rest of the event and lunch. I drank too much and refused to engage with anyone James tried to introduce to me. I sat by myself, staring at the roaring fire, while James chatted with people and the boys ran around with their friends.

I grew convinced those people hated me. It was obvious from the way Katrina flitted around the room that they all loved her, and I would never fit in with this group.

Plus, why would anyone want to befriend a cheating whore?

Eventually, James brought me my coat, but not until after Rob and Katrina left. That would become our pattern from here on out: any event we all attended, James and I always left after them. We would have the most fun. We would win, and our marriage would survive.

"You were so strong today," James said when we arrived home.

"I guess." I paused by the stairs. "I'm going to lie down."

"Okay, you rest. I'll check on you in a few."

I didn't go to bed. Instead, I locked myself in the bathroom and sliced my wrists.

Bipolar disorder. Generalized anxiety disorder. PTSD.

I told myself repeatedly that what happened to me wasn't as traumatic as what happened to James. I'd seen PTSD up close, and what had happened to me—an affair—didn't warrant a PTSD diagnosis. I was sad and hurt, and angry at myself for being involved with Rob, but I didn't have PTSD.

I sat in Dr. Sims's office, explaining how I couldn't stop obsessing over what I should and shouldn't have done regarding Rob, and how I couldn't let go of the pain I caused Katrina.

She frowned. "Your brain needs a break. I want you to start lithium. We'll use it to calm your mind down, and once you feel okay again, you can wean off it."

Lithium. I knew from my endless research that lithium was a powerful tool in combating bipolar depression and mania and stopping suicidal thoughts.

It also caused weight gain.

"I don't want to be fat." I twisted my hands. "I'm already a mess. If I get fat, I don't think it will help me feel any better."

My doctor kept her face serene. "You need to do this. You've had multiple suicide attempts and, by your own admission, are becoming obsessive. Since you refuse inpatient treatment, this is the best course of action."

Being locked up alone terrified me. James's description of life in rehab had convinced me I needed to fix myself, and I pleaded with him to never send me to a psych ward. We both failed to see this refusal to seek out help as a repetition of how disastrously we had handled James's situation after his accident.

Dr. Sims handed me a script. "I'll see you next week."

My drive home took me down a twisty, two-lane road with very little daylight. There was a tree that jutted out into the street, and if you weren't paying attention, it was entirely possible to drive straight into it. Every time I passed this tree, I considered smashing my car into it.

That day, I gunned the engine as I neared it. I didn't need lithium. I needed out, and if James wouldn't let us move then I had no option but to die.

But as I neared the bend and the perfect place to slam into the tree, my thoughts cleared. Single-driver, single-car crashes are often considered suicides. If I committed suicide, the boys wouldn't get my life insurance money, and maybe they'd feel responsible for my decision.

I couldn't do that.

I eased off the gas.

I'd take the lithium. I'd get fat if that made my brain stop going down rabbit holes. I'd do whatever I needed to do to feel normal again.

33

To my astonishment, the lithium helped even though my hands trembled and my hair fell out in clumps. I was able to get out of bed more. I engaged with the boys again and went back to yoga; I even made a few acquaintances at the club.

One woman, Samantha, took me under her wing and introduced me to her friends. I began getting invitations to jewelry parties and concerts with party bus transportation and dinners. I tentatively accepted, nervous that Katrina may be at some of these, and sometimes she was. I would leave upon seeing her, making up some excuse about the boys.

Samantha, an astute observer, noticed Katrina and I never spoke to each other, not even when in a small group, and that I often left when Katrina arrived.

Samantha confronted me about it as we sat in Panera eating salads.

"Why are you and Katrina so odd around each other?" Samantha had a serene way about her that put me at ease.

I considered lying, but the words tumbled out of my mouth. "I had an affair with her husband."

Samantha gawked at me. "Oh, lord! That's awkward."

She asked me questions, and I answered, and when I was done speaking, Samantha said, "I always thought he was a snake in the grass."

It made me feel better.

Samantha and I began spending more time together. We would go for walks, have lunches and spa days, and get together for drinks in the evening. I never mentioned my mental health issues, because I didn't want to scare her.

Slowly, I relaxed and met more people. Everyone knew me as the author who moved to town from Paris. I was a novelty, and I didn't mind. I felt almost happy.

Then, after months of improvement, while at a club event, Rob intentionally bumped shoulders with James, and I lost my mind.

I left Samantha and her daughter and stormed over to where Rob stood with a group of guys, drinking beer. I laid into him, calling him all kinds of names.

I didn't realize Samantha's husband was standing with Rob.

Later that night, I received a text from her saying she told her husband everything, and he wouldn't let her be my friend anymore. He wanted her to throw her support behind Katrina, who she barely knew, because he was friends with Rob.

I felt like a whore who shouldn't be associated with and crashed again. I found my favorite X-Acto knife and created a pattern of lines over my hips and thighs. I stared blankly at the wall and refused to see the boys. My weight dropped dangerously low again.

It took months of therapy and more medication for me to level out.

Slowly, I found my equilibrium, and one day I picked up my laptop and began drafting a story. Over the previous two years, I had received fan mail asking me to write a sequel to the teen boy coming-of-age novel I had self-published, and as I sat in my office, the desire to write hit me hard. I threw myself into the project and completed a draft in just three weeks. I sent it to the editor, made more changes, and published it faster than it usually took me to write a first draft. I did no promo for that novel—a story of love gone wrong and found again—but it found an audience and the reviews were positive.

I could write again, and I slowly reclaimed that part of myself.

A writer-acquaintance I had met at a conference a few years earlier reached out to me and asked if I wanted to submit my book to an anthology she was putting together. I agreed and spent the next two months helping her create a marketing strategy. Our goal was to hit the NYT and USA Today bestsellers lists.

We did.

With my confidence boosted, I started writing more, and James smiled every time he saw me clicking away. At night, he always asked what I worked on that day, and patiently listened as I read him my writing from earlier. Sometimes, he offered feedback, but usually he encouraged me to keep going.

He now slept with me in our bed even though every time he touched me I startled. He tried to hide his sadness, but it was in his eyes and furrowed brow. I was getting stronger, but I couldn't let myself trust James yet.

He didn't understand why I was still withdrawn. It had been three years since I discovered his affair. He had done everything I had asked, and it wasn't enough. I couldn't fully let go of my hurt. Now, I think I clung to it out of guilt. Hurting myself was penitence for what I had done to Katrina.

As my writing schedule and demands increased, so did my energy levels. I found myself doing more with the boys. Life hummed along, almost like normal, except my normal required an extraordinary amount of medicine to keep me from hurting myself. I didn't think I'd ever function without medicine again, because no matter how hard I tried, I couldn't forgive myself for James's accident, his affair, or how I hurt Katrina.

One warm, spring evening, after a long day of watching the boys play lacrosse, my family went to the club for dinner. When we walked in, I spied Samantha near the window with a group of women I recognized as Katrina's friends. Samantha avoided my eye contact, and my heart sank. Part of me wished we could be friends again, but part of me also wanted to kick her in the knees.

Normally, the women with Samantha were pleasant to me, but I caught them stealing glances in my direction, and not one of them motioned me over. I slinked to my table and tried to pretend like it didn't bother me.

"Bee, you okay?"

I shrugged. "Do you think they're talking about me?"

James glanced toward the group of women. "No."

"Then why do they keep looking at me and haven't invited me over?" I sat so my side was exposed to them, and if I turned my head slightly, I could see all of them laughing and gossiping.

I knew they were gossiping because that's what Samantha and I did, and that's what she and her friends did when I was with them. They talked about each other. Not always in a bad way, but enough for me to know that I was currently the topic of conversation.

Toward the end of our meal, as I grew more and more paranoid with each roar of laughter coming from the women,

Samantha walked over to our table. She leaned down, close to me, and whispered in my ear. "You know I love you, honey, but it's best if you don't come up here anymore."

I stiffened, and James raised his eyebrows, his curiosity piqued since he couldn't hear Samantha.

When she stood up, my eyes met Samantha's, and she nodded before walking away.

Vomit lodged in my throat. They knew. Everyone knew. How? Samantha was the only person I had confided in. Did she tell everyone or had Katrina?

I shoved away from the table and tripped over my handbag on the floor. Sweat dotted the nape of my neck.

"What happened?" James asked, grabbing my arm. The boys stared at me, but they had grown used to my strange behaviors.

"I need to go home."

For once, James didn't fight me. "Okay."

I raced ahead of my family and flung myself into the passenger seat of our car. Tears welled in my eyes, and I kept my head down. I couldn't let the boys see me like this. Not again.

It was a disaster of my own making. I had done this to myself. Me. It was all my burden to bear, and I deserved it.

At home, James followed me into our bedroom. When I curled up on the floor near the entrance to my closet, he knelt beside me and rubbed my back. "Tell me what happened."

"They all know what I did." Tears ran down my face. "I was delusional that I could stay here. You said time would make it better, but it's only getting worse."

James lifted my hand and kissed it. "Bee, sweetheart. Rob did this to Katrina, just like I did it to you. Yes, you should have ended things sooner, but you ended things. That's what matters."

I rolled my head back and forth on the carpet, knotting my hair. "You ended things for me. I was indecisive."

"You can get past this, but you have got to forgive yourself."

I blinked away salty tears. "And how do I do that? How did you do that?"

He looked away and pressed his lips tightly together before speaking. "I haven't."

"And neither will I."

Our faces were inches apart. "I hurt you. I see what I did every day. I live it every day." James paused and inhaled sharply. "But you have shown me grace, and you have tried to forgive me. Maybe I don't deserve it. I don't know."

I closed my eyes. He was right about time, but grace? I surely didn't have that in my heart.

"It's not fair," I moaned. "Why am I getting shunned, but not Rob? Why am I being painted as the whore, and he's getting away with it? For God's sake, he was all over that Ashley Madison list!"

James didn't need to explain why Rob wasn't shouldering the brunt of the disapproval. I knew. It was easier to point at the other woman and call her names than accept that maybe there were issues in the marriage. Plus, Katrina had seemingly forgiven him, and if she was okay with his bad behavior, then others would be, too.

I think that to these women, I had appeared from nowhere and swooped down to steal Katrina's husband. My presence was a reminder that seemingly perfect marriages were often anything but, and destruction hovered just beyond the edges.

These women tore me apart with nasty glances and exclusion. Their tongues wagged, and I cried—both over my bad decisions that had led me to this place and over the unfairness that Rob appeared unscathed. He smiled and laughed and refused to meet my hurt eyes. Like James once accused, I was a taker—taking and accepting both Rob's and my guilt.

I didn't fight back when called a whore or when backs

turned on me as I entered a room. Every untrue story I heard about myself was worse than the last: I had had multiple affairs; James and I had an open marriage; I was an obsessive stalker. I said nothing. I took and took and took until I broke again.

Katrina fed the rumors by screaming at me in public. My guilt caused me to let her, because I understood the depth of her pain, and I had once dreamed of doing the same to Khalie, and I still wished I had had the opportunity.

For months after Samantha whispered in my ear, I sat in Dr. Sims's office twice a week, crying over my poor life decisions and searching for answers. She adjusted my medicine and doubled down on my therapy. With her help, I realized I needed to stop swinging at Khalie's ghost by letting Katrina haunt me, and I had to stop waiting for an apology from Rob.

With Dr. Sims's guidance, I made small, daily goals to show myself grace and forgiveness. I had paid enough for the mistakes I had made, and James and Dr. Sims reminded me that those mistakes didn't make me unworthy of love. Still, forgiving myself was the most difficult thing I've ever done, but through it all, James kept holding my hand, kept promising to never leave me, and kept coaxing me from the bleakness that surrounded me.

34

Two years after I ended things with Rob, he and his family packed up and moved to Europe. It was the break I needed to fully heal, and with them gone, my panic attacks and anxiety lessened.

James encouraged me to plunge fully back into the writing world, and I started attending writing conferences with my friends again. At one conference, I found myself not dwelling on the accident or the affair, or even what I had done to Katrina. Instead, I laughed, made jokes, signed books, and allowed myself to be happy.

During a write-in session, while everyone else worked on manuscripts, I pulled up *Always Yours, Bee* and began reading older posts. Some were based purely in my imagination and some were rooted in reality, but all of them held a depth of pain I no longer felt.

Around me, keyboards click-clacked, and writers wrote, but I read. The blog was a chronology of me falling apart, and I no longer needed to revisit it or hold on to the awful memories. I had lived them and come through the other side.

I deleted my blog.

I had thought *Always Yours, Bee* was meant for James, and that it was my way of reaching out to him when I didn't know how to speak to him. But it had actually been for me. Rereading the posts showed me how I had been searching for what I had lost after James's accident: myself.

I left the conference free of my blog, but with a strong desire to write a novel again. Without telling James, I outlined a book called *Surviving the Suburbs* that was loosely based on my experiences with mental health, infidelity, and living in suburbia. I drafted it in six weeks. When I did tell James about it, he asked to read it to me, like he'd done with my other books. I hesitated, but he assured me that what happened to me was my story to tell, and I could tell it in any way I wanted.

Every night, he'd read a few chapters to me, and we'd make changes as he went. When he was done, he told me it was the worst book I'd written. My heart sank until he took my hand.

"Bee, this book hurts me, but it's well done, and it's what you need to say now."

In the end, I decided not to publish it. Even though I had admitted most of our problems to myself, I wasn't ready to publicly expose what could be seen as flaws in mine and James's marriage.

That year, on New Year's Eve, James asked me what I wanted to do for my upcoming fortieth birthday.

"Dream big, Bee. Whatever you want." He kissed me on the forehead as our friends drank and sang around us. We'd invited a few people over, and to my surprise, everyone had come.

"I want to be somewhere sunny." I no longer drank heavily,

so a few sips of celebratory champagne had left my head woozy, and I giggled. "Maybe on a sailboat." Unlike when I demanded our first trip to Nice, I didn't ask for this out of spite. James had learned that he loved the beach, and it was truly what I wanted.

"Any ideas of where?"

I drew my brows together. "The Dalmatian Coast?"

"Where's that?" James asked.

"Croatia." I often read travel magazines, and Croatia had been listed as a "must-visit" location in several of them. "It seems incredible."

James planned an extravagant vacation for us, traveling first to the Croatian capital of Zagreb and down to the coast for a week. From there, we rented a private sailboat with a skipper who made our breakfasts and lunches and acted as an evening babysitter for the boys.

We island-hopped for a week, dined in lavender fields, and swam in the Adriatic Sea's cool, clear water. We laughed and explored with our boys and played rummy under the stars.

We were a family, and it felt like our pre-accident life had returned. Even though a small wall still encircled me, the gaps in the mortar were big enough to cause the walls to fall with the right push.

One warm, starry night, James and I left the boys playing rummy with the skipper and went for a walk around Hvar. We came across a band playing in the town square, and I danced and spun and laughed.

James held me tightly. "I love you, Bee."

I turned my face toward his. The words he wanted to hear sat on the tip of my tongue, but they refused to escape my lips. "Thank you."

James sighed and hugged me harder.

Four years after discovering James's affair, I was still depressed, but my emotions had leveled. My lows didn't send me running for a knife or trying to overdose. I woke up, ran my household, and wrote. I cared for the boys, worried about how my past behavior harmed them, and started doing fun things with them again.

There were fewer and fewer steps backward and more leaps forward. The black fog hanging over me lifted, and Dr. Sims agreed to take me off lithium. Eventually, she lowered the doses on all my drugs, and I felt triumphant when I realized I didn't need an arsenal of medicine to function.

Once I felt I could be social again, I made friends easily despite my awful reputation. With Katrina gone, most people either didn't care anymore or had never heard of my transgressions, and James and I soon had a busier social life than our teenagers.

But there were still people who gossiped, and it gutted me. One day, a woman I barely knew mentioned my bipolar diagnosis. I panicked, unsure how she knew about it. When I cried to James, he sighed. He had told Katrina about my diagnosis as a way of explaining my behavior.

Determined to not sink back into depression, I wrote a Facebook post detailing what living with bipolar disorder was like for me. I laid out everything about my mental health, but after I had finished writing, I wavered. If I published it, then everyone would know, and I'd not only be a homewrecker, but also a crazy woman with a mental illness. I'd be even messier, and there would never be an opportunity to look perfect again.

"Fuck it."

I pushed the upload button and linked the blog post to my

Facebook account. If people were going to talk about my mental health, then they should at least know what they were talking about.

The response was immediate.

"You're so brave and strong!"

"I admire you so much!"

"Thank you for being authentic!"

I stared at the screen. I wasn't strong, but was I brave and authentic? I had spent the better part of six years lying to myself and the outside world. Could I be authentic? Could I live my life out loud and stop berating myself?

Supportive comments kept pouring in, but they didn't matter. What mattered was that, for the first time in my life, I was being me. Authentic, messy me, and I didn't care who knew.

That day I learned a powerful truth: I *was* brave, and I *was* strong. I sharpened my teeth, coated myself in Teflon, and learned to thrive. I confessed my sins when confronted and told myself that if I aired everything the whispers would stop because there would be nothing left to speculate about.

I stopped trying to protect my reputation and became an open book.

———

"What are you reading?" James asked one chilly Sunday morning.

I was bundled under a knit blanket on the couch with my laptop open. A fire warmed the room. "A book."

"What book?"

I lowered my newly bought reading glasses and stared at him over the rims. "My book."

James gave me a puzzled look. "You wrote another book?"

I shook my head. "*Surviving the Suburbs*. I sent it to an editor, and she had a few suggestions."

I hadn't told James that I was toying with the idea of publishing it, and he cocked his head. "You want to put it out there?"

"I don't know. I think it's good, and the editor thinks so, too." I shut my laptop and folded my hands. "It's fiction, but I'm nervous."

"Because it's ugly?" James sat on the end of the couch and darted his hand under the blanket to massage my sock-covered foot.

"I'd publish under a pen name." I put the computer on the ground and stretched out so that my feet rested in James's lap.

He stared into the distance. "I think you should do it."

"Are you sure?" My heart pounded.

"Yes."

I spent the next several weeks working with the editor to deepen the plot and often found myself picking scabs that hadn't fully healed. It wasn't unusual for me to cry my way through scenes and suffer from an emotional hangover.

By the summer, *Surviving the Suburbs* had been retitled *The Secrets We Keep* and was ready for publication. I created a pen name even though I proudly told everyone around me about the book. I had fictionalized large swaths of the story, but those who knew James and me would be able to pick out the truths.

Had I made the right decision?

As I waited for initial sales numbers to roll in, a calmness I hadn't felt in years flowed through me.

I no longer felt the shame of James's affair, and I no longer felt guilt about my affair.

I was free.

I stopped asking James if he loved me. I knew he did. His actions over the previous five years showed me. It was in the way he held me as I cried over unexplainable things; it was in the way he never belittled me for not doing enough; it was in the way he loved me when I hated myself.

But no matter how hard I tried, I couldn't allow myself to fully close the emotional distance between us. Once upon a time, James had been my entire world, and I wanted to love him wholly again. I did. I just didn't know how to escape my fear of being vulnerable with him.

"Let me love you, Bee," James whispered into my neck one night as we lay in bed. "Please let me love you."

"I want to," I said. "I'm just scared." I had never confessed my role in his accident, and I worried that if he knew, James would blame me for all that had happened.

"I'm not going to hurt you. I promise." James kissed my neck.

I closed my eyes and whispered the truth I'd kept hidden for so long. "I didn't drive you to work."

"What?"

I rolled away to face the windows. "The day of your accident, I didn't drive you. I acted selfishly, and you were hit." My chin quivered. "Everything that happened was my fault." I released a shaky breath and let the truth out. "This mess. It was all my fault."

James wrapped his arms tightly around me, and his breath warmed my cheek. "No, baby. My accident was never your fault."

345

The hardest part of that time was accepting that James's memories of the past were gone. In many ways, it was like dating someone new, and I had to let go of how I remembered us. Slowly, I realized none of what had happened mattered. I needed to focus on the now and the future, not the destruction of the past.

I stopped filling his mind with my idyllic memories and let go of who we had been before the accident. I embraced who we could become.

THE EVER AFTER

35

Pleasant warm air encircled me as I sat on a low cushion before a table. On the other side of the sand dune, a camel brayed, but there was absolutely no other noise. I was deep in the Sahara Desert, away from all man-made lights and sounds, and a sliver of purple-orange sun glimmered on the horizon.

We had arrived the day before and were greeted by our guide—a tall, dark-skinned man wearing a brilliant blue turban and robe. As he drove us through the dunes in a beat-up, air conditioning-less car, wind had whipped my hair across my face, obscuring my view. There were no roads in this part of the Sahara, just miles and miles of sand dunes and occasional nomadic Berber huts.

Afraid, I had squeezed James's hand for reassurance as our guide drifted and sped across the sand. I had been sure we were lost until the car raced up a dune. At the peak, an oasis of tents had appeared below. James smiled at me like he hadn't been worried, even though I had seen the fear in his eyes.

The camel brayed again, and the sun sat a little higher in the sky.

"We should go." James offered me his hand. "The guide is ready."

I let him pull me to my feet. Surprisingly cool sand squished between my toes as we climbed the dune to where the camels waited.

"James?"

"Yeah?"

"I love you."

James embraced me. "I love you, too, Bee."

It had been six years since I discovered James's affair, and we had traveled from Washington, DC to Marrakech, Morocco to the deep Sahara on the Algerian border. We had left our now teenaged boys with my dad, and I no longer worried about scarring them. As a family, we had sorted through our traumas and come out stronger.

The sun rose higher.

In Paris, I believed no one cheats on someone they love. It was my absolute truth. Now, I understand that sometimes we so despise ourselves that our pain spills out and hurts others.

My story could have happened to anyone; accidents happen, affairs happen, mental illness happens. James and I were a perfect storm. Yet, we survived and thrived. We were together in the desert, celebrating our twentieth anniversary.

I once scoffed when people told me time would heal wounds. I know now they were almost right. Time makes it harder to feel the specific pain, but forgiveness is what heals. It was a commitment to fixing what went wrong in my marriage and learning to love and forgive myself—no matter how difficult that became—that brought me peace.

Our desert guide said the sand and dunes shift hour by hour, but if you know where to look, you can find your way back.

Somehow, despite all the pain, we knew where to look.

ACKNOWLEDGMENTS

My boys deserve MVP awards. When I said I wanted to write about this awful time in our lives, I gave them full veto power, but each one told me that this is my story to tell and that if I needed to write it, they'd support me. They are the bravest, strongest, most resilient young men I know, and their love made getting through the darkest times possible.

Caroline Hedges. I love you. Really, full-on girl crush. From the first day we met, you've been supportive and encouraging in every aspect of my life. Your notes and feedback and brain-storming helped me take a bunch of muck and shape it into something workable. Thank you for reading early versions of all my books, but especially *Always Yours, Bee*. Plus, criticism sounds kinder and more sophisticated in a British accent.

Katie Zdybel of the Darling Axe took my third or fourth draft and made it shine with her developmental edits. Without her, I would have spent too much time describing the Paris Métro and going off on tangents about rude Frenchmen.

Lauren Donovan of The Book Foundry provided all the copy edits and proofreading, and I've never been so excited to get edits back in my life. I learned tremendously from her comments and corrections.

While Karla Kratovil hasn't read any of this book, she's watched me live a good chunk of it and is always available to hold my hand, wipe my tears, or brainstorm. She makes sure I put my butt in the chair to write every day and is only occasionally distracted by my prattling on while we "work" at Panera.

For my writing group—Phil, Kevin, Janet, Jennifer, Roopa, Dave, Bill, Eric, Magda, and Karla—thank you for sitting through my angsty readings. I didn't tell you I was writing a memoir, and you guys really tore me to shreds, but I loved it.

For my mother-in-law who passed away in July 2019 from Lewy Body Dementia after a seven-year struggle. I feel her absence Every. Single. Day. Without her, I wouldn't have started down this crazy career path, and I wouldn't have had a beautiful example of how to be the mother I wanted to be.

And lastly, Bug. You're my guy, always and forever. Thank you for encouraging me to write this book even though it's been painful for both of us. And thank you for believing in us—even when I made it difficult.

ABOUT THE AUTHOR

Mia is a notorious eavesdropper who lives in Northern Virginia, outside Washington DC, with her husband, sons, two cats, and Harlow the Cavapoo.

She drinks too much green tea, loves traveling, and has mastered the art of procrastination-cleaning.

For books and updates:
www.miahayesauthor.com

For Mia's newsletter, click here.

 facebook.com/miahayesauthor
instagram.com/miahayesauthor

ALSO BY MIA HAYES

The Waterford Novels:

The Secrets We Keep (#1)

All the Broken Pieces (#2)

Picture Perfect Lies (#3)

Coming Soon:

The Has-Beens (June, 2021)

Made in the USA
Monee, IL
03 March 2021